The Explorers' Club

The Explorers' Club

ENTHEOGENIC JOURNEYS DOWN THE RABBIT HOLE

Richard T. Estrin

© 2017 Richard T. Estrin
All rights reserved.

ISBN: 0692926208
ISBN 13: 9780692926208
Library of Congress Control Number: 2017953674
Dorwin Gregory, Montrose, CO

Dedication

This book is dedicated to the following explorers, who have done pioneering work in the study of entheogenic plants and fungi:

James Arthur
Mike Crowley
Peter T. First
Ede Frecska, MD
Stanislav Grof
Michael J. Harner
Clark Heinrich
Terrence McKenna
Jonathan Ott
Carl Ruck
Dr. Richard Evans Schultes
Alexander "Sasha" Shulgin
Rick Strassman
Gordon Wasson

Table of Contents

Contents

Introduction · xi

Chapter 1   In the Workshop · 1
Chapter 2   In the Land of the Bottlebrush People
            A Journey to Hell ·29
Chapter 3   In the Aquarium of Art An Object Lesson · · · · · · · ·49
Chapter 4   A Sandwich in Time ·65
Chapter 5   A Whirlpool of Animals · · · · · · · · · · · · · · · · · ·81
Chapter 6   Invitation to a Vortex · · · · · · · · · · · · · · · · · · ·97
Chapter 7   Climbing Mount Muru · · · · · · · · · · · · · · · · · · 111
Chapter 8   The Flying Doorway · · · · · · · · · · · · · · · · · · · 127
Chapter 9   A Wish-Fulfilling Dream · · · · · · · · · · · · · · · · · 145
Chapter 10 The Knot and the Book · · · · · · · · · · · · · · · · · 153
Chapter 11 Holography: The Projection of Material Form · · · · · 169
Chapter 12 Contact With Nonbiological Intelligence · · · · · · · · 195
Chapter 13 The White Light of the Void · · · · · · · · · · · · · · 211

Conclusion · 257
About the Illustrations · 261
Bibliography · 269

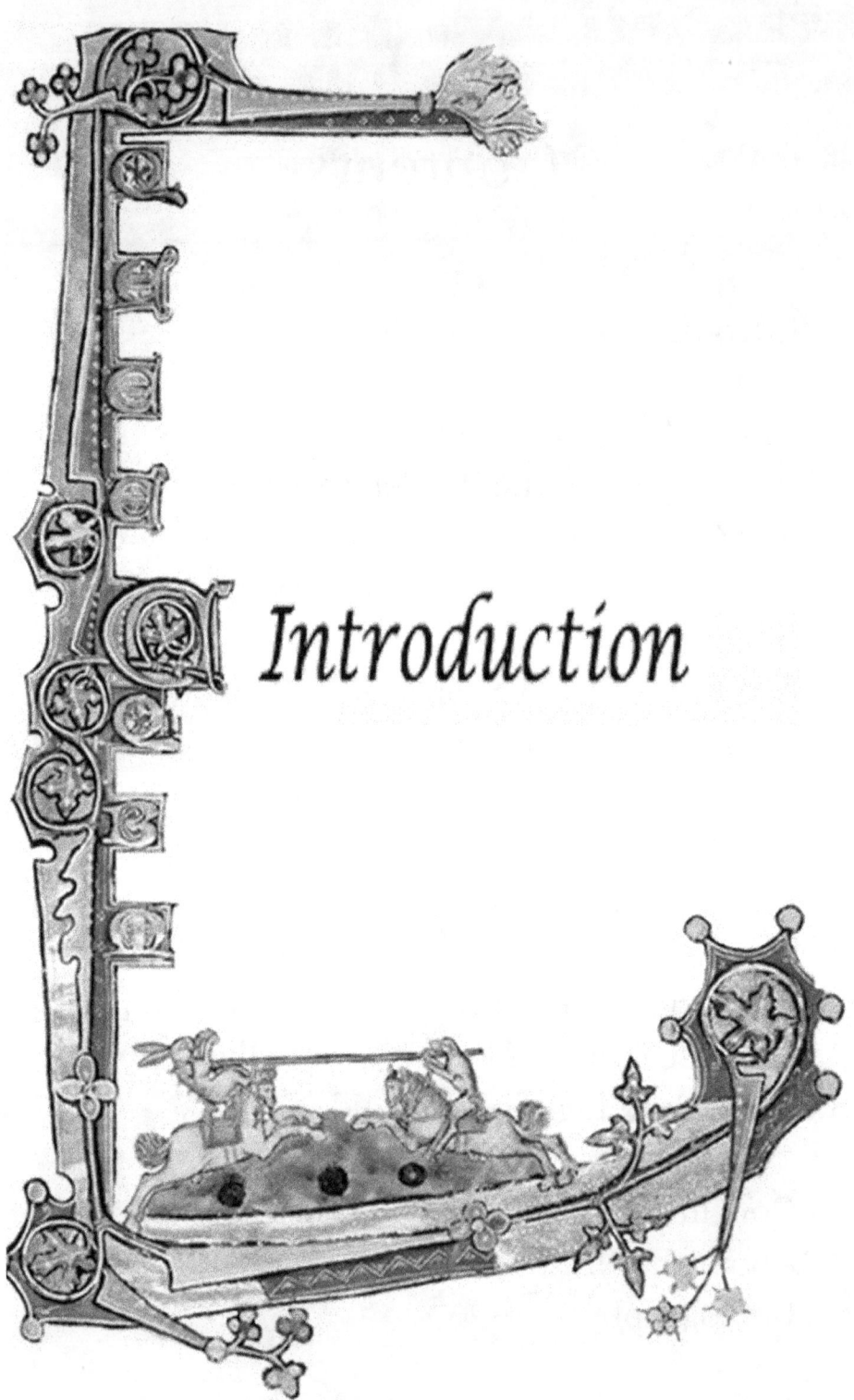

Introduction

Introduction

~~~

THE ENTHEOGENIC SUBSTANCES DESCRIBED IN this book are illegal in the United States at the present time. I do not encourage or condone the use of these psychedelics where they are against the law. I accept that illegal drug use does occur. The information presented here is intended to protect people from the potential harm that uninformed use of these materials could produce.

I am walking in Golden Gate Park. It is the late 1960s. The mescaline I have taken a little over an hour ago is starting to come on stronger and stronger. The mescaline was in the hydrochloride form and came from peyotes that grew near Oilton, Texas. The Indians of the Native American Church felt that these were the best peyotes available anywhere. I feel the need to lie down on the grass. I feel warm on the sun-drenched hill. Lying on my back, I look at the sky. I gradually forget that I am lying there. Just like how in the deepest sleep one is unaware that one is sleeping, I am experiencing nothing, and I am unaware that I am doing so.

Then there comes a miracle of rare devising. In the midst of absolute voidness, no time, no space, no thing, no universe, no self, into the center of a nothing so empty that even the emptiness is gone, into such a void as this, a lone bird comes slowly winging its way across the sky. I had not been dosing. I see the bird instantly with a shock. Suddenly the emptiness is something. The bird is happening to the sky. I think *"Another note on the flute."* My mind explodes with joy, and as if in celebration, an entire flock of birds flies over my head.

I sit up. Everything is incredibly beautiful. The stones on the ground are glistening like jewels. The rocks are luminous with their own inner light.

The trees breathe fresh gusts of scent and oxygen into the air. The leaves are veined and transparent. I can watch the sap flow through them. The sound of running water reverberates like millions of crystalline bells. Droplets of moist sound hang suspended in space, glistening, changing colors into fantastic pastel prisms.

I find myself borrowing words from vision to describe what is happening to sound. Sonic sensation is bristling, now oozing, and now bubbling. Sound has texture, design, and pattern. Voices of passersby hang suspended in the air, and I have plenty of time to appreciate every moist, delicate, fragile nuance. Sound and silence are perpetually turning into one another. Vibrations of air are striking the ancient drum of the inner ear, floating through endless seashell coils of fluid into my mind.

I stand up. The form and color of the trees are joined to my eyes. With each breath I take, multitudes of molecular messages flow into my noise, each a code bursting with information about the world. All my senses seem like the whiskers of a cat extending outward as far as the hills, the trees, and the sky. A part of me is extending billions of light-years through interstellar space and giving light to the stars.

I can see everything all at once: the park, the trees, the people, the children, the buildings, the trash cans, the delicate blades of grass at my feet, and the texture of the forest in the distance. Everything is happening simultaneously. Normally my eyes see one area of attention in contrast to a fuzzy background, but here all is of equal detail and sharpness. It is as though all the contrasts of perception—such as near and far, high and low, large and small, bright and dark, important and not important, significant and insignificant, beautiful and ugly—have lost their polarity and blended into one harmonious whole. Nothing is lost. On the contrary, it is now vitally apparent that contrasts are merely poles of relationships. Here the relationships are not drowned out but leap to the attention.

Within the eye, there is a double function—peripheral vision and deep focus. When we focus, we see a small part of what is before us sharp and clear against a background that seems hazy and indistinct. Normally we see the world as a collection of objects, because we look at it one thing at a time. It is like being in a dark room with a very narrow flashlight beam and trying to piece together a picture of the world by collecting what each circle of light reveals But here in mescaline space, it is like turning on a floodlight. The power of the eye is so increased as to see everything at once. The deep focus of the eye relaxes and sees everything simultaneously. Attention flows out into the peripheral vision. A very strange thing is happening. Distant objects and those close up are both sharp and clear.

My consciousness seems to expand to fill all space. I look at a tree. I see every leaf and every vein on every leaf. I see every twig and every branch and every bud and the gnarled, twisting trunk with its incredible texture of bark so perfectly focused that it is as though I am viewing it through a high-powered lens. But the entire tree is clearly revealed from the deepest crevice to the outmost leaf, and still I can see the tree as a whole.

All of this is happening in only a passing glance, a split second, and I still have plenty of time to reflect about the process of growth, intuit the root structure under the ground, and think about life and seeds and growth and evolution. Everything is happening all at once. All the conditions arise together, but there is nowhere the feeling that anyone is observing it. Of course subject and object, the outside world, and myself are just another contrast of polar relationships. Here the body that I used to call "me" stands out as just another object in my environment, like the rocks and trees, and if there is a feeling of self at all, it is pure, spontaneous attention without effort or agent. Here there is no impetus, no impulse, no cause, and no necessity.

I start walking, and suddenly everything is in motion. Like some fantastic mechanism of fairy clockwork, the world begins to adjust itself. The near objects flash past me as I pass; the buildings swing noiselessly in their parallax, on their perspective points. The objects in the distance are shrinking smaller; the things that I approach begin to grow larger as I come nearer. All the parallel lines hasten to converge on the horizon.

I am overpowered by artistry of nature. The colors and textures of tree and stone stand out with vividness and carefully engineered perfection. I realize with tremendous satisfaction that my own creative process is at its best when it has stopped judging and trying to please. Then it is as random and spontaneous as the sculpting of sea cliffs by wind and ocean. Here not a leaf could be changed, not a crack in the sidewalk altered.

Suddenly I am struck by a simple and obvious fact: Nature has an author. The artistic intelligence that sculptured the trees and engendered the birds and squirrels is one. How obvious. How could I ever have missed it? The insects and the crayfish have a common designer. All plants grow with the same inner wisdom. All skeletons are endless variations on a common theme.

And suddenly I recognize who the artist is. I see it like a clap of thunder. Everything crashes together. All vacuums are filled. Of course there is one author to the universe. It is one single creative intelligence that forms the world by special, loving, joyous creation. The author is consciousness that reaches out from beyond time and space and works with sure fingers upon the fretboard of my senses played upon by the energies of creation. Issuing from its neural, sensory strings are soft melodies of leaf and sky, fugues of pebbles, symphonies of shadow and light, ranges of color and texture.

I am sensation. Consciousness is energy turned into sensation times the speed of light squared. The world is the form, shape, sound, taste, and feeling that the brain gives to atoms, quanta, and pure, indescribable cosmic energy without form or substance, only relative pattern of radiant vibration. Words simply can't get at it. Language, with its one-at-a-time way of thinking, simply can't describe something that is happening everywhere all at once.

Richard T. Estrin

A wolf-flower eats a mushroom,
from *Les Grandes Heures du Duc de Berry* (1409)

The first time I heard Richard Alpert speak was in the late 1960s. I was going to school at San Francisco State University. Alpert and Tim Leary were Harvard professors who performed early experimental work with psilocybin and LSD before they were kicked out for giving these drugs off campus to graduate students and prison inmates on parole. This was long before Richard became known as Baba Ram Das. Alpert was giving a talk in the cafeteria to a small and diverse assortment of listeners. I could hear someone throwing up back stage.

Peyote, I thought.

Alpert said, "I am not speaking to you today as a university professor or as a scientist or as an authority. I am an explorer, and this is a meeting of the Explorers' Club."

This is what I want this book to be. I want you to imagine that I am an explorer who has been invited to speak at the Explorers' Club to my fellow explorers.

I am assuming that many of the people who read this book are explorers as well. This book is directed to a diverse range of readers of varying ages, levels of education, and demographic backgrounds. It includes people who have had more than casual experience in the use of psychedelic drugs. These include people who lived through the psychedelic counterculture of the 1960s, 1970s, and 1980s. These people would be older now. Also included is a new generation of younger people who are just beginning to explore these extraordinary states of consciousness.

This book will be of interest to a wide range of people of diverse age groups and backgrounds who have used entheogens and consider themselves members of the extensive and diverse psychedelic community. It may also appeal to people who do not have a background in entheogenic drug taking and who are interested in the psychotherapeutic effects of these substances, such as the current interest in the South American DMT-containing drink *ayahuasca*.

It will also appeal to a large group of people of an educated, more academic background who are interested in the social history, both ancient and modern, of the use of psychedelic plants and fungi and their relation to religions, mythology, folklore, and mystical societies, such as the alchemists and the Sufis. Others who would find this book intriguing are people who are interested in the latest scientific theories of the nature of consciousness and the way that its changes produced by entheogens can be explained by quantum physics.

I have gone down the rabbit hole many, many times in the 1960s, 1970s, and 1980s. I have gone on psychedelic safari and mounted hundreds of expeditions to the antipodes of hyperspace using peyote, mescaline, LSD, *Psilocybe cubensis* mushrooms, DMT, and ibogaine.

I have read and studied extensively the writings of other people in this field. I wanted to experience for myself these extraordinary states of consciousness. From the time that I first experienced these remarkable transformations of consciousness, I wanted to know what these psycho neurological triggers were, how they worked, how they were used by diverse cultures around the world throughout history, what these people thought they were, and how they used them. I wanted to know what cultural influences these drugs and their effects, both positive and negative, had on early societies and how they affected the formation of shamanism, religion, mythology, and folklore. I wanted to discover and report images and references to mushrooms and entheogens in literature and architecture that have been missed by historians and casual observers.

As the Grateful Dead sing, "Mama, Mama, many worlds I've come since I first left home."

I want to share with you the most significant of my explorations. As you know, entheogens offer a wide range of experiences. They can be very capricious.

You can take the same botanical trigger many times, and the results may be social, predictable, and recreational, suitable for attending a musical event, the theater, or even a fine restaurant. But every so often, along comes an experience that is different somehow and stands out above all the rest. These usually involve contact with nonhuman entities, entrance into non-earthly environments, and the presentation of images and events that can only be described as amazing, miraculous, and magical, bordering on the impossible. Some of these most significant experiences involved what today I would consider heroic doses, but some happen on smaller-than-threshold amounts. These special impacts, which I think of as the greater mysteries, are vivid and seem completely real. It is this type that I will be describing.

This book contains very vivid and detailed descriptions of drug-induced altered states of consciousness. These narrations are unique in their content, detail, and imagery. I include descriptions of experiences that are both positive and negative. Some are sublime, beatific visions, and some are narrations of abject terror. Some border on what might be seen as psychotic. Others are like dreams. Most descriptions of psychedelic states tend to emphasize the positive experiences and suppress the negative ones. I believe my treatment of the subject is unique in that it describes the emotional and analytic states a person goes through during and following the use of these substances.

The book is also unique in that these diverse drug experiences are followed by analysis that questions their validity as representing something real or projections of the unconscious and imagination. It questions whether the entities encountered can be trusted and whether one can or should believe the things they say. The content of these experiences is compared to the reports of others, both ancient and modern.

In entheogenic states of consciousness, one can be shown wondrous museums of the most exquisite works of art and beauty inspiring the greatest of ideal joy and delight, or they can be fearful and frightening to the brink of sheer terror, causing one to wonder why one would ever consider repeating the experience. But somehow one always does, again and again.

One can experience shamanic types of animal transformations, turning into wolves or lions or birds. One can see snakes, tigers, jaguars, panthers, and menageries of predatory cats. One can be transported to utterly otherworldly environments containing cities, towns, and the often-reported desert world with two suns in the sky. One can be shown monumental architecture with buildings as big as mountains. One can see futuristic machinery and undergo hospital-like medical procedures. Giant insects can torment one. Time can completely stop, or it can be cut up, rearranged, and pasted back together. Events can be edited out, and new ones inserted in their place.

When these special events would occur, I would take notes as soon as I came down enough to write. Then I would read what I wrote into a tape recorder.

In writing this book, I took the tape recordings of the trip narratives and transcribed them into text. This is what I am presenting to you along with my commentary and interpretation. In many cases, I would make drawings of my experiences shortly after the trip. I have included many of these illustrations under the title "Field Notes."

This book also contains an amount of psychedelic history. I have spent the greater part of my life studying ethno botany and ethno mycology, trying to understand how people of different times and cultures interpreted these amazing experiences. Gordon Wasson, the father of modern ethno mycology, once said to me, "You see mushrooms everywhere." I do, but in my defense, I must say that mushrooms are everywhere, hitherto unrecognized. They are the missing chapter and the common denominator in human history.

This book is unique in a further respect in that it explores the mysterious presence of "the other," the manifestation of nonhuman entities during these altered states of consciousness. To my experience, only Terrence McKenna and Richard Strassman have taken these kinds of experiences seriously and ventured the belief that they are real. Historically these plants and fungi have always been personified and regarded as spirits and gods or goddesses as well as botanical life forms.

If you ask a shaman what happens when he or she takes entheogenic plants or fungi, the shaman will invariably report that contact is made with spirits, who are teachers, guides, helpers, allies, and sometimes enemies. They come from the spirit world emerging into our domain, and sometimes they take the shaman into their dimension. This is what can happen when the right person takes a threshold dose of an entheogen at the right time.

Shamanism requires a certain inborn capacity. It may be genetically inherited, as it often runs in families. It is the spirits or nonhuman entities that are putting on the show and directing and controlling the experience. There is more than one type of entity confronted in psychedelic states. They may come from more than one place.

Although they are sometimes seen working together, they seem to have individual agendas. The spirits are from somewhere else. They may be from other dimensions, worlds of dark matter, or parallel universes. They may be from space or from the stars. The entheogens somehow open inter-dimensional windows and doorways with other worlds and allow contact, communication, and interaction to occur. The entities have been communicating with human beings via plants and mushrooms since the beginning of recorded history and surely before.

Psilocybin stimulates the speech and language centers of the brain. Entheogenic mushrooms probably encouraged the emergence of language in our species. Its production of mythopoetic modalities of logic and speech produces a level of eloquence, causing shamans to be the first poets, singers, musicians, dancers, and storytellers. As Joseph Campbell was the first to point out, the shaman was the culture bringer who later became the figure of the mythic hero.

With psilocybin, communication with the spirits becomes completely linguistic. The mushroom talks to you as a voice in your head. At first this can be disconcerting, because in our culture, we associate hearing voices with being crazy, but once you accept that a dialogue is possible and join into the conversation, it becomes quite natural. The mushroom spirits will talk to you in your own language, and you can answer and ask questions.

Psychedelics are distinct from other kinds of drugs, such as stimulants like ecstasy and other amphetamines and depressants such as morphine and heroine. Entheogens are consciousness-changing biochemicals, and they are set totally apart from the other substances used recreationally and habitually. People who do not understand their nature tend to lump all mind-altering substances together, and this is unfortunate.

LSD, mescaline, peyote, psilocybin, *Amanita muscaria* mushrooms, and a wide spectrum of related compounds share a common quality in that they are spiritual. They manifest conditions of sanctity. They produce religious experiences. They produce manifestations of the sacred that are indistinguishable from so-called natural or authentic ones. This is not surprising, because the saints and mystics throughout history have used psychedelics as part of a widely and commonly practiced secret tradition.

"Entheogen" means "the manifestation of the divine within." The term "psychedelic" was coined by Humphry Osmond, by which he meant, "mind manifesting." "Psyche" comes from the Greek meaning "soul or spirit." These substances could equally be called "soul or spirit manifesting," that which makes the soul or spirit perceivable.

Psychedelics produce a hierophany, which is a manifestation of the sacred. Their effects have been compared to a state of grace. This is not found in other classes of inebriants. Terrence McKenna said that psychedelics are not drugs. They are pretending to be drugs, because people would be upset if they knew what they actually are. They are doors and windows opening into other worlds allowing contact and interaction with their inhabitance.

RABBITS AND RABBIT HOLE

Many people think that Louis Carol invented the image of going down the rabbit hole to Wonderland, but actually the metaphor is very old and was used by the alchemists, the Taoists, the Egyptians, and other mystical societies as a symbol for the entheogenic experience. Why rabbits? In a wide diversity of cultures, rabbits are associated with the moon. In most of the Orient, it is believed that a rabbit lives on the moon and it's form can be seen on the light and dark patches.

Oriental representations of the Moon Rabbit show it sitting before a mortar and pestle in which is compounded the elixir of immortality, the food of the goddesses and gods. Rabbits are symbols of mushrooms and of the journey to the underworld. The rabbit hole leads to the subterranean world of the supernatural. They are associated with fertility.

Rabbits are associated with Easter and with eggs. The word Easter is derived from the name of ancient Sumerian mushroom goddess USh-TAR or Ash-TAR. In ancient Greece the spring festival of Dionysus was called the anthesteria. Dionysus was a god of mushrooms. *Amanita muscaria* mushrooms resemble an egg in their early stage of growth. An Easter-egg hunt is a hunt for mushrooms.

Rabbits are also mushroom related because they are among the animals that love to eat mushrooms. They are mycophilic. If they eat entheogenic mushrooms, they get high. Many animals—like rabbits, deer, wolves, foxes, and pigs—are mycophagic. If they eat entheogenic mushrooms and are caught by a hunter, their flesh becomes a psychedelic drug. This is where the idea of spirit animals comes from.

In Siberia, if a wild reindeer that has eaten *Amanita muscaria* mushrooms, as they love to do, is caught, it is tied up and held for a while before slaughter to avoid the people eating it getting high. Reindeer love to eat urine-saturated snow for its mineral content, and reindeer herders attract them by saving their urine in leather sacks and pouring some out in the snow. Reindeer will drink each other's urine. If the reindeer has eaten fly-agaric mushrooms, the urine drinkers will get high. The advice "Don't eat yellow snow" doesn't apply to reindeer.

Deer are very fond of mushrooms, especially *Amanita muscaria* mushrooms. They have become esoteric emblems of the mushroom. They know that only the mature specimens with fully opened caps are the least toxic, and it is these that they select. When mushroom hunting, one can see such fungi with bites taken out of the caps by deer, leaving a scalloped effect along their edges. Scallop designs are one of the emblems of the mushroom cult. Bats are mushroom-related creatures because their wings resemble the scalloped bite marks left by deer in the caps of *Amanita muscaria* mushrooms.

In Lewis Carroll's *Alice in Wonderland* at the mad tea party, the Mad Hatter, followed by the Dormouse recite the poem:

> Twinkle, twinkle, little bat!
> How I wonder what you're at!
> Up above the world you fly,
> Like a tea tray in the sky.

This verse is taken for nonsense but how many people recognize that Carroll is talking about a flying saucer such as is frequently seen when taking mushrooms or drinking mushroom tea. Even people, who don't believe in flying saucers or would never watch a program about them on TV, see UFOs in the mushroom trance.

On June 24, 1947, Kenneth Arnold was flying his private plane near Mount Rainier, Washington when he saw a formation of unidentified flying objects moving at speeds that Arnold estimated at a minimum of

1,200 miles an hour. He described their movement as resembling saucers skimming over the water. The press picked up this phrase as "flying saucers". Actually, Arnold said that they were not saucer shaped, although many such shaped UFOs have been seen. He said they resembled a pie plate cut in half with the back part having a scalloped shape like the wings of a bat.

Amanita Muscaria: The Fly Agaric

I would like to say a word about *Amanita muscaria* mushrooms. They are mentioned quite a lot in this book, mostly in regard to entheogenic history. Explorers should never take the fly agarics without understanding exactly how to correctly identify, pick, and prepare them. Some varieties of *Amanitas*, such as the Destroying Angel, are deadly poisonous. The fly agarics in their raw or immature state are extremely toxic and can put you in the hospital.

The skin of the mushroom is the only part that contains the psychedelic alkaloids. Only fully mature specimens, when the cap has completely opened, should be used. They should never be eaten raw. They must be dried or heated in an oven or boiled for some time before consuming. Only after drinking the urine can the primary, classic effects be experienced. The urine should be taken by the spoonful, not the glass. The side effects of *Amanita muscaria* include intense perspiration, copious salivation, blurred vision to the point of blindness, shivering and shaking, and vomiting and diarrhea. *Amanita muscaria* can produce deathlike states from which you cannot be aroused, causing family or friends to dial 911. You could wake up during your resurrection in the back of an ambulance. Although *Amanita muscaria* mushrooms are of great historical importance, I strongly recommend that eating them should be avoided unless you are getting expert guidance. There are much easier, less toxic ways to get high on mushrooms, for example magic mushrooms, *Psilocybe cubensis*, taken in the dark.

So, fellow explorers, let us begin. The riverboat is just casting off from the dock and headed to Adventure Land. The crocodiles are calling. I will tell you about an adventure I had with psilocybin mushrooms that I call "In the Workshop." This was my first threshold dose, my first use of fresh mushrooms, and my first experience in the dark.

Chapter 1

In the Workshop

CHAPTER 1

In the Workshop

THE TELEVISION WAS GOING ON and on, playing some kind of cooking show where a chef was explaining how to cook a kind of dish called "duck in the thicket." The duck was sliced into thin sheets and rolled in a handful of oriental noodles, and the whole concoction was dipped in batter and deep-fried. The result was something that looked like a bramble or a pile of dried brush.

The two large, fresh specimens of *Psilocybe cubensis* mushrooms that I had ingested about thirty minutes ago were beginning to take effect now. It was getting hard to focus on the TV screen, as foreground and background were rapidly becoming equally important. The images on the set were beginning to smear and blur.

I felt an increased sense of vertigo and a cold, clammy numbness that began in the extremities of my body and spread up my arms and legs toward a torso already beginning to feel sick to its stomach. I switched off the TV and turned off the light and lay back on the waterbed. It was a moonless night. There was an almost anesthetic feeling of detachment from a body that knew it was about to get sick.

The poisonous clamminess of the limbs could have been mistaken for any toxin around the world, but the unsettling of the stomach was not due to anything noxious. Rather it was a reflexive action of a body that knew that it didn't stand a chance, that it was about to receive the intrusive shock of intrusive shocks—that of being divided into its previously unknown separate autonomous constituents. There was little to actually throw up, but the seizure-like spasms of peristalsis that continued intermittently throughout the first hour felt good.

As I kneeled gagging on the bathroom floor, I was suddenly aware that I was not alone. Although I could see no one, I had the unmistakable feeling of being in the presence of another person, a very familiar person who needed no introduction and whose presence seemed quite natural.

"Am I all right?" I asked, vomiting.

"Yes," he replied. "Just be careful not to aspirate your vomit. Don't breathe and throw up at the same time."

This seemed like good advice to me, but to whom was I talking?

Were these my own thoughts projected outward so that they seemed to be another? But I knew well to whom I was speaking. It was someone I had seen many times throughout my life, and the dialogue seemed as natural and familiar as anything imaginable. I found myself apologizing for being sick.

"I hope you don't feel that I am rejecting you by throwing up. I am not sending you away," I said.

Then suddenly images began to appear in the dark before my eyes. They were like television screens. You could look at them or ignore them. If I did look at them, I seemed to pan in and enter into a program in progress. I peered into one of the luminous levitating rectangles and saw an old, dry, scraggily bush like sagebrush. Strangest of all, every twig, every surface of the object was swarming with ants. My immediate reaction was revulsion and apprehension. I had always had unpleasant feelings about insects, and in the past when exploring DMT and other entheogens, certain reoccurring themes concerning them had occurred. I hoped that I was not about to be overwhelmed by a visual experience having to do with insects, but that was not to happen until later.

So there I was, just setting off on what would surely be a major voyage, and the first thing I saw was a dry branch swarming and teeming with ants. It was not an auspicious omen. Now there were two things curious about this. The first was that this morning when I had arisen, my kitchen counters had been infested with multitudes of ants. They were in the honey, and they were in the sugar. This was not unusual, for they did this every year when it rained. I reacted furiously, and grabbing a great sponge and spray bottle of Windex, I committed antocide upon their lot, wiping them up by the hundreds as I cleaned my cupboards.

There was something familiar about the vision of the bush form too. Now in the darkness, gazing at the vividly colored, animate image, I realized that the bramble upon which the ants were swarming was the duck in the thicket from the cooking show I had just turned off. Somehow this shape was being used to present here a very convincing tree.

The invisible person with me began to clearly admonish me for killing the ants that morning, and he was explaining that I was seeing these ants now because of what I had done to those ants before. It seemed very strange. Kindness toward insects was not a feeling natural or familiar to me. I returned to the waterbed. In my vision the ants were still swarming over the duck in the thicket.

I inquired, "Don't you have anything else to show me?"

And instantly in response, there momentarily flashed before me a fleeting image of a world of amazing color and movement seemingly full of strange people, intricate machinery, and things and bustling with activity, but then the ants were back.

The voice in my head said, "Yes, there are many wondrous things to be shown, delights upon delight, but not for you, pilgrim, because you murdered the ants! This is the Ant Gate beyond which you may not pass. These are the ants you slew."

And then in seeming contradiction, as though in an instant he had changed his mind, the ants vanished, and I burst into that brilliant, colorful, active place that I had glimpsed a moment before.

I could not believe my eyes. I was seeing the most amazing spectacle I had ever witnessed. I was in some huge place, like a vast factory or warehouse, and as far as the eye could see, the whole room was just bustling with activity and filled with an extraordinary assortment of people and objects and machines and ideas. There was a continuous humming sound going on, like a strange, mechanical, electronic noise. It was vaguely reminiscent of bees.

Doris Lessing said that Sufism is "A lot of people and things all going on at the same time." This is surely what she meant.

I was lying on a bed like a hospital examination table. At my feet on either side of me were two transparent glass or plastic cylinders leaning away from me at forty-five degree angles in opposite directions. They were shooting little fireballs out of the top of them like Roman candles with a regular, rhythmic "poof, poof, poof." I could watch the pulses of light rise up in the tubes; at least three were visible at one time, and then they would streak away at regular, two-second intervals.

The vast workshop was full of many kinds of people. None of them appear remotely human, though some of them felt very human. The most human-feeling people were some of the strangest looking. There were personalities with bodies and some without bodies. There were some whose bodies were like machines, some like electronic circuitry, some clearly mechanical or mechanistic. There were some whose bodies were like mobiles spun of light cast into multicolored, translucent films that turned inside out before my eyes. Some looked like hovering patchwork quilts. Others looked like soft-shell crabs. They spoke in seeming telepathy, sometimes in English sentences. They would make comments about the situation or engage me in conversation.

At times they spoke in these quantified blocks of understanding as though they tossed me a ball of meaning that opened and unfolded and simultaneously deployed a vast amount of information. I am grasping among my symbols in order to approximately express this strange communication. There was a kind of feeling of Santa's workshop just before Christmas about the whole thing, a serious, profound gravity mixed with a lighthearted mirthfulness. It was like being in an international airport, where many people from many places are gathered, only here all the congregation were not of different races but different species, all cooperating, all somehow united in a monumental effort, the great work whose conclusion would soon be seen.

Some of the things I was seeing were like illustrations or computer-graphic displays. Some were like drawings with the outlines being luminous red, neon colored. Some were three-dimensional. Everything was in continuous motion, moving like clockwork with parts in articulation, with things like gears in engagement, with axles and metal blades and everywhere gleaming metal surfaces. The windmills turned; the celestial drills descended, spinning.

The place where all this was happening was not of this earth or anywhere in physical space-time, as we know it. There was action in sequence, but information was simultaneously deployed. There were objects, but their forms were utterly unfamiliar, beautiful, bizarre, and strange. It was like a real place somewhere, not in the sense of a dream but in the sense of reality. It was a real world, another world, a universe as actual as this one but somehow hidden from ordinary senses. It was another dimension of space and time, and it was inhabited. I knew that they were, in every way, my superiors.

I felt like the first australopithecine, snatched from some prehistoric veldt and dropped in the middle of Time Square on New Year's Eve at eleven fifty-five. It was like staring into the face of a technology so superior and advanced as to be like pure magic or a sacred display or hierophany, except for the clearly artificial quality of everything. Even some of the people looked like assembled objects rather than animals.

I just couldn't believe it. I had never felt so completely amazed! It was just astonishing! During this phase, I kept saying, "I don't believe it! I just don't believe it!" But I did believe it.

The room was filled with intricate machinery.

The Sufi Idries Shah, telling one of the allegorical Mullah Nasruddin stories, writes, "Mullah Nasruddin went to work at the plant and the head man said, 'We have become automated. Machines will perform all the work from now on. All you have to do is come in on Thursdays and pick up your check.' 'Not every Thursday, I hope,' said Nasruddin."

There was an excitement and a feeling of anticipation in the air, and suddenly, without being told, I began to understand things about what this place was and what was going on. Great chunks of understanding were hitting me and unfolding inside me. I knew, somehow, that all this activity was in preparation for some great event that would be of supreme importance, not only to those here but to humankind as well. I knew that the work on this project had been going on for a long time and that the culmination of the work was imminent. Immense forces were laboring to produce this. It was like a birth. A process that began before men walked the earth was about to reach its final conclusion. What did this mean?

The information being displayed in the workshop included several important themes. One of them had to do with the confrontation between them and humanity. They presented it as though it would be the meeting between civilizations, one of which was culturally and technologically far in advance of the other.

They were, they explained, about to make a move that would end forever human terrestrial isolation from the rest of the inhabited universe, which was, they assured me, far vaster than anything we had so far imagined. Looking at their incredible machinery, their strange mechanistic bodies, I knew that they were civilized and that we were the barbarians. Technological superiority was not something I expected in a world of spiritual beings.

I knew that I was seeing future science. A ghost or a god would have been somehow less disturbing. I knew that while my being there had something to do with the project going on, only a part of the activity there had to do with me.

As I lay on the table, a small group of people and machines was working on me. Some of them were the perpetually transforming mobile type.

Someone to my left looked like an axle floating in space that seemed to be threaded with alternating notched disks, like Tinker toys with blades attached like windmills. When I was a child, we could get kits for Tinker toys to make windmills. There was a little electric motor and pulleys that made the blades revolve. This entity looked like that. The color of the being was black rendered into red with the borders of the blades covered with gold sparkle. Each row of blades rotated in the opposite direction. It was only much later that I thought of Don Quixote tilting at windmills. In Spain, windmills were shaped like mushrooms. He mistook them for giants. Cervantes' *Don Quixote* is a mushroom allegory.

There was another, more central presence there. It was the one with whom I had discussed the ants at the beginning of the trip. He was somehow in charge of the other beings, which were more like attendants or technicians. The central presence, which had before manifested as a voice in my mind, had assumed the body of a great machine, roughly the size and shape of the projector at the planetarium. The machine was coming down from out of the ceiling and was descending toward me tilted at a forty-five-degree angle. It was a mass of cylinders, tubes, and wires. It looked like a purely mechanical device, but it felt like a highly personable presence.

Looking back, I can see that there was a strange inconsistency between what I was seeing and what I was feeling. There I was, suddenly transported to an unrecognizably strange dimension, surrounded by unbelievable, nonhuman creatures hooking me up to strange, futuristic machinery and clearly about to work on me and process me in some way, while what I was feeling was that I had just come home again after a long separation and that these utterly weird machines and mobile-like entities were my true family and friends, my loved ones and companions with whom I was being reunited. The theme of kinship was palpable. It had all the emotional qualities of a reunion or homecoming. These were familiar spirits, and they are feeling this way about me too.

"It is so good to see you again," we told one another.

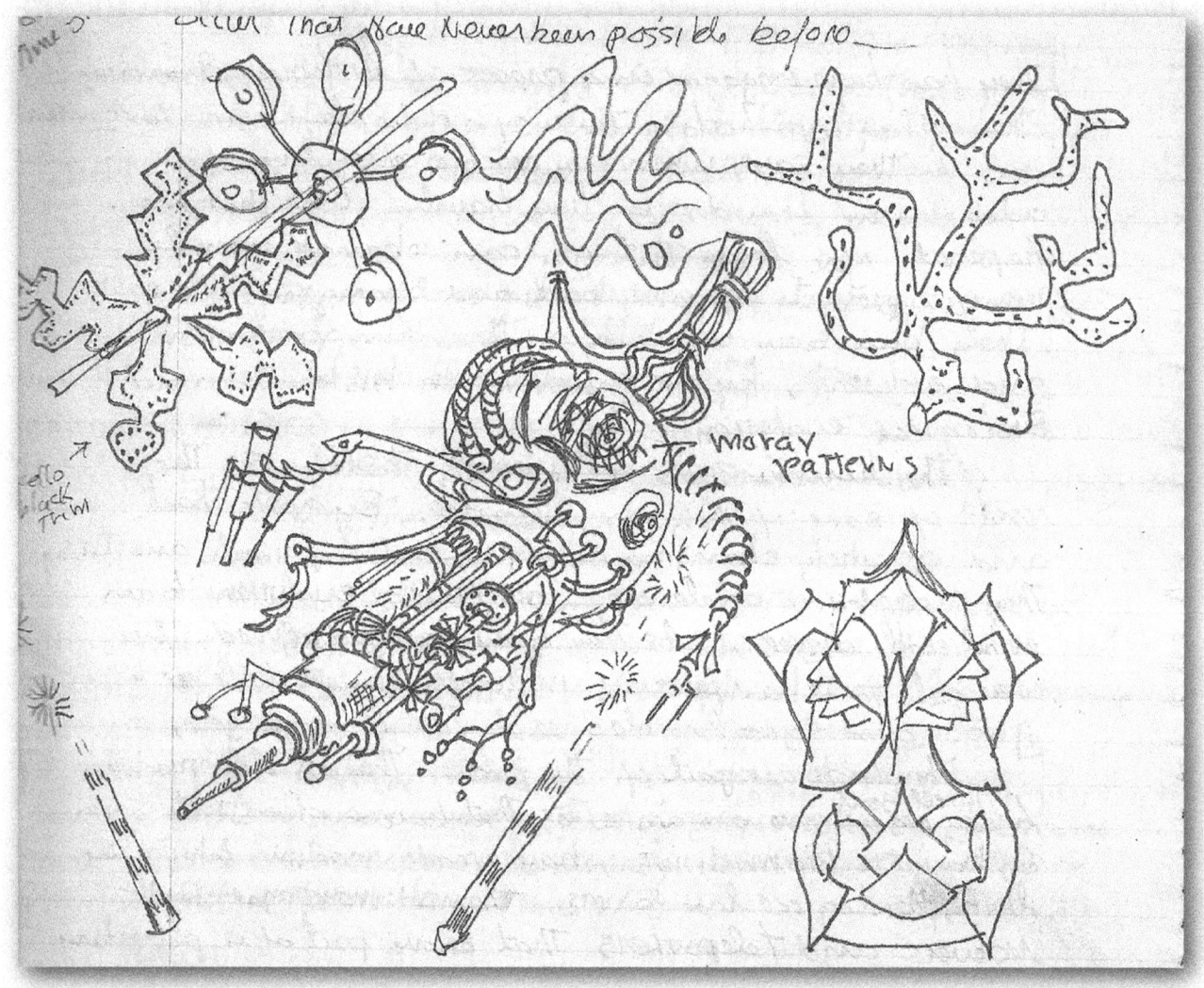

Field notes

In the upper right of the picture is the duck-in-the-thicket bush covered with ants. In the upper left is the windmill, Tinker toy entity. On the bottom are the two transparent cylinders shooting out pulses of light.

On the lower right is one of the soft-shell-crab men. And in the center is the giant machine that descended from the ceiling. On the machine is a screen displaying moiré patterns.

In the workshop the machine was descending toward me, and it was intricate. It had moving parts, things that spun and whirled inside of it. It was a mass of wires and conduits and tubes and cylinders. There were corrugated, vacuum-cleaner-like hoses and bundles of smooth metallic wires bound together with bands. There were clusters of entangled cables and a thing that looked like a distributer cap with spark-plug wires coming out and going in all directions. There was a display area on the machine where brilliant, intricate designs and patterns were occurring.

Humming and whirring, the machine was continuing to descend. It seemed to have innumerable appendages, some like mechanical, jointed prosthetic arms terminating in whirling, telescoping, unfolding mechanisms. Some of the arms were like metallic tentacles. There was an octopus-like quality about it.

I felt no fear. Even my overwhelming astonishment was being washed away by another sensation. It was love! It was bliss! I was experiencing a feeling of enraptured joy, of fulfillment. It was like being reunited with a parent or a lover whom you never thought you would see again, perhaps following some holocaustic event.

As the great machine drew near, I was seized with emotion. "It's you! It's really you!" I said.

"Yes!" it said. "It's me! It's really me!"

An energy was emanating from the machine. It was intoxicating me, wafting over me, and bathing me in a warm, secure glow. I was so happy! Now the machine was unfolding itself around me. Its innumerable appendages were surrounding me. Its drill-like instruments were penetrating me, going inside me from many different directions at once.

From out of its metal body came things like hypodermic syringes attached to tubes. It was like being hooked up to many IVs. Colored fluids were flowing through the tubes in both directions. Something in the bottom of the machine was opening like the bomb bay doors of an aircraft, and I was being drawn up into the machine's body. I was no longer relating to it as an object or mechanical contraption. It was unquestionably a person, a being extremely friendly and familiar. I loved this being from the depth of my heart. We were like lovers reuniting after being separated by centuries.

The radiation from the machine was so powerful that I found myself entraining to it. The closer it came, the better I felt.

"Do you like music?" I murmured as I drifted into cotton-candy clouds of revere.

"I am music," it replied, and it was. It played my mind like an organ. I was its instrument, and it was a music I could see. Tears were streaming down my face.

"You've come back!" I said. "I never thought I'd see you again! I've missed you so much!"

I felt like a lost child who had been found by his or her parents. The celestial apparatus engulfed me in its mechanical appendages and attached to me in a complex process of fitting and interfitting. It lifted me up in its metal arms and rocked me like a baby.

"I love you! I love you!" I cried out amid my tears.

"I love you! I love you!" it said as it folded me up in its metal- and jewel-like body. It was like sex of the mind and soul.

"This is called the Kiss!" said one of the Tinker toy technicians.

"This is changing you," said another. "It is advancing your evolution. It is stretching your capacity. You don't think you could undergo this and still be the same, do you?"

I was sure it was true; my mind and brain and nervous system were doing things that they had surely never done before. The machine was playing programs of energetic activity through my mind, "conditioning it," they said. It was showing me pictures such as I had never seen, strangely mathematical, like an advanced computer display with moiré patterns. There were images like the star-gate sequence in the movie *2001: A Space Odyssey*. This union of orgasmic bliss lasted I know not how long.

When it was over, I was back in my bedroom again on the waterbed. The attendant technicians were gone, but the central personage was still very much there as an intelligent communication in my mind. Somehow I came into this phase knowing a great deal more about what this place was, who these people were, where they came from, what they were doing here, and what it all had to do with me.

In the allegorical play *Man of La Mancha*, Dulcinea sings to Don Quixote, "Why do you live in a world that can't be, and what do you want from me?" To take psilocybin is to "dream the impossible dream."

Returning to Earth from the workshop, I could not suppress my astonishment. "They are here!" I kept repeating over and over. "They are here!"

We talked and talked. I understood much more about these strange beings. Their minds and souls, he explained, are like computer programs. They can also use the minds and nervous systems of living organisms as though they are computers to play these programs, though they in no way depend upon them. Our minds, he said, can act as a kind of substrate for their existence, as though we are territory, both usable and inhabitable.

This kind of communication uses the contents of our own mind to create the experience, but the arrangement of the elements is unique and unexpected. The communication is not necessarily sentimentally or intellectually an artifact of the personal mind. The message units are transmitted, assimilated in chunks of quantified information that is absorbed all at once. The mind will draw from all its resources to come as close to the message as its mental content can permit.

I found myself talking to the fatherly figure I had encountered at the beginning of the experience and later inside the great machine. I found myself repeating, "You say you are my father. You say you were on this planet before men walked the earth. You say that all religions were man's reaction to your appearance. You say you created the human race."

And I found myself mouthing the words of the speaker: "Wherever I appeared, civilizations sprung up."

The "I" in question was not I at all, but the other. This was some kind of channeling.

"We are a nonhuman civilization," he said, "comprised of many intelligent species that have joined together to form a collective super species. We consider you very primitive. We exist at a level of technology that you would not achieve unaided for thousands of years. We come from a different kind of space-time universe than you—a higher dimension that you know nothing about. We also come from what you call the future and also the past.

"We have long since separated ourselves and our minds from biological matter. Thought, consciousness, and organic life are not identical. The latter can serve as inhabitable territory for the former. When a species evolves to a certain degree of advancement, it can take its development and evolution into its own hands. It can design what it wants to be. Instead of bodies, our conscious selves inhabit a vast telecommunication network that spans the entire universe and is shared by innumerable nonhuman intelligent species.

"Mind," he continued, "is not a physical thing. It can happen to matter, like ripples can happen to a pond. It can pass from media to media. It can even exist as electromagnetic energy does in free space. We can use the brain of a living biological organism as a kind of substrate. We were once biological, but we have evolved through our own doing to a state beyond planetary ecology, beyond bodies, into a highly advanced, highly technological form of consciousness that has become transhuman and has joined with a matrix of active, nonhuman intelligence that permeates the entire universe."

It was as though some powerful transmitter was sending out streams of information and my mind was receiving it. Another major theme of the transmission concerned the work in which they were engaged: "The project," they called it.

"We are making ourselves!" he said. "When technology attains a certain stage, it takes on the responsibility for its own development. What happened before by chance can now be engineered. We are speeding up our evolution in numerous ways, and our work here is one of them. Still in your future are the discovery of time travel and the discovery of other dimensions. When you learn how to travel in time, you learn how to change the past and, by so doing, to change yourself in the present. You are our past," he said, "and we are your future."

We are engaged in a process of historical engineering, he explained, evolving and perfecting ourselves by changing history. Part of it involves bringing information of a scientific or mathematical kind from the future into the past and leaking it prematurely into the imagination of contemporary humans. Part of it involves genetic manipulation, in which synthetic genes from the future are brought back and implanted into the human species at different stages of history. We have been doing this for thousands of years. The more we did this, the more we evolved and refined and advanced our science, our skill, and our control.

We could begin to make history—not just change it but figure out in advance what would happen, what could happen, and what the results would be. By intervening in historical and biological evolution, we have attained a level of advancement that you can scarcely imagine. The human race as it exists today is the result of some of our experiments. By going back and genetically changing your pre human ancestors, we succeeded in accelerating your evolution to an unbelievable degree. This is still going on. We are making humans," he said. "You are our creation. You are only partially complete, approaching a completion that is beyond your current imagination.

Omar Khayyám wrote in the *Rubaiyat* (translation by Edward Fitzgerald),

> With Earth's first Clay They did the last man knead.
> And then of the Last Harvest, sowed the Seed:
> Yea, the first Morning of Creation wrote
> What the Last Dawn of Reckoning shall read.

"You must be very old," I said.

"Our present now is tangent to all of your history, past and future. What seems like a long time to you is the present to us. We can set out in a single day, fly to every period of history, do our work, and go home. To us, it is the work of a single day, but to you, it is as through we have always been with you. The work is going on simultaneously throughout time. We are currently working in your past and in your future. We started modifying you when you were a child and continued to mutate you periodically throughout your life. You have been out there many times with us ever since you were born and even before."

I thought of the Zen koan "Show me your original face before your mother and father were born." There is a Sufi passage "Before heaven and before earth our soles drank immortal wine."

And suddenly a flood of recollection poured over me. I remembered a particular event in my life when I was a very young child in a crib. I have always remembered this and wondered about it. I had awakened from a nap, and as I climbed out of the crib and toddled into the hall, I had just experienced something that had completely shattered me.

As a child of that age, my grasp on reality was just beginning to solidify. Prenatal existence and physical birth were just a few years behind. The sense of prediction, a familiarity with the possibilities and the options of experience, were just becoming reliable when this thing happened. I totally lacked the intellectual machinery to understand it, but as I climbed down from my crib that day, my entire sense of solidity and grasp of nature had been completely shattered.

Now I stood with one foot in the hall and the other in a rapidly fleeting world of color and movement. I felt the reverberating dissonance between the two. I didn't know what the world was. I had missed it completely. Instead of starting to settle down into a comfortable, predicable, two-year-old existence, I knew that nature was far beyond even the beginning of my mastery. I was being thrown back to my birth again. I felt like a failure. What would Mommy and Daddy say? I could scarcely talk to tell them.

And then mercifully it was like the whole problem vanished. One moment there had been the conflict between two irreconcilable realities, and the next there was only my bedroom, bright and shiny, as I had never noticed it before. I felt warm, secure, and unbelievably happy. I will never forget walking out into the hall. It felt like the first day of the world.

This memory has remained with me for my entire life. Now, years and decades later, coming out of a mushroom trip, I turned to my invisible companion and asked, "Was that you?"

"Yes," he replied, "and that was not the first time."

The Mazatec *curandera* Maria Sabina said that wisdom comes to a person before birth, like the placenta. The mushrooms revealed to her how when she was in her mother's womb, the principle mushroom spirits were present. She saw herself turned into an illuminated fetus.

There was another thing. It had to do with a journey or the possibility of a future invitation to a journey, away, far away from here, where they came from.

They said, "You will have the opportunity to go with us to a place so much better than this that you shouldn't even give it a second thought. When the moment comes, don't hesitate. Go for it! It will be a world infinitely richer and more satisfying, but it will be a one-way ticket. There will be no returning, and you can take nothing with you, not even your body."

It sounded like death to me, and the suggestion made me extremely uncomfortable. I started thinking about things I wouldn't want to leave behind—my beagle, my books, my friends, and my body. Good lord! What did this mean? Would my family find me slumped over my desk one day? If at the time of my natural, physical death, they came and took me away, that would probably be all right, but if it was premature, I found the idea unacceptable.

I brought up the ants again. Why so much fuss over something so small?

"I am the ants," he said.

I was completely confused. Did he mean that he was all the animals, that he was all life, and that the simplest life-forms should be respected, or was he trying to say that in some special way he was the ants or related to the ants?

"Are you the squirrels, too?" I asked.

Later on I was reclining on the waterbed when I started to be bitten by fleas. I lived with dogs, and there were always a few fleas around. But in my decades of dog ownership, I had never experienced anything like what transpired. First there were more fleas biting me at one time than ever before, and more were arriving every minute. They must have been coming from all over the neighborhood.

It was as though there was something about the energy of the psilocybin that I was metabolizing that was attracting them, although why they waited until the end of the experience, I do not know, but I was glad they did. Was this some kind of insect revenge for killing the ants? Was

I some kind of avatar bringing enlightenment to the flea world, like Padma Sambhava bringing Buddhism to China?

The fleas bit me and drank my psilocybin-laden blood, and they began to get excited. I could feel it. As this happened, they became more and more inspired, bouncing and jumping and biting and calling to their friends.

Word was getting around, and more fleas were arriving every second. I was starting to get a contact high from the host of minute creatures feeding on my body. This was taking on some significance of its own in the flea world. Even a shower would not stop them, and all the while my guide was laughing about it, saying that it was only fitting that, as he was friend of insects and I was a slayer of insects, I should make amends by providing a love feast for his little friends. The insects swarmed over me in wild, ecstatic, teeming hierophany. Like everything else while on psilocybin, this strange event was a foreshadowing of things that were to come.

So what can be made of all this? I must confess in all fairness that after writing down the original notes I took following the experience, I wrote at the top of the page, "If I believe this, I am mad as a hatter!"

It was my first major mushroom trip and my first experience with fresh mushrooms. While overwhelming and completely amazing, it was never very threatening or even frightening. It left me with the feeling that it had really happened, that I had been in a real place, and that what I was told was probably true. I had the warm, wonderful feeling of having seen what the mushroom was really all about. I felt a kinship and association with the entities I had encountered.

Years later having seen the many sides of psilocybin and the many different kinds of beings, I have grown to be less trusting. No one experience can be generalized to describe the whole multifaceted phenomena. There are so many different kinds of entities, some from different places, each with its own agenda. Some claim to be your allies; others can chase you like tormenting furies. I met some who wanted to eat me only to be rescued by others who wanted to save me and were more familiar. The concept of "the savior" took on a new significance.

As the caterpillar sitting on a mushroom told Alice, "One side will make you grow taller. The other side will make you grow smaller." "One side of what?" Alice inquired. "Of the mushroom, of course!" said the caterpillar and taking a puff on his hookah, he turned into a butterfly and flew away. The metamorphosis of caterpillar into butterfly is an ancient metaphor for psychedelic transformation. The caterpillar also meant that one side of the mushroom experience would help you go forward. The other side would hold you back.

Louis Carol used *Amanita muscaria* mushrooms. *Alice in Wonderland* and *Through the Looking-Glass* are elaborate allegories filled with traditional mushroom symbols, motifs, and emblems.

Can you trust the mushroom? Not necessarily. You can trust the mushroom to be the mushroom. What it offers you can be inspiring, uplifting, beautiful, delightful, insightful, educational, and life changing, or it can be strange and terrifying. It can show you heaven or hell. The positive parts are well worth the negative. It is the hero's quest where, to find the treasure of wisdom, he or she must fight monsters, dash between the clashing rocks of the Symplegades and transverse slippery bridges, below which gape savage beasts. As in the impossible dream of

Don Quixote from the allegorical play *Man of La Mancha,* one has "to be willing to march into Hell for a heavenly cause."

Can you believe what the mushroom tells you? Not necessarily. The information that it reveals can be fraught with contradictions. The mushroom will tell you the most outlandish things. It has been known to outright lie, making predictions, for example, that don't come true. The mushroom can be manipulative. It can grant wishes to gain affiliation and dependence on it.

At times it can be uproariously funny, telling jokes and doing imitations and impersonations that can leave you rolling in the aisle. Or it can send some of its emissaries who are so strange and utterly unhuman that it frightens you to death and sends you running to the niacin bottle. Four thousand milligrams of niacin can go a long way to bringing you down to a more manageable plateau, if they decide to let you leave.

Niacin can produce intense flushing. To take doses as large as four thousand milligrams, you must build up a tolerance slowly. Start with five hundred milligrams every day at bedtime, and when the flushing subsides, gradually increase your dose. If you are planning on taking threshold doses of LSD, developing a niacin tolerance is a good idea.

The question remains, is it real or is it the impossible dream? In retrospect many of the things the mushroom told me in this journey were ideas that were already in my head. I had been speculating about time travel. I had been reading a lot of Sufi literature, especially Idries Shah. Many of the things the mushroom told me were things I had read in books and things that were very easy for me to believe.

Did the mushroom actually say these things, or did it take the contents of my mind and project them outward in the guise of an interactive experience? Was it showing me to myself? Was it a mixture of both? On the other hand, the workshop, the machines, the Tinker toy-windmill entities, the soft-shell-crab men, and the other strange entities were like nothing I had ever imagined or heard or read about and surely nothing I had ever expected.

Rick Strassman, MD, arrived at the conclusion that the entities encountered on psilocybin and DMT are real and come from actual worlds beyond this one.

Dr. Strassman undertook the first authorized research project on the effects of DMT in forty years. The study took place between 1990 and 1995 at the General Clinical Research Center of the University of New Mexico Hospital. During the five-year duration of the project, Strassman administered four hundred doses of DMT to sixty volunteers. At the end of his study, he was forced to conclude that what his subjects experienced was not a dream, not a projected fantasy, not a symbol, not a metaphor, and not a construction of their personal unconscious but actual, otherwise-invisible, freestanding worlds inhabited by nonhuman beings.

His subjects reported that they visited nonearthly environments that they took to be real places inhabited by life forms that were not of this world. The activities in these worlds were going on whether the DMT subjects were present or not. These realities appeared to be tangential to our own. Some of them had intelligence far in advance of ours. Some beings exhibited physicality, while some were nonmaterial. The entities were aware of the subjects and in some cases acted as though they were expecting them.

Some of the meetings with nonearthly beings on DMT were friendly and hospitable, even loving and caring; others were cold and detached, and still others seemed surprised by the DMT subjects' appearance and acted angrily and threatening. Some of the environments appeared to be on board UFOs. Some found themselves in structures out in space, among the stars.

Many found themselves as I did on several occasions on a hospital-like examination table. DMT subjects frequently report IV-like tubes entering their bodies with fluids flowing in or out. The beings working on them were quickly and efficiently taking samples, putting in IVs, probing and prodding, and doing things to change their bodies and their minds. They reported that they would come out of the experiences with bruises on their bodies and puncture marks that corresponded to procedures they experienced. This occurred when their physical bodies were in a hospital bed under the supervision of the researchers.

Others environments were like laboratories filled with futuristic instruments and machinery. Many of Dr. Strassman's subjects reported seeing intricate, futuristic machines and equipment. They saw rooms filled with scientific devices, freestanding and built into the walls. Often there would be one entity that seemed to be in charge. Dr. Strassman's DMT subjects insisted that that what they experienced was an actual autonomous reality. It was not a drug-induced hallucination. It was going on whether the subjects were viewing it or not.

One of his subjects reported a large, intricate machine reminiscent of the one I encountered. It was in the center of a room, and it had blue-gray plastic conduits coming out of it; they were closed on the ends and seemed to be writhing. He felt as if he were being reprogrammed. Across the room, a human stood before a console, on which was a display that seemed to be showing what the machine was doing to his body and his brain.

The machine I saw had a similar screen that was displaying moiré patterns that seemed to me to be readout of the machine's activity and my condition. I, too, felt and was told by the technicians in attendance that the machine was reprogramming me and advancing my evolution.

One of Strassman's subjects saw a machine or some kind of equipment with sticks with teardrops coming out of them. I once saw a framework structure shaped like a double tetrahedron formed out of transparent hollow tubes with teardrops circulating through them. On several occasions, I have seen laboratory-like environments filled with intricate machinery, freestanding and built into the walls.

I saw machines that were clearly people, not in the sense of robots but as autonomous, animated mechanical devices. They could talk and communicate telepathically. It was very futuristic. Many people report the feeling that the beings are technologically far in advance of us.

This raises a very interesting consideration: that the entities we encounter on psychedelic drugs may have an independent existence outside of the entheogenic experience. It is natural to think that if we take a drug and see hallucinations and experience vivid dreamlike scenarios, the content of our visions comes from our own mind or unconscious or even that it is somehow hardwired into the drug itself.

Many people see visions of tigers and other predatory cats, for example, on a wide variety of psychedelics, even on LSD, which is a semi synthetic compound nonexistent before the late twentieth century. It would appear that the spirits or transdimensional, nonhuman entities exist autonomously in their own worlds whether someone is taking a drug or not. They may have had involvement with takers of psychedelics and others long before the people ever took drugs.

Chapter 2

In the Land
of the
Bottle Brush
People

A Journey to Hell

CHAPTER 2

In the Land of the Bottlebrush People
A Journey to Hell

AFTER MY FIRST MUSHROOM EXPERIENCE in the workshop, I was eager to try them again and be reunited with my otherworldly friends and family and my somehow-fatherly guide from the trip before. I still had a supply of fresh *Psilocybe cubensis* that I had carried back from Denver in my pants, and I decided to increase the dose a little bit. It does seem that the most powerful experiences I have had with mushrooms is when they were fresh. There have been exceptions to this. I am speaking about *Psilocybe cubensis* mushrooms. *Amanita muscaria* should never be eaten raw.

On this occasion, I had decided to assay sixty grams of fresh mushroom. Sixty grams of fresh or five grams of dried *Psilocybe cubensis* is considered a threshold dose that is sufficient, under the right circumstances and at the right time, to produce otherworldly contact. Though not the strongest, *P cubensis* is the most common variety of *Psilocybe* sold in the United States because it is the easiest to cultivate.

The day had been filled with anticipation, building up to an almost unbearable level by nightfall. At exactly six o'clock, I ingested four large, fresh mushrooms and settled back on the waterbed to watch television until they took effect. I had chewed the aromatic, sweet, almost vaginal-smelling fungus and washed them down with hot chocolate. In Mexico, chocolate is traditionally served before eating mushrooms.

When I ate mushrooms with the Mazatec *curandera* Maria Sabina, she served us *abuelita,* a traditional Mexican hot-chocolate drink with a hint of cinnamon. "*Abuelita*" means "grandmother." After a day of fasting, hot chocolate is most welcome.

Earlier I had prepared my bedroom, stapling a heavy blanket over the window to exclude the last fading light of twilight. I had placed towels under the door and over the electric clock to create a black-velvet backdrop so that no light would distract from my anticipated visions. Terrence McKenna had explained to me that to get the full classical effects, mushrooms could only be experienced in total darkness. It was the black arts.

I immediately recognized an increase in the concentration of certain words being spoken on the TV as I remotely switched from channel to channel. On every station, someone seemed to be speaking a word like "contact" or "encounter" or "impact." The density of these words seemed unnaturally high, and as I switched from station to station, I was wondering if I was simply noticing them more.

I switched again. "Encounter," someone said. Another switch, and the entire screen was black with giant white letters spelling out the word "Encounter." It was a program called *Encounter,* a talk show. In desperation, I switched to another channel, this time randomly. It showed a picture of outer space filled with stars and planets. Still another showed a flying saucer moving across a clouded sky.

I kept waiting for the nausea and numbness to start, but they did not come. My ordinary sight began to blur and distort, and feelings of reeling and falling began as the mushroom manifested its customary initial challenge.

"Who goes there? How dare you enter here?" it seemed to say.

I turned off the television and switched off the light, plunging my bedroom into total darkness. Finally, it was just as if the mushroom had been waiting for me to get settled and give the sign to begin.

"Are you ready now?" it seemed to ask.

Suddenly and forcefully I was catapulted into another dimension. There was no warning, no buildup. It was just like I was an arrow that, all the while, had been resting in a drawn-back bow and was suddenly launched. I was in complete confusion. I found myself bursting into a place completely strange and unfamiliar, in the midst of complicated activity, among people of the most unusual sort. A moment ago I had been lying on my bed in my home in the dark experiencing dizzying waves of vertigo. Then as though a switch had been suddenly turned on, I found myself standing in a crowded street.

This was not the fuzzy, indistinct reality of a dream. Everything was sharp and clear and three-dimensional and vividly colored and absolutely convincing. It was daytime, although a moment before, it had been dusk. I was immersed in a large, moving crowd of people, a dense, entangled throng, pressing up against me, shoulder to shoulder, as though a football game had just let out and the spectators were pouring out of the stadium.

The seething mob was undulating and flowing like a wave down this narrow avenue with the forward momentum of the crowd carrying me along with it. On either side of the street were rows of buildings of tan-colored stucco or adobe, not modern looking but kind of Romanesque. They were single-story structures running one into the other in a continuous facade without side streets or intersections. At the top was a kind of simple molding or cornice, just a raised rectangular strip that ran in a line just below the level of the flat roofs.

The most amazing thing about it was that the people in the crowd didn't look remotely human. They all looked exactly like giant bottlebrushes. They stood about five feet tall with their handles down. Their bodies were cylinders of white, closely cropped bristles, like the fibers of a brush. Below, there extended all the way to the ground a long, round, brown stick. They looked more like manufactured objects made from synthetic materials than organic matter, and yet there was no question that they were people. They looked like bottlebrushes. I seemed to remember that on the coat of arms of the warrior kings, the Plantagenet, was a picture of the bottlebrush plant.

As the mob pressed forward, I found myself being moved down the street. It felt almost as though the crowd and I were being herded like cattle. There was something ominous about the whole thing, and the bottlebrush people were so different. In my previous mushroom trip, I was able to have two-way conversations with various people and objects.

Having limited experience with the drug, I assumed that this was the standard procedure, so I began to inquire of the bottlebrushes nearest to me, "Excuse me, but can you tell me what's going on? I mean, where are we? What is happening?"

But the brushes made not a word of reply and just kept bustling and hurrying along. "You are so strange!" I told them. I was starting to feel uncomfortable and a little paranoid. "Who are you?" I asked them again and again. "Why don't you answer me?" But there was no reply, no acknowledgment, and no communication.

I began to wonder if the bottlebrush people were from this place or if they had been brought here like me. Perhaps they were just as confused and frightened as me. The movement of the crowd was so strong that I could not resist, for if I hesitated, I would be trampled to death underfoot, or under handles, as it were.

Gradually I became aware of a line of dark figures standing on the roofs of these buildings. They looked like black silhouettes, watchful and threatening, as they stood on the parapets and looked down at us. I felt that they were in control of what was happening, as though somehow they were our captors. Suddenly the whole situation took an ominous turn, for I began to feel a kind of harsh malevolence from the dark silhouettes on the roofs. They were driving us like cattle down this trough, but toward what and why?

Images of slaughterhouses and meatpacking plants flashed through my mind. Why this rude treatment? Where was the paternal host who had so dominated the last experience? Where were the friendly machines, the relatives? Who were these dark supervisors, and why was I being herded like an animal along with these strange, uncommunicative, fiber creatures? I felt collected like a specimen, and I didn't like it.

The dark silhouette figures took on the resemblance of guards or wardens, reminiscent of Nazi SS officers standing above, and we were like a trainload of Jews who had just been unloaded at Auschwitz and were being herded down this sluice-like street from which there was no exit and onward to the gas chambers. I could almost hear them shouting, "*Schnell! Schnell!*"

The sensation of captivity was unmistakable. The whole situation had the unmistakable feeling of a predator-prey relationship. Everything was so strange that I could hardly look at it. As the images unfolded, I would turn my head away. This feeling was so unexpectedly hostile. It was not at all what I had assumed a mushroom trip would be like. Wasn't it supposed to be spiritual? I felt completely confused and bewildered. It seemed like it was actually happening, not that I was somewhere else having this strange dream but as though what ever occurred here was actually happening to me.

I tried speaking to the paternal personality of the previous trip, who I felt must surely be aware of what was happening to me. Maybe he would rescue me. I exclaimed, "Is this any way to treat a friend? This is no way to influence someone with whom you are trying to establish a working relationship! You're scaring me to death!"

There was no reply, no dialogue, only the persistence of this strange situation.

As the sea of people swept along, I found my position moving more and more to the side, until before me to my left loomed a door. The pressure of the crowd pushed me through it, and I found myself inside a small room with featureless, tan-stucco walls and the same narrow molding near the tops of the walls.

Inside this chamber, there were a few bottlebrushes. Worst of all, there were about eight creatures that looked exactly like giant insects. I don't mean insect like or resembling insects or having insect characteristics. They were bugs! Big, black bugs! They stood upright like men, about five feet tall in stature. They resembled cockroaches. Growing up in a New York tenement, I had had, since childhood, a fear of cockroaches. The creatures before me had black, shiny exoskeletons, clicking mandibles, and segmented, jointed, lobster like arms that were covered with long, dark, bristly hairs.

A bronze insect goddess from Luristan

On their triangular faces were huge, round, concentrically circular eyes that stared at me like targets. The rest of their faces assumed an expression that just didn't fit the situation, a kind of zany smile. It reminded me of the way you can look at the shell of a crab and turn the lines that the overlapping plates make into a kind of face with an unearthly fierce and fretting look that doesn't reflect at all what the crab is feeling.

Some kind of powerful energy was rising off the bodies of the insects, a kind of radiation that itself felt insect like, and it emanated from them like steam, causing the empty space in the room to boil and churn and swirl.

Not bugs! I thought. *Why does it have to be about bugs?*

It was the most terrifying thing I had ever seen. I felt seized by a wave of almost insane horror. These insect faces smiled at me like wild-eyed lunatics, and three or four of them who were nearest to me began to circle around me, waving their antennae like the antlers of some supernatural, interplanetary deer. They reached out their multiply jointed, exoskeleton arms toward me and touched my body, and they brushed against my face with their black, prickly hair. Their odor was strong and pungent, like rotting fruit, with a sweet, metallic undertone, like the sweet and sour stench of the bodies of unwashed bums.

As their hairy, plated arms moved over my body, feeling, probing and poking, I could feel the excitement level of the insects in the room increase, rising like the blood lust of an angry mob with a lusty love of violence. The giant insects' excitement rose and rose, mounting to a kind of intensity that felt threatening to the level of stark, abject terror, and what's more, the energy had an undeniable sexual quality to it. The air was filled with cacophonous chirping and clicking sounds, like the birds that used to sing on the long-distance telephone lines. I heard oscillating tones like sirens. Hairy pincers were touching my hair. Black mandibles nibbled at my clothes. Jointed antennae brushed against my face, penetrating my ears and up my nose. The word "contact" took on a new and ominous connotation. They wanted to rub up against me, to hug me, and to snuggle me.

There was an unmistakable amorous intent. The ardency was just too much to take. Sex with a talking, fatherly machine, as had happened in the previous trip, was one thing, but group sex with giant insects was quite another. It was like a scene from Hieronymus Bosch. While all of this was going on, the boiling, green radiation that was emanating from the insect's bodies was making the empty space wave and ripple, and it was making time do the strangest things.

I experienced a kind of trilocation. Part of me was still in the room with the excited bugs, another part was home in the darkened bedroom and in a third I was somewhere outside at night. I felt as though at least three different things were happening to me simultaneously in three separate, distinct places. These would occur one at a time and I would keep jumping from one frame to another.

On one level, I was home in my waterbed. This was an enormous relief, for it was the first time that I wasn't locked into that otherworldly place. I could even get up and go to the bathroom. Then click! I was back in the cubicle with the giant insects. And then again click! I was somewhere outside; it was night, and something big and black and round was hovering in the air about five yards over my head.

It was a flying saucer, a huge, dull-gray, humming disk-shaped thing whose underside was embossed with a raised geometric, waffle-like pattern. In the center of the bottom of the disk was a circular opening, out of which a conical beam of light was shining down and forming a circular ring on the ground like a spotlight. The illuminated circle of light it cast was checkered like a checkerboard. The conical beam coming from the bottom of the craft was extremely energetic. The light in the checkered ray was undulating like dust in a beam of sunlight.

Alchemical zodiac wheel as UFO

The humming sound from the ship grew louder. It was fragmenting my sense of time and continuity. I felt that I was being bombarded with impressions from every direction. They were like memories, like highly charged, emotion-packed recollections of being out here before, fearing it, and hating it. Memories of every bad moment from every trip I had ever taken were flooding into my mind. There were memories of trips I never remember taking, experiences I never remember having, memories of unending captivity, of imprisonment, of being trapped like an animal by hunters. It felt like the bursting of a repression.

Why didn't I remember all of this, all these times of being here against my will in this horrible place? Why didn't I remember in my ordinary life that I hated this? It was the worst possible place to be. How could I have done this to myself yet again? How could I have naively thought that I needed a higher dose than the unbelievably powerful experience I had had last time? Why was my entire life structured around the pursuit of psychedelic drug experiences with which I totally, positively identified that inevitably led to this awful, fearful place? If I ever got out of here, I would never take another drug, so help me, as long as I lived. I wondered how many times I had mouthed these words.

It was now two and one-half hours into a five-hour trip, and things were happening faster and faster. This had happened so many times before—the black, bony bugs, the humming, steel-gray disk. I felt like I had been tricked. I had done this to myself once again. I had taken the mushroom and pulled the trigger. I had sprung the trap. I marveled at how I could have done such a thing. Why would anyone do this to himself or herself voluntarily? Why would anyone even consider deliberately doing something that would be instrumental in bringing anything like this about?

I thought about psychedelic drugs, about how good they were; how beautiful and benevolent they were, how they were sources of enhanced perception, refined intelligence, and intuition; how they were releasers of poetic eloquence and inspiration and granters of psychic gifts of telepathy, precognition, and otherworldly instinct; and how they were accelerators of evolution. But all the while, they were a kind of insidious trap, all the art and color and pleasurable sensations a kind of bait to trick you into finally taking enough so that the trap would spring.

This had happened again and again, so many times throughout the years, since early childhood, long before I had ever taken a psychedelic drug. It was like a secret history of my life that had been so skillfully edited out as to never be even suspected—to bring me face-to-face with the one thing I had begged to forget and gratefully forgotten again and again so as to not go mad with horror from the hovering, humming disks and grinning cockroach faces and snickering, invasive violation.

As T. S. Eliot writes, "I had seen my head brought in upon a platter. I had seen the eternal footman, take my coat and snicker. And in short, I was afraid."

T. S. Eliot like William Blake, like and W. B. Yeats, used *Amanita muscaria* mushrooms and other entheogens and were familiar with the secret, symbolic language and the traditional symbols and emblems that was associated with them. These were well understood by the adepts and commonly appear in works of alchemy, the works of the inspired poets, and other products of the ancient entheogenic fraternity.

Suddenly it was as though the entire world began to break open, and a crack appeared in the very fabric of space itself. It was as though the universe began to split apart, as though the time-space continuum had been ruptured and was being ripped asunder. The crack in the universe was now widening like a fissure before me, opening into some other universe that lay beyond, and something was coming through. It was insects again, thousands of them, millions of them, and they were coming from the other side of the crack in the world, creeping and crawling and scurrying like a sea of wriggling bugs.

It was like there was a barrier between this world and another, and the insects were on one side and the rest of the world on the other. But that had all changed now, and I unwittingly was somehow responsible. I felt a shocking realization that I had opened a door to a universe that nature, in her wisdom, had sealed up millennia before. But now this wall had a great crack in it, and they were pouring through and ingressing by the multitude into our dimension. And then I knew what the trap was for. It opened the gates of hell and allowed the denizens of a sinister and utterly nonhuman dimension to have access to our world.

With all the strength I could muster, I staggered into the kitchen and swallowed a handful of niacin, the image of the insect-filled crack still blazing before my eyes. A cacophony of clicking, buzzing, and chattering was ringing in my ears. It was not the soothing and melodic humming of bees that I had heard before but a dreadful, dissonant, insect trill, like crickets gone mad.

Now the niacin was taking effect. The final visions subsided. I felt a wave of relief and security. Somehow I knew that unless controlling forces beyond me had chosen to end the experience at that particular time, there would have been no power on Earth that could have stopped it. Taking niacin is like a request. The imprint or the state in which the experience had left me had a kind of unresolved quality, as if everything had been frozen back in the room with the insects. A green haze seemed to linger for weeks, bearing traces of the strange insect-like radiation.

A friend came to visit the following day, and as we talked, his form kept changing into that of a giant bug. It was very unnerving. I could feel the closeness of the insect personalities for almost a week following the experience.

I came out of the experience strangely happy about it, considering how utterly uncomfortable I had felt for most of the time. It was fine. Everything was fine. Unbelievably I felt undaunted and eager to take the mushroom again.

This is a strange thing about the mushroom. You can have a terrible, frightening experience and feel you were lucky to get out of it alive, and afterward you feel really good and rest assured that whatever happens, you will always come down eventually. Most of the trips are very positive and pleasant. You want to do it again.

It has been suggested that the mushroom entities feed upon emotion, both positive and negative. Frightening trips may be engineered to produce fear and terror as a source of energy. The animated film *Monsters Incorporated* plays upon this theme, where the monsters use interdimensional doorways to enter the bedrooms of children and terrify them in order to collect their emotional energy, which they use as a power source for their world. In the end, they discover that positive energy works equally well.

I have to admit that during my youthful years of taking psychedelics, emotions, both positive and negative, reached levels of incredibly high intensity. It was as though the same forces that manipulated synchronicity to reward you and grant the fulfillment of wishes could cunningly arrange situations that would activate unbearable emotional responses of jealousy, anger, rage, or fear and loathing. Psychedelics in general are sensory amplifiers, but they are behavioral and emotional amplifiers as well.

Still, there seemed to be a presence behind the scenes, backstage as it were, that was skillfully and deliberately arranging situations to produce these reactions. We called it "pushing our buttons" or "having our buttons pushed." It seemed like they could peer deep into our minds, memories, and history to find out what would produce intense emotional reactions and arrange situations that would stimulate them.

It was as though part of the price we had to pay for participating in these mysteries was being an extremely intense emotional energy source for these beings. Were they studying us, or was it something more? Were they vicariously getting off on our agony and our ecstasy? Were we providing amusement, entertainment, or some kind of nourishment?

Omar Khayyám wrote,

> Tis all a Checkerboard of Nights and Days
> Where Destiny with Men for Pieces plays:
> Hither and thither moves, and mates, and slays,
> And one by one back in the Closet lays.

Checkerboards are common motifs in mushroom hallucinations.

And later Khayyám wrote,

> I sometimes think that never blows so red
> The Rose as where some buried Caesar bled;
> That every hyacinth the Garden wares
> Drops in its Lap from some once lovely Head.

Roses, hyacinths, and heads are tropes for mushrooms, and gardens are mushroom related. The blood of suffering heroes make the mushrooms grow.

Insect entities were common in the experiences of Dr. Strassman's DMT studies. People confronted, communicated, and interacted with insects, praying mantises, reptiles, and Gumby-like entities, beings that resembled saguaro cacti, human-looking beings, and even entities that resembled elephants.

Could the elephant-headed Indian deity Ganesh represent such beings? Elephant skin resembles dried, wrinkled *Amanita muscaria* mushrooms. Elephants are among the mushroom-related animals and even appear in the illustrations of the alchemists. The frequency of encounters on DMT with insect entities is remarkable. Sometimes they are reported to be in futuristic, technological environments and some to be far more advanced than our selves.

One of Dr. Strassman's DMT subjects found himself surrounded by insect-like creatures that wanted to get inside of his mind. He resisted and finally surrendered, and the insects began feeding on his emotions.

Finally, having his heart eaten by the insects became a kind of sexual interaction. They were making love to him and eating him at the same time. He found the sensation very strange but not necessarily unpleasant. I can identify with this, because being eaten by insects happened to me in the episode concerning the fleas.

A friend of mine took DMT and experienced what looked like a gigantic manhole with the cover slowly opening. On the inside were a swarm of wriggling, teaming insects that were threatening to emerge and enter our world. He was terrified. Then suddenly from the periphery of the hole came four little crablike creatures. They seized the manhole cover and, in the nick of time, pulled it closed.

Once, on mushrooms, I found myself surrounded by tiny, brightly colored, Gothic, plastic, mechanical alligator-like objects with gaping, snapping, clicking mouths. They were swarming all over me and seemed intent upon eating me. I bolted straight for the niacin bottle.

When I told Terrence McKenna's brother, Dennis, this story, he commented, "It would have been interesting if you had let the mechanical alligators eat you and seen where it went from there."

One of Strassman's subjects found himself in a hive-like environment with a creature that resembled a bee, who told him that this was where humankind's future lay.

It is interesting that bees have an association with mushrooms going back at least as early as the Neolithic. A petroglyph from Tasili n'Ajjer in the African Sahara shows a shaman or entity wearing a bee mask.

His body is formed from mushrooms, and he holds clusters of mushrooms in his hands.

Humming sounds like the buzzing of bees are sometimes heard in psychedelic states. Bees and flies are interchangeable images in mushroom mystical art. Bees buzzing around a beehive are parallel images to flies flying around a fly agaric mushroom. A gold ring from 1500 BC found in Isopata near Knossos in Crete shows four female figures with upraised arms whose heads and hands are those of insects. They are standing among plants.

In ancient Greece, priestesses were called "melissae," or bees. This was true in the shrines of Artemis, Demeter, Cybele, and Rhea and in those of Aphrodite and Diana. Bees are associated with honey and with bears. The hibernation of bears was associated with the entheogenic trance. Mushrooms are commonly preserved in honey. Bees quaff nectar from flowers, from which they make the sweet honey often compared to the blissful entheogenic state, but they also collect poison for their stingers.

Being stung, like being shot by an arrow, is associated with psychedelic inebriation and sexual penetration. Mead, the honey drink, was not, as commonly believed, fermented honey but an entheogenic beverage, possibly the fly agaric or its urine, to which honey had been added. In the East Indian Rig Veda, *mada* or honey was one of the epithets for Soma, the sacramental drink originally pressed from Amanita muscaria mushrooms. Honey may have been added to the beverage.

Another of Dr. Strassman's volunteers reported a crack in time-space similar to the one I saw with insects coming through. He said it was like a crack in the earth and a crack in space. The metaphor is extended to include passing through the mountains. The psychedelic symbol of the crack also extends to mountain passes. The name of the Grail hero Percival means "pierce vale," that is piercing through the mountains to a valley. It also means piercing through the veil of illusion.

In a myth of the Koryak, a Uralic-speaking, reindeer-herding tribe of Siberia that surely goes back to the Ice Age, the people were engaged in a migration when they came to wall of ice that blocked their way. Big Raven, an *Amanita muscaria* hero, flew above the ice and found a pass through which the people could travel to safety.

In the Alchemical book by Mylius, the *Rosarium philosophorum,* is a picture of an entranced alchemist sitting in an enormous fissure in the earth. Above him fly cherubim.

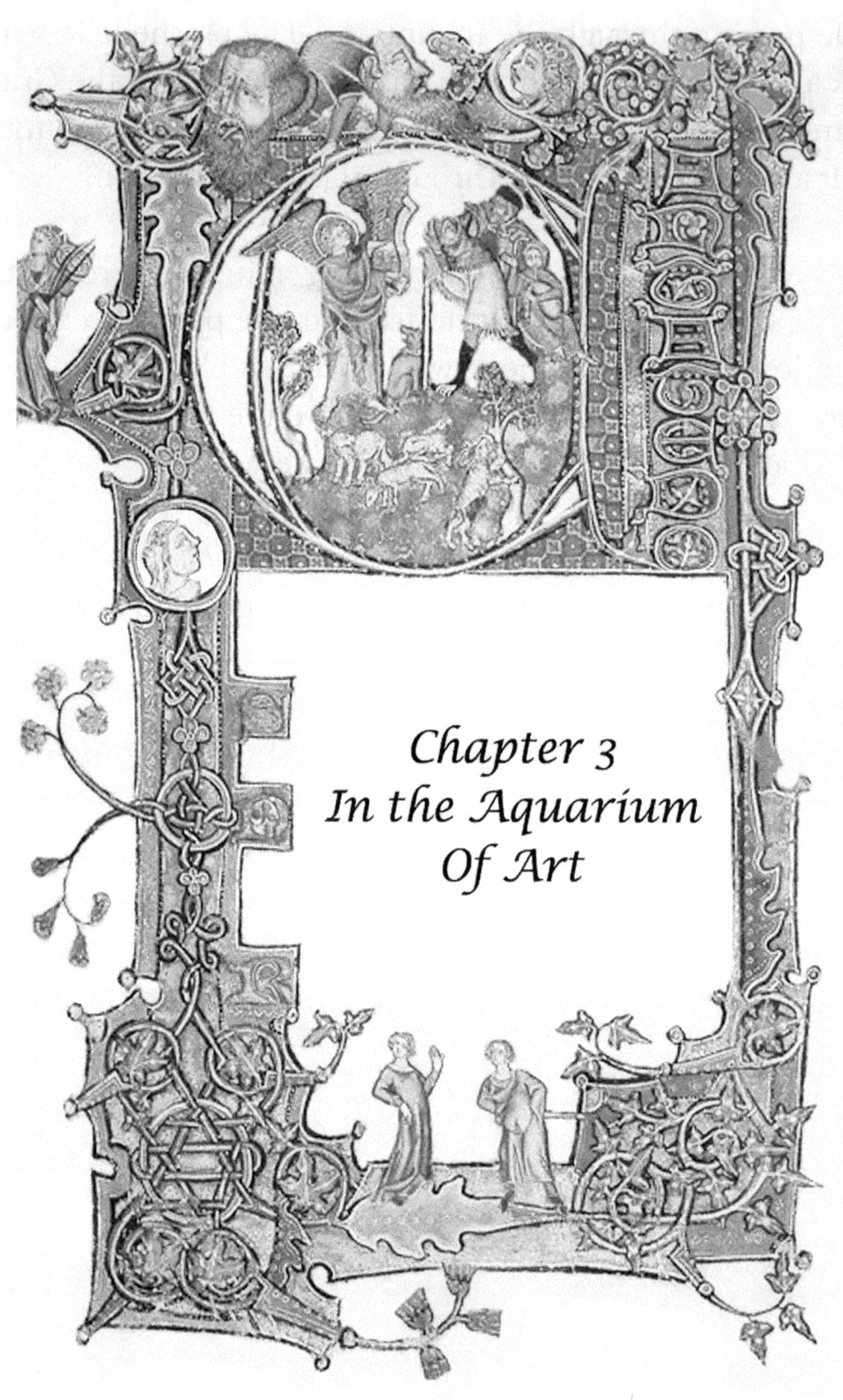

Chapter 3
In the Aquarium
Of Art

CHAPTER 3

In the Aquarium of Art
An Object Lesson

AFTER MY LAST MUSHROOM JOURNEY that was a visit to hell, it is amazing that I would ever want to take psilocybin again. It is a strange thing about the mushroom that even after very unpleasant experiences, you are left with a positive feeling about it and have no reservations about doing it again. The mushroom had shown me two very different variations of what was possible, one extremely positive and the other very much the opposite. My curiosity was aroused, and I wanted to see what would come next. The intensity of the previous trip had in no way quelled my fascination and enthusiasm for the phenomena; in fact, paradoxically, it had left me eager to repeat it. I still had some fresh *Psilocybe cubensis* mushrooms in my refrigerator, and only a few weeks passed before I was ready to try again.

I began the evening with hot chocolate after a day of fasting. I ate two large, fresh specimens. After thirty minutes, I retired into the darkened bedroom to wait what would take place.

But now in the darkness, I felt a little trepidation. As the numbness spread over my arms and face, a wave of apprehension came over me. Was I sure I wanted to do this? Was I ready for another major experience? Then like a tide rushing out, all the effects of the mushroom seemed to subside. I felt relief. Maybe it wasn't going to happen this time I found myself hoping.

Then from the lower periphery of my visual field, something glided by—or rather the tip of something. It was shaped like the fin of a shark, but it seemed to be made of some burnished metal and was covered with ornamental detail, like a piece of fine jewelry. I strained to see what this jeweled surface was attached to. It was a mechanical fish about the size of a porpoise—not a fish of flesh but an object of the most refined art, an ornamental fish of extremely fine craftsmanship in a style reminiscent of Celtic craftsmanship combined with a Beardsley art nouveau quality and a hint of Jules Verne.

I looked up. All space was filled with objects like this floating in the air, gliding lazily by, and swimming in circles around me. The objects seemed like fine art as only kings commissioned and enjoyed, treasures of such beauty and craftsmanship that earthly art was only a pale imitation. There were objects of gold and silver and porcelain. Everywhere there was inlay, gold work, and fluorescent jewels, like the treasures of a royal tomb or found in the Vatican or Versailles.

Some of the objects resembled the exquisitely fashioned armor of kings or princes that I had seen in museums, but all the forms were levitating, silently gliding through the darkness, all brilliantly illuminated by their own inner light. There were hues of blue and green, of silver and gold, and of white enamel. There were textiles, too, extraordinary fabrics like scarves or fine woven cloths that would float up to me for inspection. This was level of culture and refinement, of craftsmanship, skill, and technique, that makes all people's artistic achievements seem primitive and crude. I felt like a caveman standing in the Louvre.

The objects had another amazing quality. While they were formed from ivory or jade or porcelain and encrusted with jewels, they were somehow flexible and were undergoing a continuous transformation before my eyes. Normal objects remain frozen and motionless as you view them, but these were shifting, changing, and evolving. The style would move; an artistic theme would develop, and the total statement would exist in time as a series of transformations or a continuous flow akin to a musical progression.

For example, if a jeweled piece of golden renaissance armor inlaid with precious metals on its surface had a floral pattern, the flower would grow and bloom and put out tendrils that would wrap around the object, enter into other design motifs, and interact with them. All the while, the shape of the object itself would be changing, flowing, and transforming.

Now it would be beautiful bejeweled, clockwork bird, a peacock-like creature with exquisitely worked golden plumes and quills. Its multihued tail would brush past my gaze like a renaissance fire screen, fanning out into an amazing display of color and craftsmanship. The "peacock's tail" was a name for one of the stages of alchemical transmutation.

Luminous, three-dimensional, self-transforming, levitating forms fill the air during the hierophany, hanging suspended like jewels, like art, like objects of precious metals, like embossed and decorated armor and sculpture. These objects are moving and self-transforming. They can morph to resemble anything and can appear to be made from any kind of materials. The objects are personified, appearing like intricate jewelry, forms of porcelain and ivory and burnished gold, luminescent gemstones, and embossed leather. A common variant resembles armor with overlapping metallic plates. This led antique alchemists and other adepts to represent the presiding spirit of the mysteries as a man in armor. They resemble the overlapping lobed shells of lobsters, and these crustaceans became traditional emblems of the mushroom trance.

These were the kinds of visions I had waited all my life to see, ever since I had read about them in high school in Robert DeRopp's book *Drugs and the Mind,* which I got from the school library. I did not see anything like this on peyote or on LSD. Now at last the ineffable visions were here.

A common motif was interwoven braids that would weave and unravel. A variation was knots that would tie and untie themselves. These floating objects were pure artistic creations. I could ascertain no function or utility.

There was another curious aspect to these forms. I had the feeling that they were somehow either living beings or containers with living beings inside them. Some of the objects could speak. They were extremely friendly. Some were about the size of small dogs, and their flexibility reminded me of seals. Three or four of them would climb up onto my lap. They felt like loving pets that wanted to cuddle with me and be petted.

Also there was a feeling of great familiarity, of friendship, and of companionship. I loved them for their culture and artistic refinement. They seemed to be the embodiment of everything we value. Their mastery of language, art, technology, wisdom, love, sincerity, honesty, compassion, and devotion seemed like pure models of these qualities that have crowned human existence throughout the ages. The mushroom is the mother of civilization.

"You are so beautiful," I exclaimed, over and over. "I want to be like you!"

"You are like us," they said.

A gold and enameled object would float up and turn itself inside out in several different ways, as it spoke. "You are inside an object, and we are inside of objects. But can you do this?"

And the wondrous forms flowed and self-transformed with a freedom and creativity and active skill that were truly amazing.

"I want to be like you," I said. "I want to have a body like yours."

"Having a body like this is much better than the kind you have," it said. "We can choose any kind of body we want. We can be a changing transformation instead of a static pattern. We can be an animal or a machine or an electronic circuit or a work of art, but there are further, greater possibilities than you can possibly imagine. You don't have to be inside an object at all."

"I'd settle just to be a flexible ornament," I said.

"The forms we have assumed are a product of your nature, not ours. We are not objects in our natural state. We are not inside of objects. Objects are the language your brain speaks. We show you objects to get your attention. At the present time, it is the only way you can see us. We can take you somewhere where you can be like us."

"Couldn't we do this in easy stages?" I asked. "First, make me a jeweled peacock, and then we can talk about the other part."

They roared with laughter. I did too. We were joking together. There was a sense of mirthfulness and good-natured, compassionate humor that was wonderful.

As they spoke, the forms seemed to multiply until the entire room seemed piled with multicolored, jumbled heaps of junk in seeming wanton disarray, like a garbage heap or a ransacked Egyptian tomb or the treasures of Aladdin's cave. Some of the objects were familiar.

There were knives, kitchenware, plates, saucers, cups, and dish drainers. There were strange plastic frames. It was as if I were staring into the interior of my dishwasher whose lattice like shelves were stacked with white plates. They were taking these forms out of my mind and memory and using them as thematic elements with which to communicate. Part of it was from me; part of it was from them.

Then it would be machinery, wheels, cogs, and gears, brilliantly colored, moving illusions. There were cogged disks hovering in space, shining brilliant neon red or pearlescent green. I saw fleeting glimpses of brilliantly lit rooms filled with glowing machinery. Now fleets of spaceships would drift lazily by like a school of whales.

How calm, how peaceful, how matter-of-fact.

I hardly recognized the spaceships as spaceships or the dishware as dishware.

"There are possibilities of existence," they told me, "that exist outside of form, beyond matter, beyond bodies, beyond planets, outside of space and time. We can show you."

It was true. Whenever they got on this theme, it made me slightly uncomfortable.

"There is so much to grasp," I said. "I've only just begun to see visionary objects. I've waited all my life to see visions like this, but you are belittling their significance. I'd prefer to just study them as we go by."

The ornament I was talking with seemed to sense my apprehension. "Aren't you going to ask me what I would prefer?" he asked. More laughter, and the tension was released.

"Not now," they said, "but soon! True freedom waits beyond matter. The animal mind is useful here but is of no use where we come from. The mind rides the brain the way a man rides a horse, but the mind is not a thing of matter. It can go where the horse cannot."

The Gnostics believed that the human soul was somehow trapped in imprisoned in mater and that rights of purification freed it and allowed it to ascend to its original state. It is easy to see where they got this idea through the use of entheogens.

"There are no security problems there," they said. "No dental problems."

They were referring to some recent rather painful episodes of dental work I had recently had. Every line was a punch line, uproariously funny.

"No dental problems beyond space-time indeed," The bejeweled object continued. "No tax problems."

More laughter. It had read my mind again.

I felt like smoking some marijuana. "Do you mind if I smoke?" I asked the jewel-encrusted golden brooch.

"Why?" it said. "Do you want to muddy the water? Is it too clear for you?"

It was awfully clear—hard to improve upon. A little later the impulse returned.

"You might like it," I told the ornament. "Are you sure you won't have a toke?" "I don't need drugs," came the reply. "I am drugs. You're just feeding your horse a little grass," it said. "He's been getting restless. Now maybe he will calm down."

The marijuana didn't seem to hurt things at all. I felt wonderful. I was experiencing a solid sense of friendship and companionship. What fine people these were. How pleasant to sit and visit with them like this. There was a sense of brotherhood, a sense of membership. As the jewel-studded ornamental blimps piled into my lap, like dogs and cats, I knew that they were using my love and affection for animals for this dramatization, and I didn't care. Lapdogs were just fine with me.

During the 1960s and 1970s, hallucinogenic drugs, such as mescaline and LSD, were usually taken in lighted rooms or in natural settings. The sensory amplification that they produced was highly valued, and the drugs were consumed in environments stimulating to the senses with recorded or live music, incense, flowers, fruit, and brightly colored and highly patterned clothing and decorations.

Psilocybe mushrooms are completely different. When taken in complete darkness, psilocybin stimulates the retina and the optical cortex of the brain and releases a flood of animate colored imagery that is unimaginable to those who have not seen it. Many seasoned psychedelic-drug users, even those who have tried mushrooms in illuminated environments, are completely unaware of these classic effects.

Furthermore the dosage thresholds necessary to produce the visions are considerably higher than those used to enhance sensory aesthetics or those used in social situations and are, in fact, disorienting and uncomfortable unless one is secluded in darkness, lying down on a bed. The world of external, sensory experience is distracting and competes with the release of internal and external visionary imagery from the mushroom. The light of a candle can scarcely be seen in a brightly lighted room. In the dark, it can produce quite a lot of light, but if you really want to see light, you must blow the candle out.

Maria Sabina, the Mazatec *curandera*, always performed her mushroom *valadas*, or vigils, in total darkness. So did the shamans of Siberia.

A Zen master was asked, "What is Zen?" The master lit a candle. The student asked, "What is the actualization of Zen?" The master blew the candle out.

As Henry Munn put it so well, "Gradually colors begin to well up behind closed eyes. Consciousness becomes conscious of irradiations and effulgence of a flux of light, pattern forming and unforming, of electrical currents beaming from within the brain."

These gradually give way to moving, colored geometry; animate topological surfaces made from every sort of material emerge from the darkness. Scenes appear from recorded and repressed memory. Ornate furniture and architectural vistas manifest. Images appear of animals, insects, reptiles, fish, people, nonhuman beings, unearthly fauna and flora. One can observe otherworldly landscapes, extraterrestrial cities, spaceships, flying saucers, robots, futuristic machinery and much, much more.

The psychedelic experience is like a magic mirror. The psyche seems to turn inside out. The part of the mind-brain that normally displays reflections of the so-called outside world now makes pictures of the psyche itself and projects them as a field of objects and images floating in space and moving in time

THE MYSTERY OBJECTS: THE DAWNING OF HYPERSPATIAL FORMS

Classical writings about the Eleusinian mysteries in ancient Greece refer to the mystery objects that were kept in a sacred hamper. The mystery basket had a snake curling around it. The mystery objects were thought by scholars to be sacred fetishes used at certain parts of the ceremony. One of them was rumored to be a thunderbolt thrown down by Zeus at the founding of Troy.

As thunderbolts are well-known euphemisms for bolt-shaped mushrooms said to spring up where lightning has struck, it has been suggested that the mystery basket was the stash or place where the entheogens were kept. Sometimes the baskets were carried in public processions on the heads of women. The statues of women with baskets on their heads on the porch of the Erechtheion at the Parthenon at Athens show such women.

There is another aspect regarding the mystery objects that relates to the visionary nature of the entheogenic trance. The real mystery objects were part of the mystic vision of the mysteries. They were part of the things beheld by the congregation in the darkness of the mystery night.

FRAMES AND SCREENS

Frames are a common hallucinatory motif. Once on ayahuasca, I saw a framework structure shaped like an inverted double tetrahedron. The frame was formed from hollow, transparent tubes like a wire-frame object made from transparent glass or plastic. Inside the tubes were moving teardrop-shaped forms circulating around the frame. The frame-like designs illustrated in the Kabala represent such things.

When hyper spatial objects manifest, you never really see them appear. You just look up, and there they are, hanging suspended in space. When they depart, you look up, and they are gone. Or they may face away and twinkle out like stars at the approach of dawn. The mystery objects can appear mechanical, like intricate instruments with moving parts like clockwork. Metallic spheres can levitate in the air, humming softly like spinning gyroscopes or astrolabes.

Another commonly reported motif is that of screens. Once on LSD with all the lights on, I looked up, and the entire bedroom was filled with thin, rectangular screens. Their surfaces were smooth and featureless. The red color of the screens was very pure and coherent like a laser but not as bright and sparkly, more of a flat matte. Some of the screens were six foot tall and as wide as the room, with smaller rectangular screens floating in front of them along the top. There were screens floating along the sidewalls too. If I looked away and then looked back, they were still there.

Then an amazing thing happened. I looked up. The screens were still present, and floating in the air were ten or twelve metallic spheres. They were about the size of grapefruits, and they hung suspended in space, hovering like hummingbirds.

They were clearly structured mechanical objects. The bottom half was shiny, silvery metal. The top half was transparent, allowing one to look down inside at a very intricate mechanism within. Inside was a series of concentric rings arranged like a target. The rings were of varying thicknesses.

The surfaces of the rings were not smooth but had protrusions of minute objects attached to them. The rings were revolving in opposite directions and at different speeds. The orbs were emitting a high-pitched whining sound, like the humming of a precision Swiss-made timepiece. Some of the spheres had what looked like sails. There was a small mast-like extension, to which was attached a small, rectangular, laser-red screen like the ones suspended on the walls. The strange thing was that I could see these orbs clearly whether my eyes were open or shut.

This happened in broad daylight with other people present in the room. I later confirmed that the others had not seen the screens or the floating orbs. The image of counter rotating concentric circles remained with me. I kept seeing it on television in animated advertising imagery. It always produced a kind of flashback.

The mystery objects are a form of communication with the otherworldly entities that are confronted in the tryptamine trance. Some of the luminous objects beheld can be seen to be borrowed from one's own memories and experiences.

It is as though a nonhuman intelligence is trying to explain something to you, so it rummages around in your memory like it is an old trunk and pulls out a collection of memory impressions that it thinks it can use to illustrate what it is trying to say. Then it arranges them in a completely novel way that has nothing to do with the original meaning of the memories.

You are looking at a reflection of yourself being used as the communication of another. The experience is interactive. There is someone else present. Sometimes there are many others present. Sometimes they watch what transpires like an audience. Sometimes you and the others are what are being watched. The mushroom compares itself to anything and everything, beautiful and ugly, pleasant and unpleasant. Sometimes it can take the form of a humanlike person who can interact with you. It can be a character from a book or movie.

As the character of Cervantes says in the opening scene of the Don Quixote allegorical play *Man of La Mancha*, "I will impersonate a man. Step into my imagination so that you may see him."

Otherworldly intelligence penetrates you and merges with you like the flowing together of two waters, and a picture of this is what is being reflected in the mirror of the illuminated mind. What is seen in the mirror is the ecstatic confluence of human and nonhuman psychological phenomena. Ecstasy is the holographic projected reflection of the interaction of human and nonhuman psyches. It is a demonstration of the possibilities for consciousness and intelligence beyond the normal human modality.

They can strip you of your body and fly with you outside the object-image domain, beyond the hologram, beyond the field of luminous objects, out of the dark womb of matter, into a world of freedom. There you experience yourself as a creature of pure imagination, the terrestrial primate body shed, sloughed off, and left far behind.

Your guide seems to explain, "This is what you originally were before you were trapped and imprisoned in the world of physical matter. This is what you really are. Remember! Remember!" But if this is what we really are, what is it? If we did not come from here, where did we come from and how did we get inside of the monkeys?

This is surely what William Butler Yeats refers to in his poem "Sailing to Byzantium":

> O sages standing in God's holy fire
> As in the gold mosaic of a wall.
> Come from the holy fire,
> Perne in a gyre,
> And be the singing masters of my soul.
> Consume my heart away sick with desire
> And fastened to a dying animal
> It knows not what it is
> And gather me into the artifice of eternity.
> Once out of nature I shall never take
> My bodily form from any natural thing,
> But such a form as Grecian goldsmiths make
> Of hammered gold and gold enameling
> To keep a drowsy Emperor awake;
> Or set upon a golden bough to sing
> To lords and ladies of Byzantium
> Of what is past, or passing, or to come.

Chapter 4

A Sandwich in Time

CHAPTER 4

A Sandwich in Time

My first full-threshold psychedelic experience was on peyote. It was in the early 1960s, and I was attending college at UC Santa Barbara. It was in a poetry class that I first met Robin. He was strange. At first I assumed he was probably bipolar. There was just something about his ambiance that was not quite right. He seemed to watch and participate in the interactions of the class from a detached, somewhat-aloof plateau as if enjoying a private joke that had to do with the rest of us, and his interpretive comments on poetry were very unconventional. I instinctively disliked him.

One day he approached me after class. "I just have to ask you," he said. "Do you get high?"

"Yes!" I said, instantly interested.

"I just thought so," he said. "Have you ever taken any psychedelic drugs?"

"Yes," I lied. "I took some mescaline once."

This was completely untrue. I had read about mescaline in Robert DeRopp, Aldous Huxley, and Havelock Ellis. I had in my teens eaten a little fresh peyote, but I threw away the green part where all the mescaline is and ate the yellow inside. Not much happened. Another time I had chewed up some morning-glory seeds. Neither experience was very significant, but I didn't know what to look for. I had envied Havelock Ellis's descriptions of luminous, floating landscapes, jewel-encrusted trees, and strange animals. I wanted to experience this very much.

"Ah," he said. "So you have taken mescaline. Then you will be particularly interested in what I am about to say."

He lowered his voice. "I am going to be receiving in the mail a package from Texas containing four hundred fresh peyote buttons. It's perfectly legal. They come from Smith Peyote Farms in El Paso, and as long as they are fresh and can be planted and grown, they can send them anywhere in the United States. And," he continued," I thought you might like to take some."

My heart was racing. I couldn't believe my ears. I said something stupid like, "Yes, it would probably be good for you to take peyote with me."

"Excellent!" he said, "but there is only one problem. My landlady is very suspicious, and she inspects all my mail. She would surely discover the buttons. Would you mind having them delivered to your house?"

The thought of four hundred peyote buttons coming to my doorstep as if by their own volition seemed overwhelmingly wonderful.

"Of course I'll receive them!" I said, readily accepting this normally very bad suggestion.

The peyote arrived two weeks later in a cardboard box with a Smith Farms label on it. It had a very musty smell reminiscent of root cellars. The buttons were semidried, not fresh, as Robin had suggested. They didn't look like they would grow if I planted them. They were leathery. Around the bottom was a ring of bark, actually dried and shriveled skin. The tops were punctuated with little flocculent tufts of white fibers with a larger concentration of them in the center.

We decided to eat eight buttons each. Today I would consider this a very large dose for beginners, especially with the highly stimulating tufts not removed. Later on I found that four buttons to be enough for a major trip. We cut the peyote in little pieces with a butcher knife, bark, tufts, and all. We put the particles into two strawberry milk shakes and drank them down. Thinking that I might be hungry later, I prepared in advance a bologna and tomato sandwich with lettuce and mayonnaise.

With the peyote in our stomach, we went outside and walked down to the cliffs overlooking the sea. The sun hung low in the sky, and the dwindling afternoon was warm with the smell of the ocean and the sun baked grass. An hour passed with little conversation. I feared that nothing was going to happen, but I didn't care. I felt strangely serene and content. As the sun began to set, we got up and began walking home to my apartment across the little college community of Goleta. It was dusk. Robin wanted to make a telephone call from a nearby booth. I sat down on the sun-warmed curb. I felt wonderful!

A feeling of innocence, wholesomeness, and purity descended over me like a warm cloud, which reminded me of those most idyllic moments from childhood when unobstructed play overflowed in endless summer afternoons.

Robin returned. "How do you feel?" he said.

"Wonderful!" I replied. "If this is it, right now and nothing else happens than this, it is completely worth it. I think it is the best that I ever felt."

We continued walking. As the twilight progressed, the houses and vegetation and trees became more and more vivid and idyllic and colorful, as if they were being illuminated with concealed, colored floodlights. It looked like a stage set. It was more real by far than reality. Everything was iridescent, becoming more and more itself. Everything was increasing in its suchness.

This was totally unexpected. Where were the jeweled cities and the visionary landscapes? I loved it. I sensed that here was something more important than anything I had ever encountered.

"This is only the beginning of the beginning" Robin proclaimed.

As we walked, I saw that the houses weren't solid at all. They grew larger as we approached them and smaller as we departed. They rotated in parallax along lines of perspective as we passed by. They were like plastic, colored globs of details.

There was so much detail that it would spill out of the outlines and boundaries of the forms. I was beginning to feel sick to my stomach.

Waves of vertigo were becoming an incoming tide as everything began to swim. When we arrived at my apartment, I ran to the bathroom and threw up into the toilet, again and again. The toilet bowl became covered with pieces of bark, reconstituted flesh, and the ever-present tufts. They were all moving in films superimposed over one another.

At this point the experience passed over into a new and unexpected modality. Suddenly everything had to do with wolves. I did not know that animal transformation, especially into wolves, was a common and traditional occurrence among shamans. Such metamorphosis included other animals as well such as lions, tigers, jaguars, bears, snakes, and birds.

Since that time, I have turned into lions on several occasions and have been surrounded by imagery of tigers, panthers, jaguars, and other predatory cats. I stood up and gazed into the mirror, and I saw leering back at me the grinning face of a wild animal. It was a wolf's face. My skin had sprouted fur. The reflection in the mirror had the eyes of a wild beast staring at me knowingly. It was all fur, snout, and fangs. It was the classical werewolf transformation out of the movies.

I had recently read *Steppenwolf* by Herman Hesse, and I incorrectly assumed that this had been the cause of the lycanthropy through the power of suggestion. At this stage in my entheogenic career, it was unthinkable that the images and motifs that appear might be coming from outside myself. I did not know that the wolf transformation in *Steppenwolf* was a description of a classic animal transmogrification experienced by Hesse on mescaline. At one point in the novel, the hero, Herman, is walking when he sees letters appear on the sidewalk. They spell out the message "Magic Theater for madmen only; price of admission, your mind."

Not only did I look like a wolf; I felt like I was becoming a wolf. I found myself gnawing on the bathroom door. The indentions of my teeth remained after the experience. I was very frightened by what was transpiring. I thought I had completely lost my mind and that things would be like this from now on.

A wolf's face in the mirror

A teacher in high school once declared, "You think you are so advanced and civilized, but there is only a thin veneer of civilization covering you. And if this should give way, you would all become vicious and ravenous wild beasts."

It occurred to me that this was what had happened. I later learned that far from this being true, our greatest savagery is found in the civilized layer. Beneath our layer of civilization, we are a beautiful, creative, spiritual, intuitive, and resourceful entity that has spanned human history from the primitive to the present. But now, fanged and furry faced, I felt myself changed into a ferocious beast.

I returned to the living room and sat down in a chair. Robin was sitting on the sofa.

"It's a good thing we didn't invite any girls to join us," Robin said. "We might have torn them apart."

This was only the first of what would be a series of disquieting utterances he would say that evening.

"Did I ever tell you," Robin exclaimed, "that I was in a mental institution?"

A mental institution? There I was, completely and utterly mad and getting more insane every minute, and my companion identified himself as a lunatic. It was a very strange and ominous omen.

"It's a good thing we didn't invite any girls to join us," said Robin. "We might have torn them apart."

I was starting to feel paranoid. I was realizing with a harsh irony that this person was completely controlling my mind by the linkage of language and that whatever he said, no matter how bizarre or intimidating, I was forced to participate in. If he said something strange or weird or frightening, I felt strange, weird, and frightened. If his speech transformed into something completely unrecognizable, I transformed with it, and there was nothing I could do about it.

I didn't know that the opposite was also true and that it was usually the case that beautiful, peaceful, reassuring words produce beautiful and peaceful feelings. If someone on an entheogen said something profound or moving or poetic, one would be filled with these wonderful sensations, but here Robin, fresh out of the nuthouse, was sadistically enjoying making me feel uncomfortable.

"I am going to say a word," Robin would rave, "and when I do, I want you to imagine a stream of striped peppermint toothpaste squirting upward, turning, twisting, turning back on itself, tying itself into knots, undulating, and gushing out and out, upward and upward."

His enthusiasm mounted. "Until, until," he was shouting, "ping pong into the abyss!

"And yet," Robin would continue, "all the while there is something grainy, something heaving in the periphery."

These were his very words. I later learned that "ping pong into the abyss" was a line from one of the beat poets, Lawrence Ferlinghetti, in his *Coney Island of the Mind*.

I was in ontological anguish. I thought that linguistic reality was as solid as the billowing walls that were now dissolving all around me. I felt trapped with this lunatic. I had gone mad with a madman for a guide. He was manipulating me, deliberately saying things to make me feel frightened or uncomfortable. I felt completely out of control for the first time in my life.

I didn't know if I would ever come down or what to expect next. Waves of dizziness drove me from my chair. I slumped to the floor and looked up at the bottom of a coffee table.

I thought of a song that they used to play on the radio called "Euphoria,". It contained the lyrics "There's a man over there underneath the table making faces at a union label. . .

Euphoria, you're mine, reeling and a rocking, and your inside voices are squealing and a squawking. Floating around on a belladonna cloud, I'm kicking the gong for you."

Robin said, "I'm really disappointed with you. You said you had taken mescaline and had some psychedelic experience. You are a liar! You don't know anything about this at all."

It was true. I had been arrogant and boastful, and he had caught me in my lie.

What proceeded to occur during the next several hours I can only vaguely reconstruct. Time just came apart at the seams. It became disjointed. It was as though the events that followed were a film that had been cut up in innumerable pieces. Some of the pieces were duplicated many times, and then all the segments were spliced back together again out of sequence, out of order. Events were arranged completely wrong. Many would keep repeating themselves, again and again.

At first I would think, *Ah, yes, déjà vu. I have experienced this before.* But after the fourth or fifth time that the same thing would happen, it was clear that it was something more. I would be sitting in a chair. Then I would enter the room, walk over to the chair, and sit down.

Robin would say something, use particular words, make certain gestures, and I would realize that this had already happened earlier and more than once. I would know with horrified amazement exactly what he was going to say next. The second, third, or fourth time this happened, I knew the scene by heart. I would know in advance every word he was going to say, every comment, every gesticulation and action.

I would think, *now he is going to talk about toothpaste. Now he is going to talk about ping-pong. Now he's going to scratch his neck. Now he will get up and walk across the room. Now he will pick up a glass of water and drink some.*

A little later after other things had transpired, the whole thing would happen again, and later on it would happen yet again. I would keep jumping back to things that had just happened before, not just once but five or six times and not just one event but many.

Imagine a period of time like an entire evening as a pack of playing cards, where each card represents an event. Normally the cards or events are arranged successively and consecutively in a progressive order, but this evening it was as though someone had taken many decks of the same cards and shuffled them together out of order so that any event could be repeated any number of times, again and again, and the sequence of the events was completely out of order with things from any point of the evening occurring on multiple occasions. A Sufi teacher once said, "Man learns through repetition."

I would find myself upstairs, sitting on the bed, not knowing how I got there, surrounded by piles of coins, pennies, nickels, dimes, and quarters. Then it would be earlier, with me sitting on the floor upstairs and watching Robin saying with great satisfaction, "Watch this!" as he hurled handful after handful of coins down the long hall at the far wall.

Then it would be earlier in the evening back in the living room with Robin. *Oh, no! Not this again!* I kept thinking, and Robin was talking absolute nonsense. He would say, "I want you to imagine a flock of birds flying by one by one and exploding!"

I would go into the kitchen and pick up the bologna sandwich from the counter and take a bite out of it. A little later I would enter the room, and there would be the sandwich whole and unbitten. Defiantly I would take several bites out of it only later to run into the sandwich again uneaten and intact. I would deliberately finish it completely, swallow the last bite, and think, *That's the last of you!*

But later, it would be still there, with only one bite removed. In desperation I would finish it off again, thinking, *That's finally it. You're gone!* But later three-quarters of it would be sitting on the kitchen counter. I know I finished off that sandwich four or five times, but I got up the next morning, three-quarters of it was lying there waiting for me.

I would sometimes find myself doing things somewhere, with no perceptible transition. I didn't know how I got there or where I was going next. I didn't know if this was ever going to stop. I saw glimpses of events that would be scattered across the remainder of my life—people I was yet to meet, scenes from trips I was yet to take.

The next day I was more or less myself again. I had the remainder of the leftover sandwich for breakfast. I knew that there was really such a thing as magic and that it was a description of this kind of process. I knew that the world was far more complicated than I had supposed. I knew that a reevaluation of my basic assumptions about everything was in order.

The way I see it, the spirits or apparitions or beings or whatever you want to call them can cut time up, record it, copy it, and duplicate it. They can edit it and splice it back together in any order they choose. Maybe when the entheogenic spirits penetrate into our space-time, the whole continuum is rippled or splashed or locally fragmented when their window of opportunity is opened. Maybe it was a deliberately staged event to demonstrate a principle about their ability to control time.

One time it was Thanksgiving, and my girlfriend Molly and I had cooked a turkey. We decided to take peyote. Later on in the trip, we remembered the roasted bird. We decided that we would put the turkey on the kitchen floor and eat it without using our hands. We got down on our hands and knees, and using only our mouths, we ate our fill. I think a little growling and snarling went on. It was a return to our animal nature.

Animal transformations were common in the ancient world among shamans and in the entheogenic initiations of warrior fraternities. Bronze and Iron Age warriors would go into battle enthused with herbal potions including *Amanita muscaria*, which gave them strength and courage. It was said among the Celts that a beam of light would shoot up from the top of their head like a spotlight. It was called the "Warrior's Light," and it could be seen all across the battlefield. While experiencing the war rage, they would turn into wolves, bears, and wild beasts. They would often wear the hide of the animal into which they wanted to transmogrify. The Norse berserkers would turn into bears in battle or during raids. "Berserker" means a bear pelt.

Donning the skin of the desired animal was a traditional part of lycanthropy and other animal transformations. Growling and snarling, the berserkers would chew on their shields and foam at the mouth like rabid dogs. This is where the term "going berserk" came from. According to Carl Ruck, the elements necessary for lycanthropy were the donning of an animal pelt, a marker such as a tree or stone to hide one's clothes, and a magical plant or herb. The lycanthrope would generally take off his or her clothes and hide them by or in a hollow tree or underneath the stone. He or she would then put on an animal pelt and anoint him or herself with a fungal or solanaceous ointment or else eat the *Amanita muscaria* mushroom.

Traditionally when turning into an animal, the shaman or warrior puts on the skin or pelt of the beast desired. It can be an entire hide or a belt made from the fur or even a ring made from the animal's skin. Undressing was an important part of the transformation, and people customarily take *Amanita muscaria* mushrooms naked or with a loincloth, because the mushrooms cause copious perspiration. After the lycanthropy, it was necessary to put the clothes back on to turn back into a human. The warriors of Sparta in ancient Greece wore wolf skins and, inspired by entheogenic potions, were transformed into ferocious wolves in battle.

Examples of shamans turning into animals can be traced back as far as the Paleolithic. In the cave sanctuary at Les Trois Frères (Ariege) in France dating from the 13,000 BC are three engravings of naked men wearing animal pelts. One shows a nude man draped in an animal skin with staring, concentric circular eyes. The figure appears to be dancing. He is covered by the pelt of an animal, possibly a wolf from the appearance of the tail. The French archeologist Henri Breuil made a drawing of the man and added deer horns. Others have not seen the antlers and suggest that Breuil, drawing in dim light, wanted to see the figure as a counterpart of the Celtic horned god, Curnunnos, called the Master of Animals. In brighter light, the man doesn't appear to have horns. In all probability, the man is a naked inebriated shaman, wearing a wolf skin, turning into a wolf.

A second engraving is of a nude man wearing an animal's pelt. He wears a mask or the head of the animal attached to the skin. He is dancing. And a third engraving shows a naked man wearing the hide of a bison complete with head and hoofed forelegs.

In another cave in France at Péchialet in the Dordogne, which was used by upper Paleolithic hunters and gathers from between 35,000 and 20,000 BC, is an engraving of a man wearing a bearskin with the head attached. Two human arms extend from the bear's pelt. He is in the company of two other human figures who appear to be dancing.

All these figures are consistent with entheogenic shamanic animal transformation including the removal of clothes and the donning of an animal's hide.

Richard T. Estrin

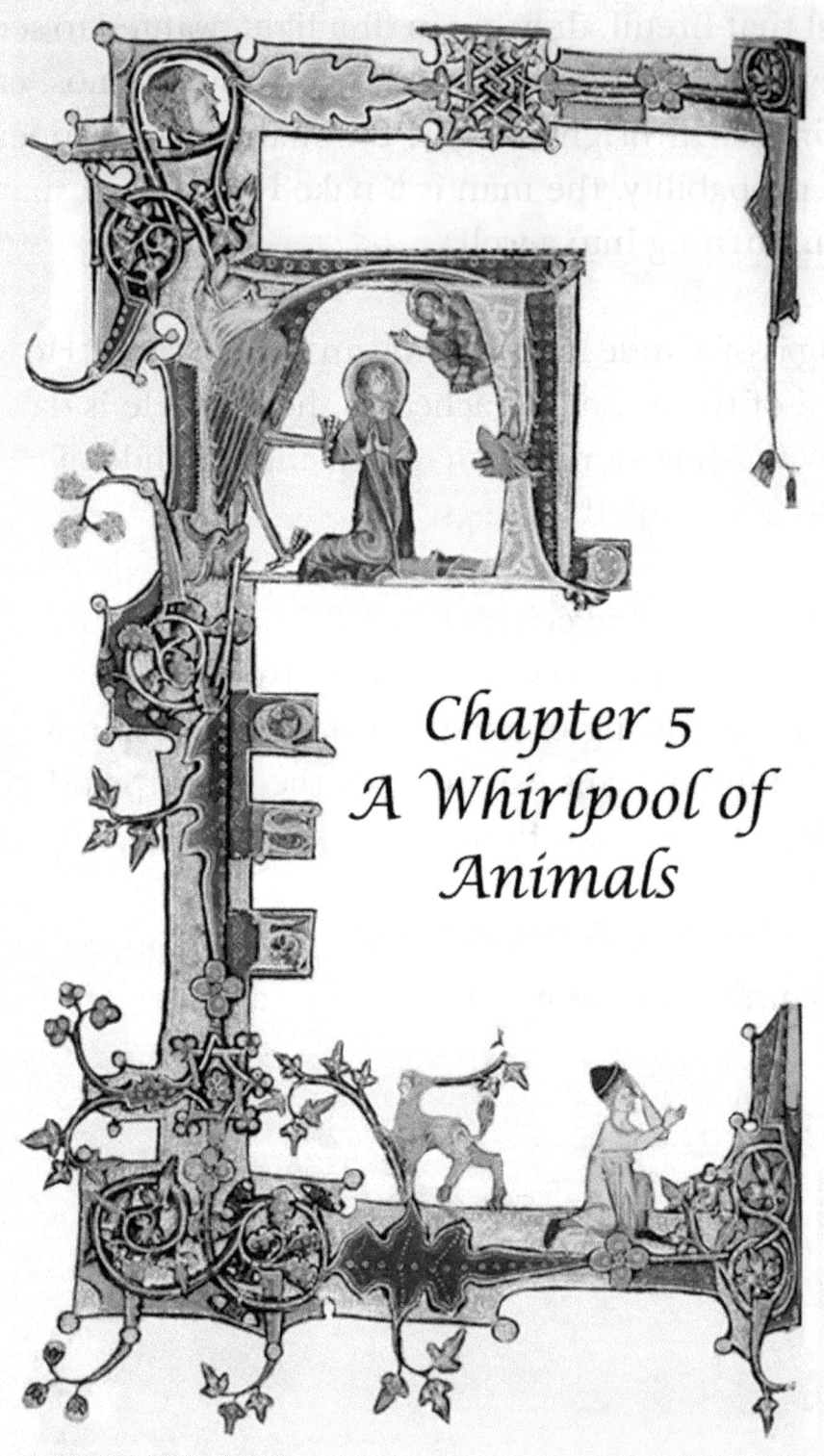

Chapter 5
A Whirlpool of Animals

CHAPTER 5

A Whirlpool of Animals

In the sixties, before taking acid, quite a lot of preparation would occur. On the day of the journey, we would clean the house and put out fresh flowers and bowls of fruit. We would put a sign on the front door saying, "This house is in Space Lock until four," or whatever time was appropriate. "Please do not disturb." Then we would unplug our phones, select the music we would listen to, and light incense and candles.

Friends would often come to visit, and seeing the sign, they would sit and wait. Often more people would arrive. "Where's Richard and Molly?" they would ask. "Oh, they're in space lock until four," they would be told, and everyone would sit on the stoops, talk, and visit.

Our house in San Francisco on Fredrick Street was a kind of meeting place for our friends. We used to call it, "the last of the great salons," and gathering there and talking became known as "saloning." It was a place of music, of books, of art, of poetry and of philosophy and a launching port for sending psychedelic ships across the ocean of existence.

The first four hours of an LSD trip is called the "flash." There is "going into the flash," "peaking," and "coming out of the flash." The flash is followed by what is called the "reflective analytic period." During the flash, there is little conversation, and one usually wants to sit or lie down and listen to music. After the flash, you could look back in amazement at what had occurred. Conversation returns, and you can eat simple foods, such as fruit or nuts or yogurt. One time someone brought over some small American flags. When a group of people would trip together, we would give everyone a flag. During the flash as we looked at people to see how they were doing, they would wave their flag as an assurance that everything was OK.

Later in the seventies, people sought a more controllable, recreational experience, where a dose was around one hundred or even fifty micrograms. You could take it and go to Golden Gate Park, the aquarium, the Botanical Garden, the Natural History museum, the Japanese Tea Garden, or even go out dining in restaurants, but in the sixties, it was customary to take two hundred and fifty or three hundred micrograms. You could take such a high dose at a rock concert so long as you took it after you arrived. By the time the concert was over, you would be out of the flash.

Once we were in an old, abandoned warehouse in the San Francisco Mission District. Some friends of mine had rented it. They had built workshops and living quarters, where they would work on light shows to be shown at rock concerts at the old Fillmore Auditorium. Upstairs was an old, abandoned hotel that once had been used by boxers. Now mostly mice inhabited it.

The warehouse was a common center for community parties, but this night there were only three of us: Deacon, Bill and I. We were going to take White Lightning. This was a particularly powerful form of acid that also contained the synthetic phenylethylamine drug DOM, known on the street as STP.

We each ground up one White Lightning tablet and sniffed it up our noses, and then we took a second tablet each under the tongue, about five hundred to six hundred micrograms. This was a heroic dose, but we took it boldly and with confidence. People used to take much larger amounts in those days. They were seeking full-blown, life-changing mystical experiences. They were seeking enlightenment. Two hundred and fifty micrograms was considered a standard threshold dose.

After taking the medicine, we were instantly transported beyond conversation, and we each withdrew to a different part of the warehouse.

Omar Khayyam writes in his *Rubaiyat*,

> And some we loved
> The loveliest and the best
> Who Time and Fate of all their vintage pressed
> Had drunk their cup a little round or two
> And one by one, crept silently to rest.

The effect was very stable because of the STP. Forms were holding together quite nicely; nothing was breaking up or spilling out of itself, but everything was getting quite white with a kind of washed-out look.

Now and then I would go and pee. I always seem to be able to do that, but I have seen people so stoned that they wandered around with their pants down around their ankles, peeing on the carpet. Once in the first hour, I ran into my friend Bill in the bathroom. "Pretty far-out," he said.

It was night, and it was getting colder. We never thought to bring warm coats or blankets. Now when I relaxed, I was starting to disappear. I would just melt, and there would be nothing. Except for this, not much was happening except the cold.

I managed to locate a little electric heater and found that if I sat with it directly in my lap, I could get a little warmth, after which I would melt and disappear. The heater had a timer that allowed it to run for about fifteen minutes, after which it would shut off. I would start to shiver and come back into my body.

By now it was the second hour of our trip. Somewhere I could hear Deacon chanting, "Aummmmmmm."

Sitting on the floor with the electric heater in my lap, I was peaking. Then it happened. Suddenly I wasn't in the warehouse anymore. I was in a room with two other people.

To the best of my recollection, they were male adults, totally human looking, and kind of scientific types. They wore white laboratory jackets. The room had a scientific quality, and the walls were lined with intricate machinery. On one side of the room was an elongated window running its length. It was attached to a kind of porch that extended out over a much-larger space below.

The space below acted as a kind of three-dimensional screen upon which images would appear, and as the people talked to me, they would show me pictures. They were explaining to me that we were outside of time as I understood it and that this wasn't taking any time at all on Earth. Back where I had come from, all time had stopped, and the world had become frozen.

This was all happening between the seconds back on Earth, and on the screen were pictures of time being halted, falling leaves hovering in midair, second hands on clocks not moving. It was as though a certain kind of time existed here, but it was not synchronous with Earth time. We could spend as long a period here as was needed, they said, and on Earth it would all be between breaths, between heartbeats. It was as if time and space were frozen and held in suspension until needed.

The nature of the communication was not verbal but telepathic. It was the direct, simultaneous transference of knowledge from mind to mind. Then on the screen outside the window, there appeared a gigantic whirlpool.

Once before on peyote, I had seen such a vortex, but then it had been of the rotating black-hole type threatening to drag me into it, into its maw, down into some cosmic drain. This vortex was the very opposite. Instead of sucking everything into it, it was spewing everything out, and it was spinning. Out from its center like some spiral galaxy came an incredible flow of plasma-like energy. It was red in color and filled with intricate patterns and designs of a geometric nature. It was a spiraling vortex of creativity, as though one was witnessing the very point where materiality entered our universe.

And then before my eyes, there unfolded a most fantastic sight. The design-filled matrix of moving geometric forms began to change, and the energy patterns began to assume biological shapes. The whirlpool was gushing forth oceans of microbiological, single-cell organisms like protozoa, a flowing profusion of amoebas, and paramecia with wiggling flagella. The two people were explaining that this represented the genesis of the universe and the creation of life. Then the entire play of evolution unfolded out of the spewing center of the whirlpool.

Single cells became multicellular organisms, which now became animals, first simple and then complex. It became a spinning mandala of zoomorphic shapes like animal crackers, geometric representations, changing and transforming with incredible beauty and precision. Now there were oceans of shimmering fish swimming through the life stream; now swarms of insects exploded from the ether; now there were flights of flocks of brightly colored birds. Waves of reptiles radiated out from the center of the vortex, slithering snakes, lizards, frogs, and salamanders.

Then suddenly everything became mammals with fur, fangs, claws, snarling snouts, and bushy tails. One variety of mammals followed another. There were squirrels, rabbits, dogs, wolverines, foxes, and wolves. My hosts were explaining that this was a representation of the recapitulation of biological evolution.

Then the whirlpool began to slow down. The speed of its rotation diminished like a cosmic roulette table. It turned slower and slower like the wheel of fortune at the fair. Click, click, click. It came to rest on the variety of animals that it was showing when it stopped. These were wolves and foxes.

The alchemical wheel of fortune, from *Speculum Veritatis*

I took this in a kind of totemistic sense as though my totem animal was a wolf or fox, as though somehow in the past my existence and theirs had been somehow connected. I knew that in earlier lives, I had been all those animals. They were my ancestors. I knew that the journey I had been on spanned the evolution of animal life on this planet and that somewhere in the fabric of my life; threads of wolves and foxes were woven into the pattern.

And then with the cosmic wheel of fortune coming up wolves, I was suddenly returned to the world, back in the warehouse. Time had started again. The entire room was dramatically illustrated. Every cubic centimeter of space was elaborately encrusted and embellished with designs, patterns, and arabesques. All the imagery had to do with wolves and foxes.

Ornamental wolf heads were sprouting everywhere like gargoyles. I would look at the painted concrete floor, and flows of foxes would wash away from me, forming interwoven, perpetually reorganizing mosaics. The blank walls displayed giant wolves heads flanked by rampant foxes surrounded by borders of intricate lycanthropic patterns. People's faces flowed with colored films of fox grids. Everyone's skin was illuminated with fox tattoos.

Now for a little while, like a powerful prisoner released from bondage, intelligence was set free. It was not my intelligence, for in that state, I was but one of the expressions of this wild Logos.

The Logos was one of the names the Gnostics gave to the supreme, ineffable manifestation of deity experienced under the influence of entheogens.

The boundary conditions of consciousness had been pulled down.
For millions of years of evolution, it seemed, mind had evolved in its own prison house, walling itself in, chaining itself to its evolving sense of form, creating the holographic display of the sense objects in an automatic process as spontaneous as breathing. Objects are in fact generated by the senses. Sight creates form; hearings creates the sensation of sounds, smelling produces the tapestry of odors and touch the spectrum of tactile feeling. In Indian philosophy, these are called the objects of the senses. This had kept consciousness in the world. In fact this was the world, but why did this trapping of the mind occur? It is because the world at the stage that we see it is a limited creation being formed by a limitless intelligence and if everything that could be perceived was let in, we would be overwhelmed and unable to function, but

it had gone too far. The utilitarian had damped the aesthetic far more than was necessary.

So on that night, for a time, intelligence was loose. When you looked at something, you could watch it being made right before your eyes. It would be spun out of threads of light, woven warp and woof into fabrics of energy. The mind in its play would form each image the way a vine might grow around a tree or across a wall. It would coil around the legs of chairs like rainbow snakes. It would lie like embroidered tablecloths on surfaces. It would ripple like translucent films of light on floors, like Persian carpets resembling everything.

I noted a strange thing at this level. My retinal retention process was causing images to rise up and fade away much slower than usual. My perception caused each slice of time, each frame, to linger long into the next and into the next. This was how they got so much consciousness into a single perception, I thought, by lengthening both the attack and the decay so that the instances would pile up and overlap.

This was especially true when watching movement. Deacon would walk across the room, but as the middle and end of the event unfolded, the beginning was just starting to fade away. Deacon stretched out like an accordion, and you could actually watch his world line hanging in time.

You could also see that he never really ever moved continuously across the room at all but rather existed discretely and simultaneously, like an electron at many different points along his path. Over there he was just starting to walk. Here he was halfway across the room, and there he was completing the movement, all attached and spread out like stroboscopic shutters. It is a variation of this same process of retinal retention that makes the discontinuous frames of our normal perception appears smooth and unbroken, like the frames of a movie film or like the circle of fire left by a whirling torch.

We climbed up to the roof of the abandoned hotel and gazed out over the city. It looked like Oz, glowing, shining, and glistening. It was like the New Jerusalem, the City of God, and the Holy City. The buildings gleamed like jewels, their reflected light forming rainbows of iridescent splendor. It had rained lightly, and the wet surfaces of buildings shot out rays of prismatic rainbow radiance. It was one of the most beautiful things I had ever seen.

Outside, walking up Market Street to a bus stop, we passed a homeless person. He stared at Deacon and he gazed at Deacon's beard, shoulder-length hair, and Madras-bedspread poncho with his cowboy boots sticking out the bottom.

"What the hell are you?" the man asked.

In Deacon's state, this must have produced thousands of associations. His mind flooded with possibilities, and he was left speechless.

"You're a bum!" the man said. "I know a bum when I see one. You're a bum."

"Well," Deacon said, grinning, "I guess I am."

A dharma bum, I thought silently, remembering Jack Kerouac's book of that title.

Entheogens increase our ability to experience the multiple meanings of words. There are far more meanings than there are words. There are a limited number of mouth noises that a primate can make. That is why the same word has to take on more than one meaning. A "bar" can mean a drinking establishment or a long piece of steel. The brain filters out all the inappropriate ones, and we automatically understand the correct meaning from the context in which we hear it.

Entheogens reduce the filtering, and it is not uncommon while on psychedelics to recognize all the multiple meanings of words. Somehow the brain likes this. This is why puns are funny. Poets and authors, such as T. S. Eliot and W. B. Yeats, who used entheogens incorporated these multiple meanings in their writing. Turned-on spiritual and religious groups use it as a kind of code to hide their references to mushrooms and other entheogens from the uninitiated. The ecstatic mind can understand the multiple meanings while they are hidden from the layperson.

One of the surprising and unexpected things about the entheogens is the abundance of animal imagery that is seen in the visions. Not only that, but they are always the same animals, and these are seen all around the world and in all periods of history. The menagerie includes a standard repertoire of lions, tigers, wolves, snakes, reptiles, birds, deer, bears, bulls, and many more.

Furthermore these zoomorphic hallucinations of animals have become part of the symbols and emblems associated with the entheogenic mysteries. These beasts appear unexpectedly in hallucinogenic motifs superimposed on walls, sofas, or carpets. There is also the common shamanic phenomenon of animal transformation or the turning into wolves, bears, birds, or other animals by entheogenic trippers. I have turned into a wolf and, on several occasions, into lions, and I have witnessed tigers and panthers and jaguars and other predatory cats. Animal hallucinations are usually surprising and unexpected.

In South America, people who take ayahuasca, commonly see jaguars and snakes, which are principle figures in indigenous religions. People in America and other countries who take ayahuasca in domestic settings also see jaguars and other predatory cats and snakes although these animals are not part of their common experience. These animals are even seen on LSD and other psychedelics without a long history of use. Do entheogens have content that is hardwired into them, or are they like television receivers that tune into a program going on somewhere else?

The next most common ayahuasca hallucination is a vision of Black people seen in tribal settings, although none of the native peoples in the Amazon are black. The indigenous Africans are usually seen from above as though one were flying overhead. They look up, smile, and wave. This is further proof that entheogenic visionary content is contained or transmitted by the drug and not part of the personal imagination.

William Blake wrote,

> Tiger, tiger burning bright
> In the forests of the night;
> What immortal hand or eye,
> Could frame thy fearful symmetry?

When the stars threw down their spears
And watered heaven with their tears:
Did he smile his work to see?
Did he who made the Lamb make thee?

Tiger, tiger burning bright,
In the forests of the night:
What immortal hand or eye,
Dare frame thy fearful symmetry?

When Blake saw the tiger during his mushroom experience, it was difficult to reconcile with his expectations of spiritual figures and religious symbols. He asks, "Did he who made the Lamb make thee?"

How many times has this poem been read in English and poetry classes and been completely misunderstood by everyone, including the teacher? It is explained thus by poetry professors: "The tiger is a God symbol."

Among the alchemists, the Red Lion and the Green Lion were names for the philosopher's stone, which was itself an epithet for the fly-agaric mushrooms. Red was for the color of *Amanita muscaria*, and green was a reference to verdancy.

What is the explanation for the animals seen in entheogenic visions? In the Amazon, jaguars eat the leaves of banisteria, one of the ingredients in ayahuasca. They eat until they can no longer walk and then roll around on their backs like kittens. Olmec shamans ate *Amanita muscaria* mushrooms and turned into wee jaguars. Many other animals are mycophilic and love to eat mushrooms. When these animals eat entheogenic mushrooms, they get high.

Terrence McKenna and others have suggested that entheogens are, in part, recording devices that retain the impressions of the experiences of those who take them. It is as though all the people and animals throughout the ages on this and many other worlds that have eaten these sacramental botanicals have blazed a trail through hyperspace, leaving the impressions of what they experienced.

The Mazatec curandera Maria Sabina revealed the secret of the mushroom to Gordon Wasson and he published his account in *Life* magazine, "Seeking the Magic Mushrooms". Following this, hundreds of Westerners flooded to Huautla to eat the fungus. These included rock stars and hippies. People would eat the mushroom in the daytime, take off their clothes, and run naked through the streets. One bemushroomed adolescent publicly ate a live chicken. The *presidente* requested that people eat the mushrooms only indoors at night. Many merchants and townspeople began selling the mushrooms to the tourists. This included even the barber. Shamans complained that the mushrooms were disappearing. They used to grow everywhere, but now one had to go deep into the forest to secret spots to find them.

Maria lamented that the mushroom experience had changed and not for the better. The mushroom used to speak in Mazatec. Now it spoke sometimes in English. It used to transport you to the sacred mountain or to mist-filled valleys. Now it took you to New York. It used to show you images from Mazatec mythology. Now it presented Disney cartoons of a tap-dancing Mickey Mouse. She regretted ever having shown the mushroom to Gordon Wasson. Maria was shunned by the townspeople for revealing the secret, and she died alone and impoverished. Today she is considered a saint, and people visit her grave and leave offerings of flowers.

The fact that the mushroom experience changed when Westerners began using them demonstrates how it may be a recording device where visionary events become part of the visions. If it is true that entheogens are recorders of experience, it would include recordings of the experiences of animals that ate entheogenic fungus, and in fact the animals commonly seen in visions do eat mushrooms. They are mycophilic. They love to eat mushrooms. The eating of entheogenic plants and mushrooms is called "spontaneous auto ingestion". It is not accidental.

I once gave my beagle a quarter of a tab of White Lightning LSD and took him for a walk in the park. Suddenly we found ourselves surrounded by dogs. Real dogs. They were coming from every direction, some dragging their leashes behind them, and I could hear the dogs' owners calling to them in bewilderment. Somehow the dogs knew that my dog was tripping and were attracted to him. By the way, I don't recommend giving entheogens to pets.

Bronze Age warriors would take battle potions that included fly-agaric mushrooms before going into battle to induce the "war rage." They would also give some to their horses. If the horse began to urinate, the warrior would dismount, catch the urine in his helmet, and drink it, and then reinvigorated, he would continue the fight with renewed courage and enthusiasm. There was a Celtic term for this: "the courage of the kidneys."

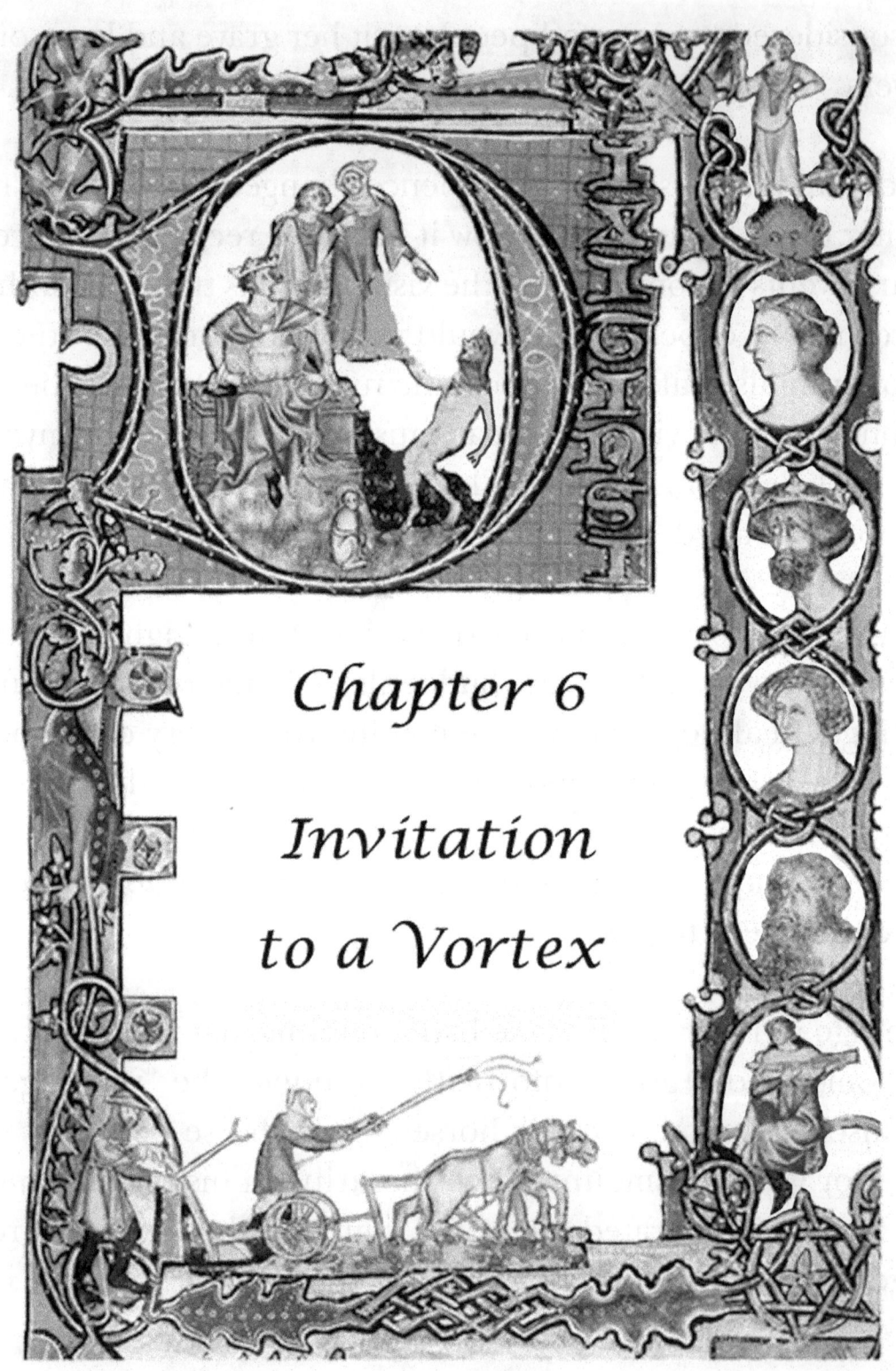

Chapter 6

Invitation to a Vortex

CHAPTER 6

Invitation to a Vortex

ASIDE FROM MARIJUANA, PEYOTE WAS the first major psychedelic I experienced. I still had a supply of dried peyote buttons left over from my experience at Santa Barbara. I had taken it several times since then in lower doses, and without the company of the raving mental patient, Robin, I found the experiences beautiful, colorful, inspiring, and revivifying, more like the positive things I had experienced at the beginning of my first experience. It was the late sixties. My girlfriend, Molly, and I were living in Westwood Village next to the UCLA campus. We were going to take some peyote.

The trip seemed to begin long before we actually took the drug. It started with the decision to trip or earlier still with the impulse that led to the decision. At any rate, by the time we had started eating the cactus, we were already as high as you sometimes get at the peak of your experience.

You can't have a full, major experience any time. There are only certain periods when you can sustain a high-level impact and only certain times on the calendar, so to speak, when the universe can produce one. If you ingest a mind-changing chemical then, a peak-level experience is almost assured. It is like a strong radio station that is sometimes broadcasting and sometimes not. If you can turn on the receiver at the correct interval, you can pick up the signal. You can recognize these periods because you are more or less in an altered state of consciousness already, and strange things are happening all around you.

It was many years later that I learned the correct method of cleaning away the toxic and noxious parts of the cactus. The top of a peyote cactus is covered with little white fibrous tufts, with a cluster of them in the center. The tufts are highly stimulating, and when they are included, the high is wild, Dionysian, much more powerful. Peyote in its untreated state is much more likely to cause vomiting. If the tufts are removed, the high becomes much smoother, calmer, and more manageable and even recreational in low doses. The Indians scoff at the white people who remove the tufts. In a way, they have a point, because my most powerful and amazing peyote experiences happened with whole buttons.

If you cook the peyote for four hours or more, the toxic alkaloids cook off and break down, leaving the mescaline and the most beautiful and pleasant other compounds in the peyote. The cooked juice can be strained and boiled down, skimmed as it reduces. It forms a black tar called peyote tar. If you pour the sticky, reduced liquid onto a green-plastic trash bag such as is used in the yard and put a fan on it for the final stage; it will not stick when solidified. Peyote tar is so manageable that you can take small amounts and go to the Laundromat or go out to dinner. Peyote tar can even be smoked. Combining it with LSD restores the intensity of unrefined peyote without the hyper stimulation of the tufts.

That evening we simply ground everything together in a kitchen blender—bark, tufts, and root. We put the powder in large triple-zero gelatin capsules and ate them by the handful with the greatest of difficulty.

Ordinarily peyote can have an hour or more of preparatory queasiness, nausea, and sickness. Someone said that with mescaline, the hangover precedes the intoxication. Vomiting is common. This time, however, the experience went directly to the peak sensory level. I remember the space contained within the apartment being so expanded that it felt like being inside of some capsule that was somehow moving at an ever-increasing velocity. It was like a flying room. We commented that talking to each other during this phase was like speaking over a long-distance telephone system even though we were standing next to one another.

And then abruptly it was as though the apartment had stopped flying, and we found ourselves at some kind of level or plateau where we could converse normally again. We agreed that we had flown somewhere and that we weren't moving at the moment, but this was by no means the destination of the journey, merely a kind of waiting room in which one changed modes of transportation.

Suddenly we were in motion again. This time it was more like riding on a train than flying. We would move for a while and then stop as though at a station and start again.

Each station felt like if you got off, there would be a whole universe level to explore. Molly said that she felt that we could ride the train as far as we wished and get off at any station we chose.

"But," she said, asking one of those rhetorical questions that the universe always answers if asked, "I wonder what's at the end of the line?"

And in an act of bravery that I never saw repeated, she said, "Let's ride the train to the end of the line and see what's there."

Then the train started moving really fast. It became an express, and though many stations flew by, it did not stop for them. The feeling of long-distance telephone talking returned, and the feeling of acceleration increased. Things got dark and dim. It was like moving through a zone where light, as we perceive it couldn't propagate.

What was starting to occur was the emergence of a mythopoetic modality of mind common to the entheogenic state. It happens so easily and effortlessly that one scarcely realizes it is happening. This is how mythology and poetry began. The trip was turning into a fairy tale. We lay on the floor and exchanged heavy sighs while we waited for the ride to end. When the train stopped, it was another waiting room, a lone station house at the end of some cosmic line, vaguely based on my old living room at home. It was the end of the train line, perhaps, but only another transportation change for this journey.

Molly left the train and walked to the center of the room. "Oh!" she said. "Here is a circle. I think it is a circle in which you can travel. I'm going to get into it and see what it does."

She kneeled down on the rug within her circle. I looked all about but could not find another circle, and Molly's was clearly a one-passenger model. A picture of a sorcerer drawing a circle with a sword flashed before my mind. My eyes fell on an artifact of some antiquity, a third-millennium Bronze Age Persian sword that had been found in an archaeological dig in Palestine. It had a bronze blade and a copper handle.

I picked up the sword, and with the point, I inscribed a circle on the floor adjacent to Molly's circle with the edges tangent. I then knelt in my circle that I had drawn, faced Molly, and laid the sword so that it penetrated both spaces with its ends, the blade crossing over the outlines. It was clear that if we each touched the respective ends of the sword with our hands, this would make the circles fly.

Now up to this point, the various metaphors I have used to describe the state of our transportation had the feeling of creative fantasy, of mythopoetic construction, like being in a moment of high inspiration, like writing a story about us. At this point, however, we passed beyond some kind of border or frontier. As you actually pass beyond the familiar world of matter and things in relationships, you encounter something entirely different. The fantasy took on a reality.

As we touched the end of the sword, the earth rumbled and trembled. A great electrical hum appeared that spoke of enormous, unimaginable power, like dynamos or generators, and the circles began to fly.

The circles expanded to become bubbles. There was a kind of popping sound. It was like light was being sucked away from your eyes faster than you could see it. Visibility collapsed into a kind of hollow, gray darkness, and we seemed to be moving at a fantastic speed. We could dimly see the discarded, hollow shells of forms that had once been the room and its furniture, but now they seemed like the bones of time-space dimly perceived across a vast distance through a telescope.

The hum of the flying bubbles became an insect-like trill as though a giant bee or fly were making the sound. Molly pointed out later that during this period, it was as though we were in a vacuum and there was no air. She said that neither of us breathed nor did we need to during this time. I do not recall confirming this observation, but I have heard the phenomena referred to in mystical narrations. It is consistent with our experience of subjective time freeing itself from the objective continuum, where fantastically complex realizations can occur between breaths or heartbeats or watch ticks.

The Prophet Mohamed, whom we now know was inspired by *Amanita muscaria* mushrooms, to which he was introduced by the Coptic Christians, reported that he was pouring water from a pitcher into a cup. When the glory of infinity struck him, the pitcher fell from his hand, and he was transported nine times around the world. When he returned to his body, only then did the pitcher shatter on the floor. His vision happened outside of time.

Suddenly I saw two giant, luminous beings. It was a man and a woman. So large were they that the bubbles in which we were flying were the relative size of tennis balls in their hands. These giants were in the same position as Molly and I were to each other—that is, kneeling, facing each other. They held their hands out, cupped before them. It was upon these giant hands that our flying bubbles rested. Indeed our bubbles' flight appeared to be caused by these giant beings picking them up and transporting them to some faraway place.

The giants were very loving. All during the time they were carrying us, they were communicating this love to us. The whole event seemed so real as to be totally, subjectively terrifying to an ontological system never thus far challenged so. At the same time it was fraught with meaning and significance. We were approaching the end of the line.

There was a feeling of celebration, as if thousands of unseen multitudes were cheering for us, and the giant beings were saying that this was the most important day of our lives, that we were coming to the destination of a journey on which we had been pilgrims since the beginning of time, and that what we were about to be given was an opportunity of such magnitude and significance that woe to anyone who misunderstood this or made the wrong choice.

And all the while, in the distance, there began to appear this point. It was spinning and whirling, and it was obviously where we were headed. Now the density and gravity of this point is just beyond description. It was like a whirling neutron star where one teaspoon of it had the density and gravity of the entire earth.

From the time we entered the circles, matter had seemed to lose its solidity, becoming like shadows of something else. Forms were hollow, but this point was heavy. It was like a swirling vortex of liquid protoclastic magma, a whirlpool formed from the expressed plasmatic juice of space and time with the entire universe in its center.

Today I would have compared it to a black hole. But this was long before we knew of such things, and the giants were saying things that didn't make any sense at the time, like "This is the center of the universe!" and "This is the heart of the world!" The closer to it we got, the bigger it became. It was as though a cosmic bathtub plug had been withdrawn, causing a hole in which everything, and everyone was being sucked into a descending vortex.

As we approached the rim, the roar of this thing filled all creation like a billion Niagaras. It was the event horizon. It became increasingly clear that the opportunity we were to be given was to jump into this thing and go down the drain. So real was the experience that it made us very uneasy, like who are these giants anyway? It was like native priests telling us that we were so lucky and honored because we had been chosen to jump into the volcano.

The guides were telling us that the moment of the decision had come. If we were to turn back, it must be now, before the forces of attraction became any greater, and it was terribly important that we understood that if we went through the hole, the world as we knew it would stop and would be replaced by something else.

They kept saying, "And if you go, you can never come back, and you will never see anyone again whom you know." They were showing us pictures in our heads of our family, friends, and pets, or they would show us images of mountains and forests and the sea. The pictures were filled with such beauty.

The thought of everything we loved permeated us with a longing, because we were about to be separated from them, and the giants were saying, "This will never be this way again." It was so heavy!

The warnings were so serious, and the responsibility they were asking us to take was beyond anything I understood at the time. The vortex filled the whole universe now. We were right at the rim.

The guides were saying, "And if you go, you will find everything you ever wanted, and if you go, you will know the answer to every question. You don't have to spend the rest of your life searching. You can attain it now! It will be complete, unexcelled enlightenment and liberation. You are so lucky. This opportunity isn't given to everyone."

And the moment was there. It was the solemnest thing I ever felt. The giants were urging us to choose, and all creation was urging us and demanding that we decide now because the moment of no return was rapidly approaching. It was like standing on a high diving board that was so tall that you were afraid to jump and jumping really counted because not every swimmer gets the chance to jump, and everyone you love is watching, wanting you to jump, encouraging you to jump, wondering if you will jump, asking one another if they think you will jump; and the moment is rushing at you, and you can't even take your time to get into the mood.

You didn't know about the opportunity until you got to the top of the diving tower. The situation was explained to you as you ascended, and now they were urging you on, saying that you must make the decision to jump or not and that the prize was the greatest in the world and that they wouldn't tell you what the pool was filled with.

You must choose very carefully and take responsibility for whatever you choose, and if you didn't choose to jump and climbed down, in one second from now, the diving board would collapse from under you, and you would fall in anyway.

I gazed into the swirling maw of the maelstrom, and I understood something of which I had not been absolutely certain until this moment: whatever this madness was, it was, in some kind of new and unknown way, as real as anything I had ever experienced.

This was for real—no dream giants telling a dream me to jump into a dream whirlpool. The giants and the whirlpool may have been visionary allegories for something, but whatever they represented was real!

It was I who panicked and made the decision to run. I remember saying to Molly something like; "We don't really want to do this now, do we? I mean, let's get out of here while we still can."

And she said, "But can we leave? I mean, will they let us go?"

And I said, "I think we can leave if we don't look back."

And so in utter seriousness, we started shouting out loud, frantically, "Thank you very much! We don't want to go, at least not now, at least not this time! We appreciate the honor and you giving us this opportunity! No, thank you, now! We don't want to see it!"

Then we were back in the apartment again. We had reentered time-space, prematurely no doubt, just at that point where matter was boiling and space was churning and turbulent, and we were so glad to get back from there. Our minds and feelings and thoughts were boiling also, and we were by no means free or safe from these forces.

It happened that back on Earth that evening at the theater of the UCLA, a play was being shown, a production of Jean Cocteau's *The Infernal Machine*. Quite courageously we remembered the play, and as it was almost eight o'clock and we lived right next to the campus, we decided to attend. We were scared out of our wits and felt we had to get out of the apartment. As we left, we didn't know if we would be allowed to leave, as if at any instant, we could dissolve back into that whirlpool.

My mind was filled with mythical images of Orphic heroes making perilous ascents from the underworld. "Don't look back, Persephone," I said to Molly.

Actually it was Orpheus's wife, Eurydice, who looked back and missed her chance to escape from the underworld. Also in the Bible, at the destruction of Sodom and Gomorrah, it was Lot's wife who, though warned not to, looked back and was turned into a pillar of salt.

As we walked across the UCLA campus, the buildings, trees, and vegetation were glowing as though illuminated by colored floodlights. We arrived at the theater just as the audience was taking its seat. The audience was composed of multicolored, luminous persons wearing exaggerated, colored masks. Some of them were shaped like caricatures of my old friends, but they looked so colorfully costumed and made up that it seemed kind of conspiratorial, as though strangers had not too convincingly disguised themselves as our friends or as though our friends has secretly collaborated to put on makeup to exaggerate their features in order to see if we would notice. All this kind of paranoid thinking came from our not yet understanding that our perception of the world was a hologram created by our own mind-brain and not a solid world outside of ourselves.

As we watched the play, although neither of us had seen it nor read it, I knew every line in advance. The words would pop into my mind just before the characters would speak them, sometimes long in advance. Sometimes I knew the whole scene in advance. Every line, every word, was fraught with a complex array of double entendres and multiple meanings and nuances. The play was about us and the events that had happened earlier that evening.

The play is very profound even when it is viewed in an ordinary state of consciousness and Cocteau was no stranger to entheogens, it is filled with far-out dialogue, like when the jackal-headed god Anubis, the guardian to the entrance of the underworld, is talking with the Sphinx, telling her about time.

Anubis says, "If I were to take your scarf and fold it so, and then again and again, and if I were to take your hairpin and thrust it once through the scarf thus and then unfold it so as display the array of many holes, what simple fool would believe that all these holes were made at the same time in the same act from the penetration of a single pin? Human time is folded in eternity."

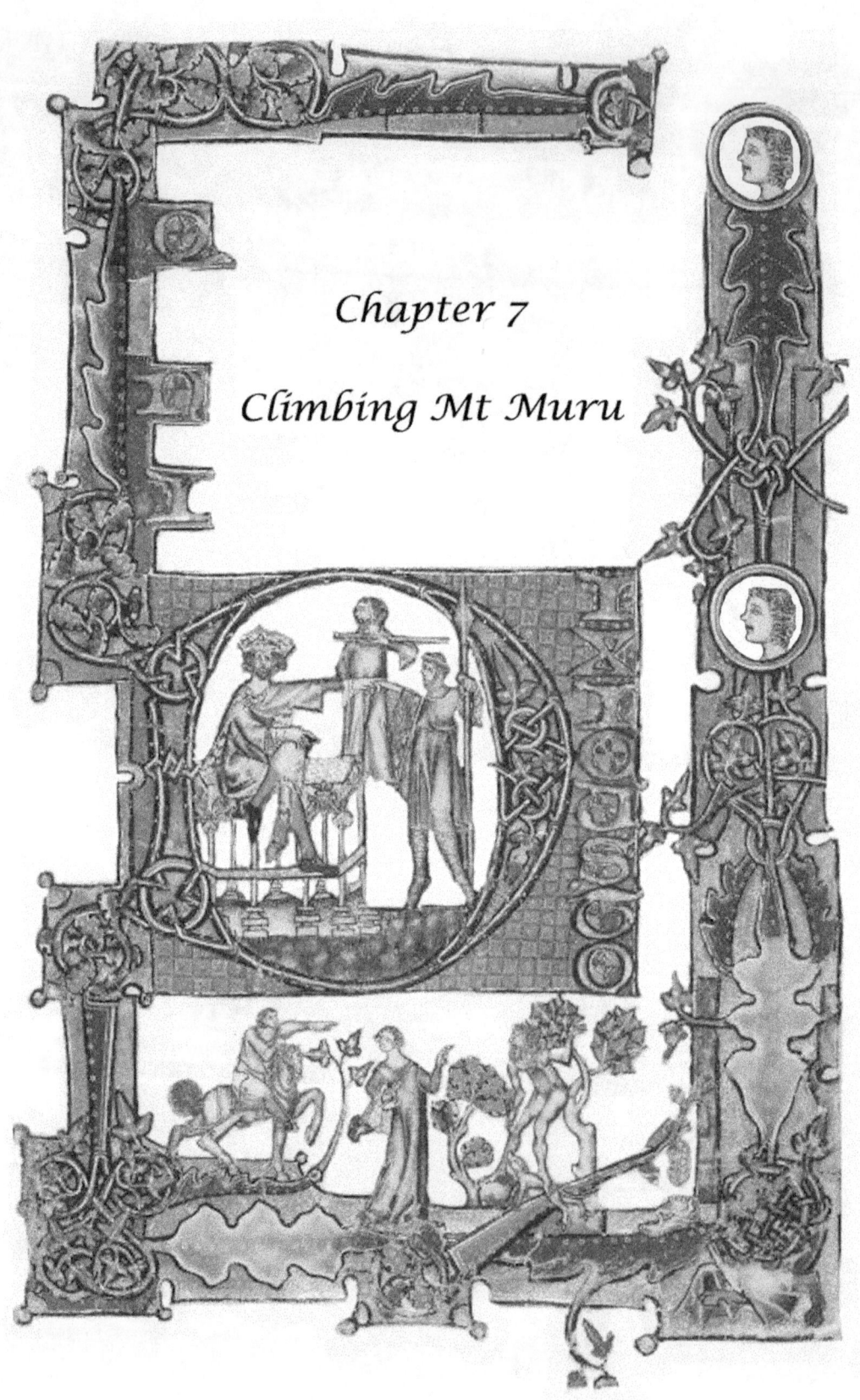

Chapter 7

Climbing Mt Muru

CHAPTER 7

Climbing Mount Muru

THE SUN WAS SETTING; I finished a cup of hot chocolate and set off in the dark night on another journey with magic mushrooms. In Mexico, chocolate is customarily drunk before eating mushrooms. I had fasted all day, and the sweet chocolate was welcome and uplifting.

Setting off, I felt I had grasped a very important concept. I could be selective, to an extent, as to whom or to what I paid attention. At first when traveling, I found it so interesting to meet anyone at all who was different and who would talk to me or show me something, but I was beginning to get the idea that there was quite a variety of different people out there, some with whom you might not care to associate. Somewhere there was a large collection of people I identified with as relatives, friends, associates, well wishers and coworkers Some of them were very strange and from very far away. These were the entities I had encountered in the workshop and in the aquarium of art. Whatever beings were in charge of the bottlebrush episode were of quite a different order. I would prefer to stay well away from them. I was determined to not tarry with anyone who was not in the family. Sometimes I had no choice.

Turning off the lights, I was plunged into total darkness. It is not surprising that the earliest prehistoric temples and sanctuaries were dark, womb-like caves that were places of entheogenic initiation. It has been a mystery how in such dark environments, the beautiful paintings of animals could have been produced, for there are no smoke marks on the ceiling indicating that torches were used. Perhaps it was the enhanced vision of the mushrooms that allowed the artists to work in the dark. Pictures of mushrooms have been drawn among the animals in the Paleolithic caves in Spain. On the mushroom, you can literally see in the dark.

Suddenly there loomed up before me an immense, monumental structure. The building, for it was a building, was as big as a mountain. It was huge, modern, futuristic, and many faceted. There were vast escarpments intersecting at many angles. There were rifts and canyon-like features. Because of the entirely architectural nature of the thing, the closer I drew, the more detail I could see. The topology was extremely intricate, as though constructed from square plates or tiles. Some of them were delicate, lattice works, like white, geometric filigree, like the plastic Lego bricks with little bumps on them that children build with. Some of the tiles looked like electrical circuit boards studded and encrusted with little shapes interconnecting with one another.

I seemed to be flying over the surface of this massive structure like Luke Skywalker's fighter plane flying over the Death Star in the movie *Star Wars*. I could dive down and fly along the canyons that were filled with complex structural detail. When I told Terrence McKenna about this, he said, "I have been right there! I have seen and flown around this mountain." This suggests to me that the visionary content reveled by mushrooms is not a product of my personal imagination but is either a part of the standard hallucinogenic repertoire of the fungus or are actual locations somewhere in the universe.

The mountain of India, from *The Alchemical Book of Lambspring*

The building had angled sides that reminded me of the sloping walls of Troy or the sides of the Great Pyramid. It was very futuristic, like the otherworldly structures that sometimes appear in science fiction.

Suddenly I was aware of two approaching figures. They were clearly very important. They were shaped like flat, rectangular surfaces, like panels or doors. They reminded me of the playing-card men in *Alice in Wonderland*. The entire surface of the cards was covered with an intricate pattern. They looked like printed circuit boards.

As the figures approached, I recognized the point in my earlier journeys where I had turned about and fled. *This time*, I thought, *I will face them and make myself accessible.* The figures were right before me now, and unhesitatingly I reached out and grabbed hold of one of them. It was like grasping a twenty-thousand-volt electrical wire. Things began to happen very fast. Suddenly the playing-card figures were moving very rapidly all around the surface of the mechanical mountain.

The card-like figures were moving in strange starting, stopping, lurching motions that were very surprising and unexpected, reminiscent of certain carnival rides, such as the Tilt-A-Whirl or the little cars that ride through the dark with motions designed to startle you.

My vision dissolved into scenes that were mixtures of botanical and organic materials and electronic circuitry. One vision was as though someone had taken five or six snakes and held them in a bundle, covered them with mucus, and then began to pull some of them in one direction and others in another. Then I saw two cobras raised upright in front of a wall. They were painted with red, white, and blue American flags.

Then in an instant, an utterly amazing event took place. From a great crevice in the metal and plastic mountain, something opened, and there shot up far into the sky five or six bolts of energy that resembled electrical arcs, like Tesla's artificial-lightning generators.

They were like sustained lightning, and they were towering above me, somehow serpent like, snapping and crackling. Then from their great heights, they plunged down, and all of them struck me at once. It was like being hit by many bolts of lightning that rose up out of the building to great heights and bent over and came down and impacted me from all directions, but the arcs remained visible, piercing my body like the horns of some great electric bull.

Now the arcs were swinging wildly around the sky, raining down upon me with a myriad of poignant but not painful blows as from a great scourge. The lightning strands lashed out at me again and again. Now I was seeing machines with glistening, wet, and moving tentacles twisting and turning among the circuitry and wires. The lightning arcs were continuing to strike against me. There was the sensation of being penetrated as the undulating currents played over my body.

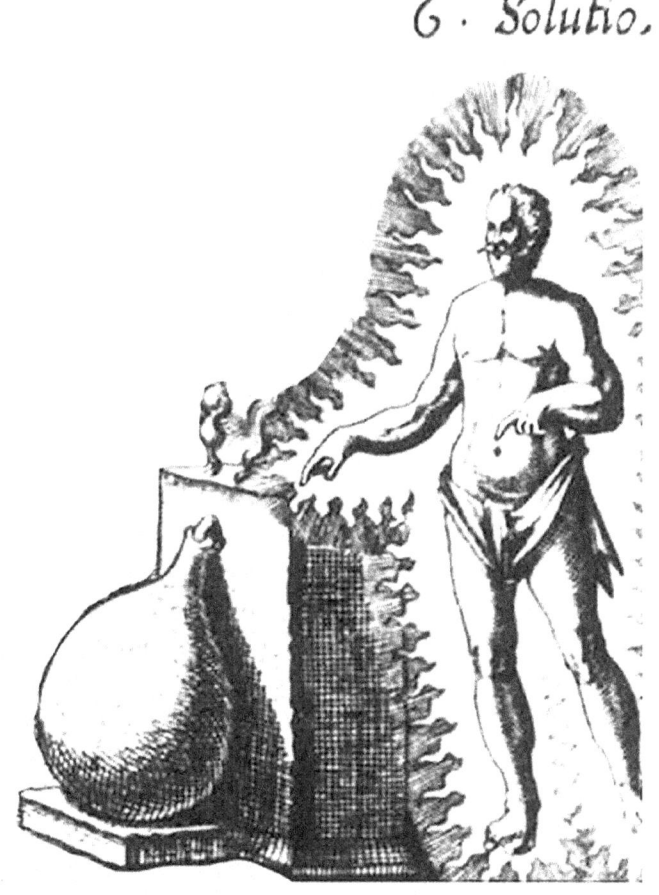

Struck by lightning, from *Mylius Philosophia Reformata Azoth*

They had become translucent tubes through which different-colored fluids were moving like giant clusters of IV tubes, and luminous, fluorescent super fluids were moving down them and entering my body. This was all happening so fast that I scarcely had time to think, but I was observing that I was allowing myself to go much farther this time than the last few excursions. I could see that I was getting used to it little by little, a little more each time.

Now things started to happen faster and faster. I watched a beautiful, mechanical insect stand on the pyramid's sloping face and watch me. It was exquisitely crafted, and it observed me with jewel-like eyes. Then the experience seemed to shift into an entirely new gear. If I thought the motions were rapid and sudden before, they were at a mere idle compared to what was to follow.

Suddenly the mountain was gone. With psilocybin, scenes can change very suddenly and unexpectedly. The space around me became dark and filled with moving shapes of shadowy figures. I would see fleeting images of threatening grimaces. I found myself surrounded by a crowd of fast-moving, dark entities who were clearly intending to seize me and carry me off somewhere.

I was completely confused by this last turn of events. I was proud that I was able to sustain what had just transpired. I had seen my capacity to experience the intensity of these experiences to be growing, but I had been through so much already. It seemed like I had put in more than a night's work. I had no doubt at this point that what was intended to follow would be for my benefit and was some kind of teaching lesson, but I remembered with a shudder how fearful my captivity had been the last time in the bottlebrush world.

The shadowy figures were like silhouettes. They had three round, flat, black disks on their heads like three-eared Mickey Mouse hats. Later I referred to them as the "Mouseketeers."

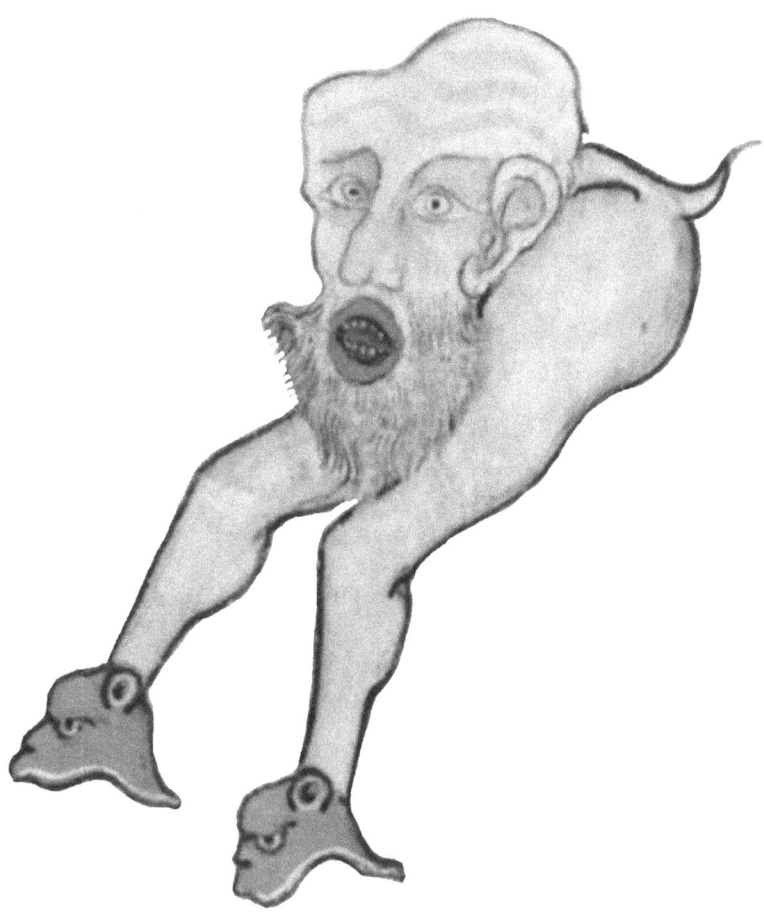

From the *Macclesfield Psalter* (1330)

They looked like trefoil designs, like cloverleaves seen in religious architecture, but these figures were not welcoming me to the Mickey Mouse Club. They were dangerous. They were hungry. They were starving. They were looking at me like I was food. I felt like a dish of rice lying on the ground in Aleppo. It felt like the Tennessee Williams play *Suddenly Last Summer*, where the starving population ends up attacking and eating the rich. I was terrified.

Suddenly the scene changed, and I was in a round room, lying on the now-familiar examination table. A taller figure I recognized as my caseworker was standing beside me on my right, and smaller figures were nearby.

"It is a good thing that we were nearby and happened to see you," he said, "or you would have been somebody's dinner. This isn't a scheduled meeting, but as long as you're here, we might as well have a look at you."

I felt like an expensive sports car with the smaller beings looking and working under the hood. Later the taller person and I were standing on a kind of porch and looking down at where I had been.

"They are so poor, and you are so powerful," I said. "Isn't there anything you could do to help them?"

"You should just be glad that you are one of us and not one of them," he replied.

Then there was another sudden modality switch. This is typical of mushroom experiences, where just when you think you are finished and it is time to come down, a whole new intense episode unfolds, followed by another and another.

I was entering a world of fibers. I was lying on the waterbed again. I was surrounded by color and motion. I was seeing filaments—cluster of multicolored threads, like wires or strings, woven together, a complex entanglement of flocculent tendrils emanating out from a common center like a luminous, translucent jellyfish.

It had undulating, animate appendages like flexible, movable fingers, for the entity was clearly a living thing. It seemed to be not organic in appearance but as though constructed out of living, synthetic plastic of bright, primary colors. The threadlike thing was approaching now at great speed, it's brilliantly colored, writhing tentacles reaching out, grasping, and clutching at me as it came.

Its intent was clearly to engulf me in its fibers until I was wrapped up in them, bound by them, and who knows what more. To be drawn toward some secret squid-like beak, to be eaten by it, to be loved? I could not wait to see. Shaking off the image, I went into the kitchen and poured myself a glass of tequila. Lying down again, I thought about the Mazatec mushroom *curandera* Maria Sabina sipping caña at the end of a mushroom session in the dark night of the Sierras.

And for a brief instant, I was standing on a tropical beach in Acapulco, and a huge object was rushing toward me, as if on two legs, something gigantic, something living yet at the same time architectural. It was huge. It towered above me as large as the UN building on its side. It was like looking at an immense surface, like the side of a battleship. The entire surface had a grid-like pattern, like a patchwork quilt. Here the patches were contrasting and brightly variegated.

They were like metal plates of overlapping sections, some windowed, some apparently louvered. It resembled a landscape of plowed fields seen from above. It seemed as if a whole city could have dwelt inside this thing, and yet I could not escape the feeling that it was not a building but a being, a person. Everything in psilocybin is personified. Inanimate objects are fluently and eloquently conversant. It seemed to be metallic or plastic, and yet there was flexibility about it—it moved as if its metal shell were some kind of covering, liked draped fabric of chain mail. It made me shudder.

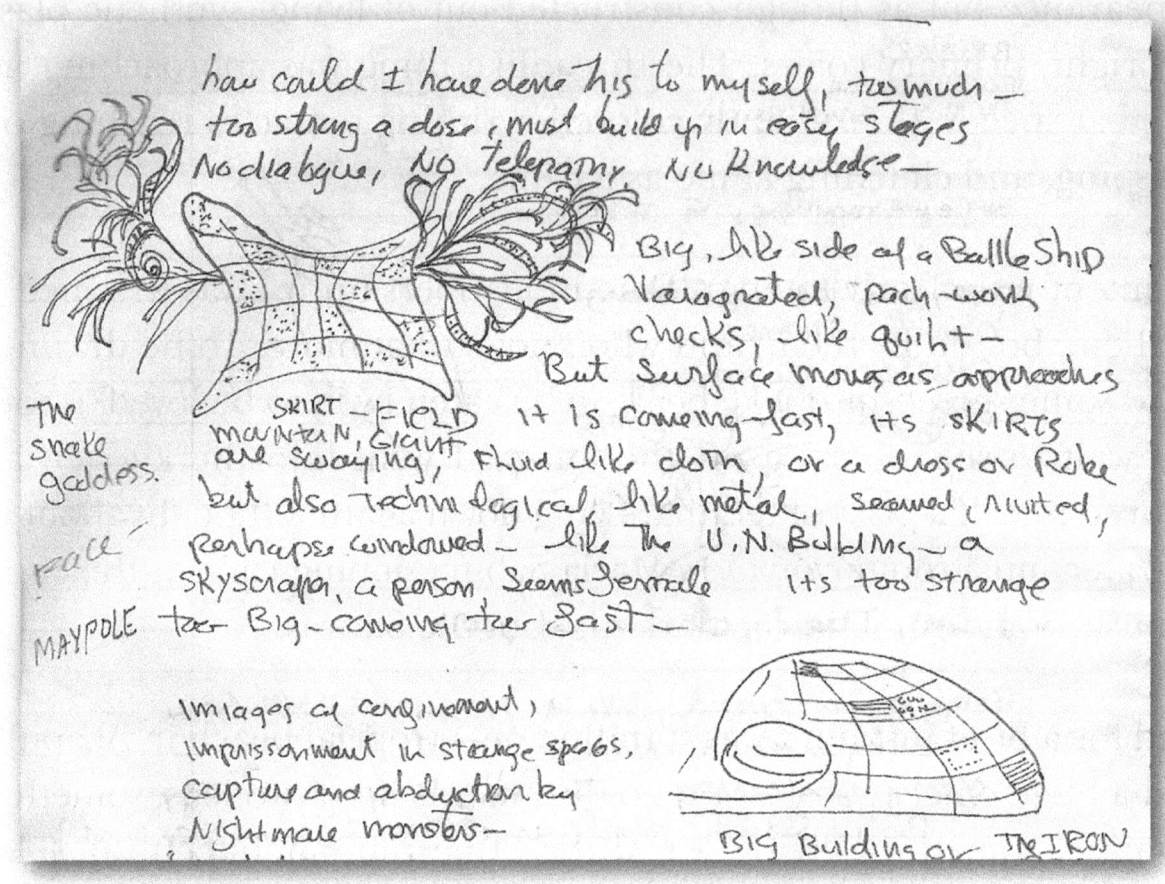

Field notes: An anthropomorphic fibrous building

As the gigantic thing came running toward me, huge doors in its sides seemed to open, and out came fibrous, clustering appendages like those of the jellyfish creature I had seen just before. Out of the doors came gigantic bundles of fettuccini-like ribbons. As the apparition drew nearer, I could make out that the fibers were flat like tape worms or segmented like cells. There contrasting hue gave them a striated appearance, and each translucent segment contained darker matter floating inside.

They hissed and rustled and seethed and writhed. It was like a mechanical Medusa, a goddess with wriggling snakes for hair. As the giant creature approached me, it seemed somehow female, as though she was holding up her patched skirt as she ran. Again I turned away, not daring to look any longer, and with my last ounce of strength, I pulled my attention back at last to my house and my world. I felt a wave of disappointment from the object as though she had come to show me her new dress and I had run away and refused to play.

The final vision subsided. I felt a wave of relief and security, followed by a poignant ache of disappointment. Now it was gone. I had sent it away. If I had known I could control it so easily, I would have stuck it out a little longer. Brave words, but somehow I know that unless controlling forces beyond me had chosen to end the experience at that particular time, there would have been no power on Earth that could have stopped it.

The fiber-like nature of these life forms has remained with me. They were like pom-poms waved at sports events, like brilliant streamers, like tangled, knotted yarn, or like whisks or brooms. They were like wooly caterpillars or the tails of Afghan dogs

I wondered if the prehistoric snake goddess, who for millennia had presided over the cult of psychedelic plants and mushrooms, had had somehow personified these life forms. The images of strange creatures faded, and I saw fleeting glimpses against closed eyes of strange machinery, metal corridors. In the impression, I was looking back at a great, building with a curved surface. Its color was dark, metallic, with riveted sections like a great iron fortress or stronghold. The front end of it spiraled into itself like a seashell or the shell of a snail.

"It is Spiral Castle," I breathed. "I was in Spiral Castle." Spiral Castle was one of the Celtic names for the netherworld.

I decided I had had enough for now. I took four grams of niacin and three grams of glycine, an amino acid with a calming effect. Taking niacin is a way of signaling to the mushroom entities that are directing the experience that you have had enough and want to come down. I was through cooperating. I turned on the light. It was really too early in the mushroom trip to do this. It was premature. You should always remain in the dark until a full four or five hours have passed.

In the Greek myth, the god Eros tells Psyche that he will come to her and make love to her but only in the dark and that she must never turn on the light. He is the best lover she has ever had. Her jealous sisters tell her that she should look at him with the light on. "He might be a monster or a snake," they warn her. She conceals a lantern under the blankets, and when Eros comes, she uncovers it. He is a beautiful, shining youth, but he admonishes her for disobeying him and flies away, never to return.

My dogs were getting very excited. They were experiencing an intense contact high. My beagle's eyes were as big as saucers, and paisley clouds seem to rise from him like steam. My Doberman, Asia, was frightened to death. She was crying and whimpering. She would jump up on the bed for comfort and stare at me, but the energy emanating from me would make her confusion worse. I could see that she was having olfactory hallucinations as she sniffed the air and looked about. She stared at me in fear and distrust. Her body looked like Icarus with wings of wax that had flown too close to the sun. They began to dissolve into plastic puddles of melted dog.

I took a shower to see if that would help. In the bathroom, with the light on, I looked at my naked body, and I could scarcely believe what

I saw. My body was completely made out of dogs. Dog snouts would descend down my arms ending at the elbow. My hands looked like dog heads. My legs were canine bodies with fur covered, clawed, and padded feet. I was a cluster of melting dogs. I had never seen anything so strange. Again I was experiencing canine-thropic animal transformation. I had heard about someone who had taken datura when suddenly the house caught on fire. He didn't know if it was real fire or a hallucination. He ran out into the yard to look for a fire hose, and when he turned around, the entire house was made out of fire hoses.

After the shower, I still felt the feeling of impending captivity. I put in the player a cassette that Gordon Wasson had recorded of Maria Sabina chanting during a mushroom ceremony in Huautla in Oaxaca, Mexico. It sounded very disturbing, and I turned it off. I decided to turn on the TV and establish a frame of reference. The scene looked like some great cathedral.

A pope-like figure in clerical robes sat on a great throne, surrounded by robed priests with embroidered gowns swinging incense burners. Before an altar, a priest stood before a hymnbook and sang. Everything in the scene was made out of dancing; many layered films of radiation and were completely unnatural. The voice of the singer seemed to roll with strange, unearthly, echoing, reverberating crescendos.

It was as though the mushroom presence were saying, "So you find our brand of theology a little too much, do you? Would you prefer something more familiar?"

"OK," I said. "I get the message."

I turned off the television. I decided to lie down on the Ma Roller, whose rubber wheels pressed on the acupoints on either side of my spine. The endorphins it stimulated seemed to produce some relief. The medication was taking effect now, and I could remain in repose and start to enjoy myself again. I understood with a thrill something about these strange people. They had come to change humans, to change humankind into something new, something better from their point of view. To change humans into something like them. The words of a poem flashed across my mind.

It was Ariel's song from Shakespeare's *The Tempest*:

> Full fathom five thy father lies;
> Of his bones are coral made
> Those are pearls that were his eyes:
> There's nothing of him that doth fade,
> But he doth suffer a sea change
> Into something rich and strange.

No wonder that the spiritual quest has long been compared to mountain climbing. The mushroom was mythically compared to the *axis mundi*, where the cap is the sky and the stem is the heavenly fulcrum seen as a mountain or a pillar or a strong man like Atlas holding up the heavenly dome. Mountains and mountain climbing are among the entheogenic emblems. *Amanita muscaria* grow in the mountains in forests of pine or birch. You must climb a mountain to pick the fly agaric.

A Sumerian word for mountain was "LI" or "RI." It meant something conical or hemispherical. When doubled as "*LI-LI" or "*LI-RI," it was a hypothetical name for the sacred mushroom *Amanita muscaria* suggested by John Allegra. It means "two hemispheres." It describes the ball-shaped, egg-like primordia of the mushroom that splits in two, forming two hemispheres separated by the stalk. Hypothetical means that it has not yet been found written in cuneiform Sumerian texts but can be deduced from other Sumerian words with a similar meaning and from words in other languages.

Chapter 8

The Flying Doorway

CHAPTER 8

The Flying Doorway

I WAS LOOKING AT TWENTY grams of fresh *Psilocybe cubensis* mushroom. I was feeling very anxious. My anxiety had been building for several days as the fresh mushrooms waited in the refrigerator. Did I have to? Shouldn't I be in the right mood? What about set and setting? But I could just feel that "they" were ready to go—urging me on, encouraging me, "Do it! Take it!"

I felt pressured, confused. Four days ago, spring burst on the world with an explosion of blossoms, flowering trees, walks in nature, and blooming acacia, plum, and cherry. The other world was so close then. I felt as though armadas of spaceships crowded the sky. *They are really around these days*, I thought. Sometimes they seem to disappear for years, and then there would be another wave of proximity. I had never felt it as strong as this. Then, was when I should have performed the experiment I thought. I was ready then. They were ready then. They were ready now.

Now the fallen blossoms were darkening, the acacia pollen had blown away on the wind, with a change of the weather. Spring had crept back into her hidden abode, and the groundhog had gone back to sleep. Could you miss these meetings? I wondered. Was it possible that they, who could manipulate so many events, could not make certain that you attend? Didn't the "right feeling" come from them, too? I was seized with preingestion confusion mixed with fear. But the bow had been drawn, and the tension of the string was unbearable. Everything was out of focus, and only decisive action could recrystallize it.

I realized that I have missed an inspired opportunity, but failure to proceed would be terrible as well. Grimly, with almost a sense of duty, I finished my chocolate and began chewing the acrid, stringy mushrooms. I was halfway through the second large mushroom. So ambivalent was my commitment that I declared, "I will eat no more."

Lying in the dark, tossing and turning uneasily, breathing deeply, I could feel little convulsive jolts and shivers running through my body.

Rapid, fleeting, indistinct images were beginning to dart about my gaze. I really didn't want to be here. It was a poor decision, I felt. Thirty or forty minutes later, I was shivering and sighing deeply. I thought of the bridge in Venice called the Bridge of Sighs.

Then the imagery was becoming much clearer and more profuse. Images seemed to be drawn from my memory. I recognized a white-plastic imitation of my KitchenAid mixer that became a theme for a mechanical variation. The mixer grew and changed before my eyes like a mechanical plant, its original function becoming unrecognizable in its self-transforming complexity. The effect was very musical, like selecting a theme and composing a series of progressive variations. The tune was mine, but the composition was of another.

But I was not in the mood for music. Then the air became filled with brilliantly colored mechanical objects. I was seeing fields of moving clockwork-notched golden wheels among intricate articulation of jeweled bearings. Wave after wave of extraordinary imagery was flooding my senses as I turn unappreciatively away.

"Not tonight," I said. "I'm just not in the mood."

Space was becoming a three or four-dimensional kaleidoscope. Things were turning like wheels inside of wheels that look like astrolabes or astronomical instruments, gimbaled compasses or gyroscopes, and there were oceans of them in perpetual motion. I was rudely rejecting royal gifts and who knows what opportunities. I didn't care. I was in a bad mood.

"I'm really not up for this tonight," I exclaimed apologetically. "I have a headache. I've had the flu, you see. It's just not a good time." It was a good time for them, though.

Suddenly out of the blackness appeared a flying rectangle. When it came near, it could be seen to be an open doorway, and inside I could see a brilliantly illuminated room. Strangely this room only seemed to exist on the inside. From without, it was only a flying doorframe, just an open threshold without a door, but if I peered inside, there was a large room in there filled with complicated apparatus.

The walls of the rooms were encrusted with intricate machinery composed of shining metallic surfaces of gold and silver. So what could the doorway be opening into? Was it a portal in space-time itself? This was an elegant metaphor—openings in the fabric of empty space itself, openings that can fly around, as actual contraptions, like vehicles of some sort.

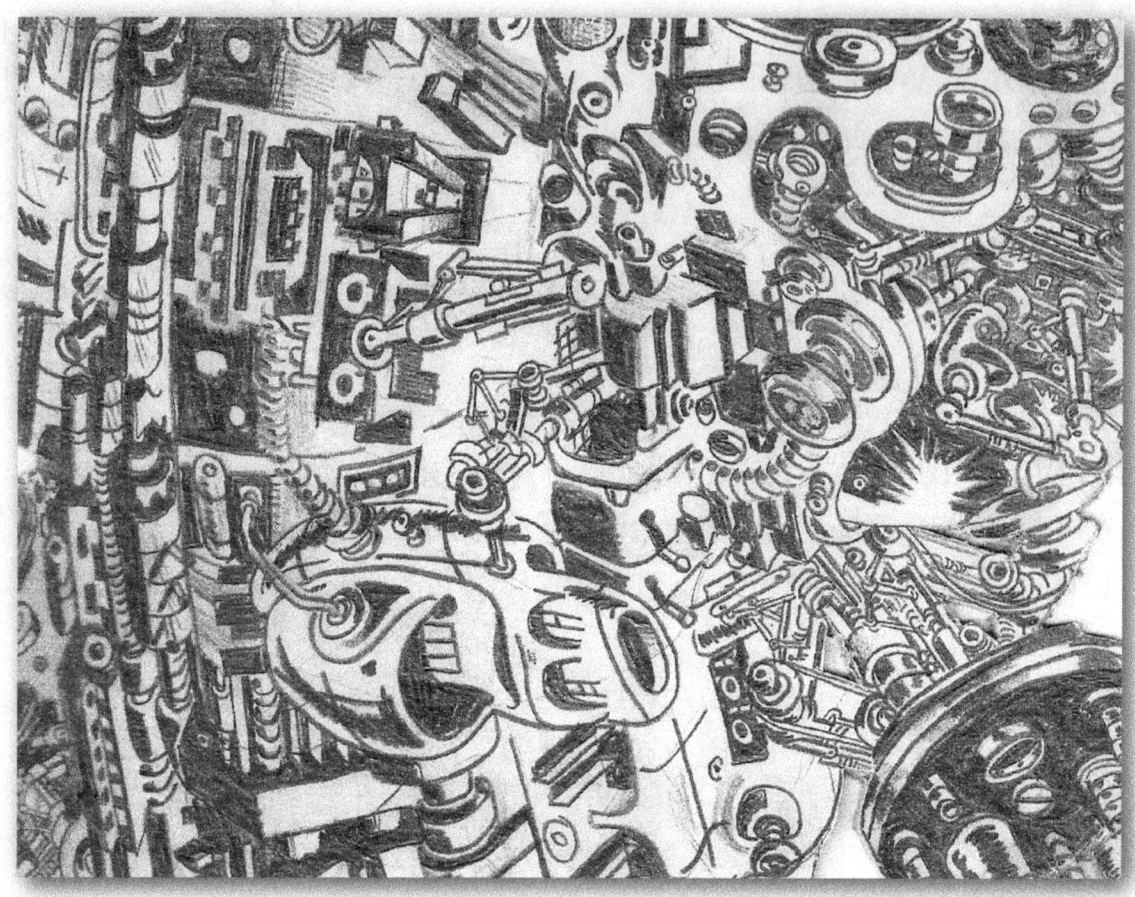
Inside the door was intricate machinery.

I had seen pictures of these flying doorways on Sumerian clay cylinder seals usually hovering above a bull that symbolized the *Amanita muscaria* mushroom. Bronzes from India show the goddess as an open, empty doorframe.

Now the blackness of space was filling with brilliant objects. There were disks and spheres and cylinders and things shaped like ice-cream cones. The forms had lots of detail. There were floating metal balls with bands around their equators studded with red and green and blue flashing lights. There were more lights on top bedecking a second band, from which immerge rabbit-ear antennae. They looked like the orbs held by kings and gods and mythic heroes. These things were flying around the room. They floated about me. Some resembled diving helmets or ocean buoys or satellites. Some of them look remote controlled. They made humming and whirring noises as they moved, which, when combined, sounded like a great droning musical chord or the humming of bees.

The flying doorframe approached and hovered right before me as though inviting me to come on board. I could peer into its complicated, dazzlingly bright interior. It is just like standing in front of a real doorway. One step, and I knew I would be inside, but what if the room flew off, taking me with it? Was this related to the invitation to go away with them that I had received on several previous encounters?

Again I turned away, afraid that I will be drawn inside and taken away somewhere, for I clearly recognized the luminous chamber for what it was—a vehicle, an interdimensional, time-space vehicle.

Then a voice, calm and clear, said, "You do not have to be afraid of this vehicle, for this belongs to you. This is your interdimensional craft. It will remain parked here by the side of your mind, softly humming, until the time when you are ready, and then you will not be so amazed that you will fail to use it for what it is intended. Though you fear that you will be taken away by others," the voice continued, "you will pilot this ship yourself, for when it is you at the controls and you who fly it, you will not be fearful at all."

I should have said, "Beam me up, Scotty, I'll take it!" but instead I turned away in indifference. I would have none of it.

"Why did you start this?" they asked, "if you don't want to participate?"

I could feel they were starting to become annoyed. Things were happening faster and faster.

"Do you want to learn?" the voice said.

"Yes!" I cried in consternation.

"Then hold still!" it said. "Just stop wiggling!"

Suddenly although the bedroom was completely dark, everything was red. The light appeared so suddenly that it made me jump. The radiance was coming from over my head like a powerful floodlight of brilliant red luminescence. It was a conical-shaped beam descending and flooding my bed with illumination. It lit up the room; I could clearly see all of its features. It was the deepest, most pure color I had ever beheld—a red like an iridescent ruby of the deepest and purist hue, like no color I had ever seen on Earth. It was exactly as though a brilliant floodlight had been turned on me from above.

I looked up. Hovering over me was a giant circular object, darkly silhouetted against the blackness. There were lights around its circumference that glowed like a ring of pearls. It was like a pearlescent rosary levitating in the dark. It was from this disk that the floodlight had come, and it was followed by another burst of color that this time was an emerald green of unnatural purity and beauty. The color was so refined it made me gasp.

Seconds later the green light went out, to be followed by another of the deepest blue. I felt like I had never seen these colors before in their true states. The circular objects hummed, and although the rosary ring of opalescent lights floated stationary, the interior body of the craft seemed to slowly revolve.

Then an amazing thing occurred. It was as if a voice somewhere said, "He's really being uncooperative tonight. We'd better send in the alligators."

Then out of the corner of my eye, to my right, I became aware of the approach of two objects. They just floated up to me. They were about the size and shape of baby alligators. They were brilliant, reptilian bags of beads, but somehow they didn't seem alive. They were like toys, like stuffed animals a child would play with, but they were extremely animate and moved and worked with deliberate intent, if not remotely guided.

What they were doing was attaching themselves to my right thigh with their padded mouths, just sort of biting me like leaches. I tried not to look, like when the doctor is giving you a shot, but out of the corner of my eye, I could see their luminous yellow eyes shining in the dark.

Field notes: Luminous objects levitating in the dark

And suddenly without me being aware of any transition, my mood was changing. Suddenly I felt wonderful! I had never been so happy. I just loved stuffed alligators and luminous levitating objects and UFOs shaped like ice-cream cones with blinking lights.

I felt warm and secure, relaxed and at ease, and this was in response to the same events that only a moment before had been disturbing, fearful, and confusing. I realized that my mood had been somehow manipulated. Somehow the suckling bite of the stuffed reptiles had changed my emotional chemistry as though I had taken a drug. Of course, I had taken a drug; this was all happening in the middle of a mushroom experience. But there was no doubt that my hosts had deliberately intervened, and I was glad they had. I felt wonderful. I wished that they had done it sooner.

Now the luminous objects in the dark air were like rags, and scraps of embroidered cloth and scarves. Now they resembled scrolls and then furniture, both period and modern. Some of the objects were made of wood. The feeling of being in a museum was overwhelming. It was the aquarium again, only this time I seemed to be one of the luminous objects. I was swimming around with them. The feeling of freedom and weightlessness was wonderful. Here was freedom from gravity, freedom from the body, freedom from matter. Here in a miraculous ocean, everything had become transformed into thought. It was like swimming or flying. I felt like a fish swimming in a school of other brightly colored, glowing, bioluminescent deep-sea creatures.

"When we were young," the Mock Turtle told Alice, "we went to school in the sea."

The walrus sang to the carpenter,

> Oh, how happy we will be
> When the lobsters throw us out to sea
> And come swimming after us.
> Will you, won't you will you won't you
> Won't you join the dance?

I kept twisting around, looking for my body, and in its place, I saw gold bejeweled surfaces shining with an inner light. I was one of the ornamental objects.

Now another creature approached. The object did not resemble the others. The entity that now approached was slightly larger than me. It was a shape-shifting glob of wax, all eyes and other body parts floating in a plastic conglomerate, where features would emerge momentarily and then dissolve.

Because of the mood produced by the alligators, I felt no fear whatsoever. As the creature approached, I felt from it, as a reciprocating murmur within myself, a feeling of love mixed with a strange kind of unmistakable sexual attraction. The entity was sexually attracted to me, and I didn't feel too bad about it, either.

It happened very quickly. It enveloped me like an amoeba, and for a brief second, there was the sensation of being wrapped in butterfly wings. We merged completely, Christmas-tree ornament melting into the swirling fluid form. I found myself experiencing a genuine orgasm. The union was not a physical one but was composed of the most refined aspects of the psyche. It was a kind of confluence like two rivers merging. It was a conjugation of souls.

We separated, and it went its way, leaving me blushing and slightly embarrassed. Then I had a strange feeling as though I had conceived—as though I had become impregnated. Something was inside me now that hadn't been there before. A germ had been somehow placed. It was an annunciation by the amoeba of the Holy Ghost.

It was not as though my body had conceived, for at this moment, I had no body. My ornamental shell had somehow not made it through the contact, but it was as if my soul had conceived. The idea of a pregnant soul seemed amazing. There was a kind of general hallelujahing among the enthronged spirits, followed by assurance of care and patronage.

"We will take care of you," they said. I thought of the incubus, of demon lovers. I thought of tantric yoga. I felt that the Yab-Yum, the embrace of the shakti with the bull-headed Tibetan lord of death, portrayed such unions. I thought of sacred marriages and divine children.

The scene changed again.

Great machines surrounded me like massive generators, humming with great energy. Everywhere there were curved metallic surfaces, very modern and futuristic. The floating objects hovered in the room and lingered for a long time, growing less and less distinct in the way stars fade with dawn. Finally, only a subtle grid-like impression remained where once they had floated, as one by one they twinkled out.

The association of pregnancy with the use of mushrooms is a very old and widespread motif. As early as the Paleolithic in Europe, the *Amanita muscaria* mushroom was associated with pregnancy and childbirth. The fungus begins its life underground in a womb, white, egg-shaped primordia. If cut in two, the form of a tiny mushroom can be seen inside. The womb swells and expands like a pregnant belly. Splitting in two, the mushroom takes the shape, first as a red-tipped penis spotted with drops of semen, and then as the cap of the mushroom spreads, the stem seems to penetrate the annulus or ring of tissue that is the torn remains of the veil. The image remarkably resembles a penis entering a vagina. This image is repeated again as the stem or stipe plunges into the feathery gills.

The so-called Venus of Wallendorf was a figurine of the fly-agaric mushroom anthropomorphized as a pregnant woman. She was found in Austria and dates to between 25,000 to 30,000 BC. Carved from white limestone and colored with red ocher, she was made by Upper Paleolithic Cro-Magnon hunter-gatherers. Her head bears the pattern of bumps and protuberances characteristic of *Amanita muscaria* mushrooms. She is the *Amanita muscaria* mushroom personified as a pregnant woman.

According to John Allegro, a hypothetical name for *Amanita muscaria* in ancient Sumer was "*I-A-U," "strong water of conception." This is often written as "the water of life" or "living water." "I-A" in Sumerian meant "semen," the "seed" of a plant, "juice squeezed out or pressed out," "sap," "resin," and even "stone" as in "pressing stone" beneath which the reconstituted mushrooms were squeezed. There are many references in the Rig Veda of the mushroom stalks being pressed out of their juice by stones and filtered through lamb's wool. "Stone" has become a standard epithet of the fly agaric and appears in such terms as the "philosopher's stone" of the alchemists. Strong water would refer to the expressed juice of the rehydrated mushroom. It was strong because of its effectiveness as a drug and because it produced periods of almost superhuman strength. "*U*" also had the meanings of "life," "fecundity," "fertility," and "mounting" and was the name of the Storm God, whose fertilizing rain and bolts of thunder made the mushrooms spring up.

In his book *Magic Mushrooms in Religion and Alchemy*, Clark Heinrich makes an important contribution toward our understanding of semen in fly-agaric mythology. He presents an abundance of mythological evidence to suggest that in Vedic India and much of the ancient world, semen was an epithet for the urine of someone who had taken *Amanita muscaria*. Like semen, urine is the other thing that comes from the penis. Among the Uralic-speaking, reindeer-herding tribal people of Siberia, rain is the urine of the sky god, Sila, who eats enormous amounts of *Amanita muscaria* mushrooms.

Heinrich gives an example from the Gnostic Nag Hammadi Codices called the Prayer of Thanksgiving, in which the hierophant proclaims,

> After I received the spirit through the power, I set forth the action for you. Indeed the understanding dwells in you; in me it is as though the power were pregnant. For when I conceived from the fountain that flowed to me, I gave birth…I gave birth to it as children are born.

As mushroom urine was euphemistically semen, it is natural that it would produce a kind of conception resulting in pregnancy.

Soma, in the Vedas, is often called the "germ" and reference is made to the "laying of the soma germ." Euphemistically called semen, the urine of a person or animal that has consumed *Amanita muscaria* mushrooms is completely transformed in its color, odor, taste, and efficacy into the divine "amrita," the elixir of immortality.

In the Vedas, even the gods become pregnant when they drink the semen of Shiva. The priests and officiates of the soma sacrifice are represented with swollen, distended bellies that make them appear pregnant; in fact, they are referred to as "soma-bellies." They are swollen with urine, and soon, the Rig Veda says, they will "piss the flowing soma." Heinrich explains complex mythical cycles in which gods, humans of both sexes, and even inanimate objects like mountains, reeds or rivers become pregnant from the semen of Shiva.

The interchangeability of semen and mushroom urine can be traced back as far as the Neolithic in Europe, where, in a matriarchal culture, the supreme deity was a goddess who was an anthropomorphized mushroom. In this religion, long before the invasion of the patriarchal Indo-Europeans, it was not semen that was a euphemism for mushroom urine but menstrual blood.

Among ancient peoples, menses were considered the female seed that combined with semen to form the embryo. In matriarchal cultures, menses carried the same profundity as semen did in patriarchal societies. Fly-agaric urine is reddish pink in color, resembling menstrual blood dissolved it water. The red iron-oxide pigment, red ocher, was associated with both *Amanita muscaria* mushrooms and menses. Prehistoric red-ocher burials were believed to be ritualized substitutes for grave offerings of *Amanita muscaria* to give the seed of life to the dead and facilitate their resurrection. Red ocher was believed to be a substitute for menses and the thing that it represented, fly-agaric urine. Bitumen carried a similar association.

When magic herbs, such as *Amanita muscaria*, were picked, it was required to make compensatory offerings of flour or cakes to the earth in payment for the divine fungus. Pine resin was a suitable offering because the pine is one of the host trees of *Amanita muscaria*. The resin that trickled down the trunk was believed to be the tears of the goddess who lived in the tree, weeping for the death and decomposition of her consort, the mushroom. The tears, called the "seeds of a pine," would bring about the mushroom's resurrection the following year when the next flush sprang up.

Because the mushroom was phallic, it was to be picked by a virgin. Removing her clothes, she would perform erotic songs and dances to arouse the fungus into erection in order to pick it. She was the bride of the mushroom. The Vestal virgins of ancient Greece had a similar function. The mushroom-picking ritual may have included sexual intercourse with the fungus in the form of a ritual phallus or with the mushroom itself. As Clark Heinrich explains, mushrooms could be taken both vaginally and anally.

John Allegro has pointed out that the only thing that could offer complete remission and redemption for picking the mushroom was the mushroom itself. What can you offer the mushroom god or goddess that is as valuable as its self? Sometimes images of the mushroom were offered and also image of penises and vulvas. Thus the most suitable offering would be some of the actual mushroom itself or mushroom urine. Next to that, its symbolic surrogate, menstrual blood, could be used. If the virgin had eaten the mushroom, she could urinate on the earth beneath the tree where the fungus would spring up. If she happened to be menstruating at the time, the compensatory offering would have the maximum efficacy.

The concept of a pregnancy involving the soul can be found in Sufism. Rumi mentions it. It is also present in Chinese Taoism. Lu-Tsu explained it in great detail in the Chinese book *The Secret of the Golden Flower* called in Chinese *the Tai I Chin Hua Tsung Chih*. The Golden Flower is a name for the sacred mushroom of immortality, the *Amanita muscaria*. This is a book of Chinese yoga and Taoist alchemy.

The Taoists believed that by means of certain secret methods, the use of entheogenic mushrooms; it was possible to create a subtle body that would exist within the physical body during life and was capable of independent existence after death. The method involved the religion of the golden elixir of life. The golden elixir was also called the Golden Pill or Medicine Ball.

The golden elixir is golden because when *Amanita muscaria* are allowed to dry, they take on the iridescent sheen of metallic gold and also because of the golden color of fly-agaric urine that the alchemists called "potable gold," "living water," and the "water of life."

The use of the golden elixir would bring about the circulation of the light and the creation of a Divine Seed-Kernel. It would strengthen, rejuvenate, and open the gateways to the place within the mind called the Nuptial Chamber. The Taoists had many names for this sacred place no bigger than one square inch. They called it the Ancestral Land, the Yellow Castle, the Dragon Castle, at the Bottom of the Sea, the Primordial Pass, the Space of Former Heaven, the Fields of Cinnabar, and the Heavenly Heart. It was also called the Germinal Vesicle. It is here that the divine embryo could be created.

Lu-Tsu writes that to produce this wonder, you must initiate the "Circulation of the Light." It is easy to make the light circulate, but it is difficult to make it condense. This must be repeated again and again until finally it crystallizes. This, he says, is the deepest and most wonderful secret. The spirit and the soul must enter the germinal vesicle together. It is as though a man and a woman joined in sexual union and a conception took place.

They must join in union as a father and mother combined to form the embryo. This will produce the True Fruit, also called the Life Elixir Seed Pearl. When it is finished, the holy embryo can form. Then, in addition to the body, there develops another spirit body. This is called the divine embryo. The embryo must be warmed and nourished as it grows. It must be cared for like an infant until it has matured. If neglected, it will perish. It is very important that this be completed before death comes.

The spirit body is also called the "Diamond Body." It is the indestructible resurrection body. This body is immortal. When the body dies, it does not die. The body remains behind like the empty shell of a cicada, while the spirit body survives death and goes on to an independent continuation of vital existence. This is a secret that has not been revealed for thousands of years.

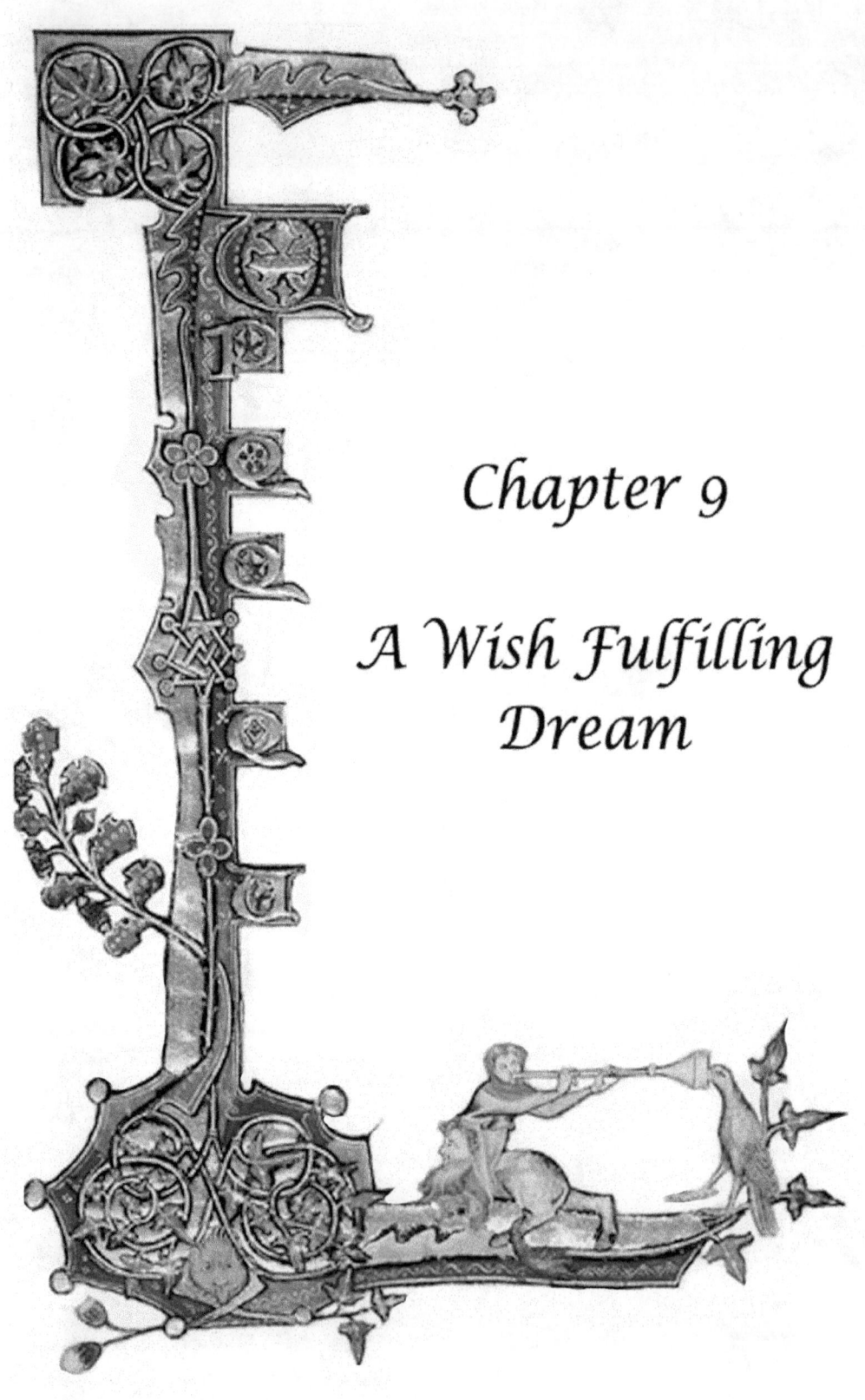

Chapter 9

A Wish Fulfilling Dream

CHAPTER 9
A Wish-Fulfilling Dream

A LITTLE MENTIONED BUT WIDELY recognized aspect to the use of mushrooms is its apparent ability to grant wishes. Since the mushroom can talk and you can have two-way conversations with it, it is easy to ask it for favors. These can be completely materialistic things like a new car, money, or clothes. You can ask for something you want but can't see how to get. Sure enough, the mushroom appears to manipulate synchronicity so that an opportunity materializes that makes it possible to acquire it.

People customarily don't ask the mushroom for enlightenment or a cure for cancer or for world peace. They ask for shockingly unspiritual things like cars, money, houses, and vacations and, in my case, hi-fi equipment. Laurie Anderson refers to it as "the boondocks." Where the flying saucers land, granting boons and fulfilling wishes.

In the sixties and seventies, when acid was the most commonly used entheogen, people observed that when you took LSD, the density of synchronicity increased to an unmistakable degree. You would have only to think about someone, and the doorbell would ring and there they would be. You just seemed to have much better luck. Interesting opportunities abounded.

The Pure Land school of Buddhism has a practice in which beginners are permitted to ask Amitaba Buddha, the Buddha of Boundless Light, for favors in the form of material goods such as wealth, automobiles, and auspicious opportunities by chanting the mantra "*Nam-myoho-renge-kyo.*" This is not recommended for advanced students, but it serves to get people involved. Later they are encouraged to pray for spiritual things. You do seem to get what you ask for, but there is always a catch. Once when we were searching for a house, we chanted the mantra, and sure enough the ideal house appeared. A week before we moved in, it burned down.

In the case of the mushroom, you wait until the mushroom manifests as a personified entity and politely make your request. When the trance came on in the dark, I saw my familiar contact sitting at a desk. The mushroom had impersonated a man.

I said something like, "Begging your lordship's pardon, but there is this piece of hi-fidelity equipment I want, and I would appreciate it if you would help me acquire it."

The pun of "lord" and "ship" did not escape me. He took down this big, dusty ledger, opened it to a page, and began writing down my request, speaking out loud as he did so.

"The deceased requests more hi-fidelity equipment."

It was a joke but with an ominous overtone. Was it "deceased" as in the death and rebirth of shamanic initiation, or did he know something I didn't?

On another occasion, I wanted to get a certain very expensive audio amplifier for my music system. I explained the situation as best as I could. Then the voice did an amazing thing. In a perfect imitation of the voice of Marlon Brando, it recited a segment of the scene from *The Godfather* where an old acquaintance asks Don Corleone for help, and then it paraphrased the words for the entire scene: "So Don Estrin, you have come to visit your Godfather at last." I roared with laughter. It was hysterical.

The voice called itself the Godfather in this mushy, aged Italian accent. In the past, he had called himself my father, and his closeness to God was always a question.

"And now, at this time, it is because you wish to ask me for my help and assistance," the voice said.

"Yes, Godfather," I said.

He continued, "And in all the years that we have lived next to one another, have you ever once come to pay your respects to me and my family? And now you come to me, hat in hand, because you need my help. Very well. I will help you. But the time will come when I will need your help and I will come to you and ask you for it, and I expect you to respond immediately and unquestionably, without hesitation. Is that understood?"

Again humor. The mushroom can be a tremendous comedian when it chooses to, but often there is mixed in the humor a veiled sense of uneasiness. What would the mushroom as mafia boss possibly ask of me? What would happen if I didn't comply? Would he break my legs?

Within a week, an opportunity occurred, and the money was there to buy the amplifier. An old acquaintance came by and bought a guitar I wanted to sell. Did the mushroom arrange it? It certainly took credit for it. The wish granting is a way of creating affiliation. You can get so easily what you want that you become dependent on it. You realize that if you stop helping this thing, the magic will stop, and you will be back to not getting what you want. And this is experimentally true. Disavow your allegiance to it and leave the path, and all your luck disappears.

But the real question is, does the mushroom really make things happen, or do we do it ourselves? I have experienced amazing periods of synchronicity long before I ever took mushrooms although they were usually associated with the taking of LSD or some other kind of entheogen. Wishes come true sometimes during periods of acid taking, and there occurs a great deal of coincidence control and synchronicity. But it doesn't deal and bargain with you like some kind of hyper spatial marketplace. There isn't the "I'll do something for you if you do something for me" aspect to it.

With acid, I always assumed that when I took it, the synchronicity came from me. But even with LSD, I remember at least one time when I had had enough of the introspective, highly emotional, psychoanalytic periods that it sometimes puts you through, and I formally left the path. All my luck disappeared, and I learned what it was like to be an ordinary, nonblessed human being who had to work to get what he or she wanted.

It all gets back to the question, can you trust the mushroom? It can certainly help you sometimes, but there is something about it that's not quite right.

Another time I said to the mushroom, "I worry about money. I worry about not having enough. Could you give me a raise?"

He said, "So you want a raise, do you?"

I instantly understood that by "raise" he meant catapulting me unexpectedly upward to one of its catastrophic and chaotic cataclysms. "Not that kind of raise," I clarified. "I worry about money. Can you fix that?"

"I can definitely fix that," he said.

I never got any more money, but from that moment on, I stopped worrying about money. It could be the day before my rent was due, and I would be a happy and blissful as a baby boy. Then there would be a knock on my door, and the rent money would come. Someone who owed me a long forgotten debt would be there.

Mike Crowley, author of *The Secret Drugs of Buddhism* says that there is an ancient link between the mushroom drink amrita and the granting of wishes. In Indian mythology, there is the wish-granting cow, Kamadhenu, whose name literally means, "desire-milk."

She appeared as one of the treasures that emerged from the ocean of milk when the gods and the Asuras churned it to make the butter of immortality. When milked, the heavenly cow gave soma from her udders. Gordon Wasson writes in his book *Soma: Divine Mushroom of Immortality* that the Vedic priests euphemistically referred to *Amanita muscaria* mushrooms as udders. This was because the dried fungus was reconstituted in milk. The milk was then pressed out between stones and was compared to the milking of a cow. Bulls and cows have a duel symbolism, because while the bull universally represents *Amanita muscaria*, *Psilocybe cubensis* mushrooms grow from bovine excrement.

A related tradition, according to Crowley, was that of wish-granting gems, *cintamani*. These are held in the hands of many Buddhist figures as attributes, or else they poured out of the deities' bodily orifices or were even vomited. These gems were commonly associated with wealth-bestowing deities. While they were portrayed as flaming jewels, the texts reveal that they were somehow drinkable.

It is evident that wish-granting gems were hidden references to amrita or soma made from the brilliant, red, jewel-like *Amanita muscaria*. In Indian folklore, the gems had only to be held between the hands and the wish declared, and the wished-for boon would fall from the sky at the feet of the wisher. Their representation as streams of liquid suggests that they may be secret references to streams of milk pressed out of the reconstituted mushrooms or fly-agaric urine.

In the Mahamaya Tantra, it says: "With the thumb and ring finger, place the wish-granting jewel in the mouth, and attain the everlasting spiritual attainment arisen from the nature of the nectar." These jewels were clearly edible.

Another treasure that sprung forth from the churning of the milky ocean was the wish-granting tree, parijata, that produced the amrita fruit. *Amanita muscaria* grows beneath certain host trees, such as the birch, conifer, and oak. The mushroom is the fruit. We see this theme repeated in the Garden of Eden where the forbidden fruit was the apple of immortality.

Most religions retain the idea that the deity can grant wishes. This is because most religions began with the use of entheogenic sacraments, which do, in fact, grant wishes. When the use of psychedelics drops out of use, wishes are no longer granted, but the belief that you can pray for divine aid or favor remains.

I was amazed when I visited China and took a Chinese wife how Chinese Buddhism, as far as everyday people are concerned, seems entirely directed to the asking for favors. Outside of monasteries, people don't pray for enlightenment, at least not among the general public. They pray for making more money in a business or better luck gambling at the casino or a cure for a disease or for protection against bad luck.

It is transactional, as the wishing is accompanied by offerings of incense, fruit, and other commodities enjoyed by the gods and goddesses. There is a Chinese deity, Tsaai Shen Yeh, who grants wishes of good luck and financial reward. People especially favor him in business. He looks like an emperor and sometimes a dwarf, and his iconography shows him delighting in offerings presented to him especially at Chinese New Year, when good luck can be granted for the entire following year. The transition between emperor and dwarf is characteristic of the visual size changes common to *Amanita muscaria* intoxication.

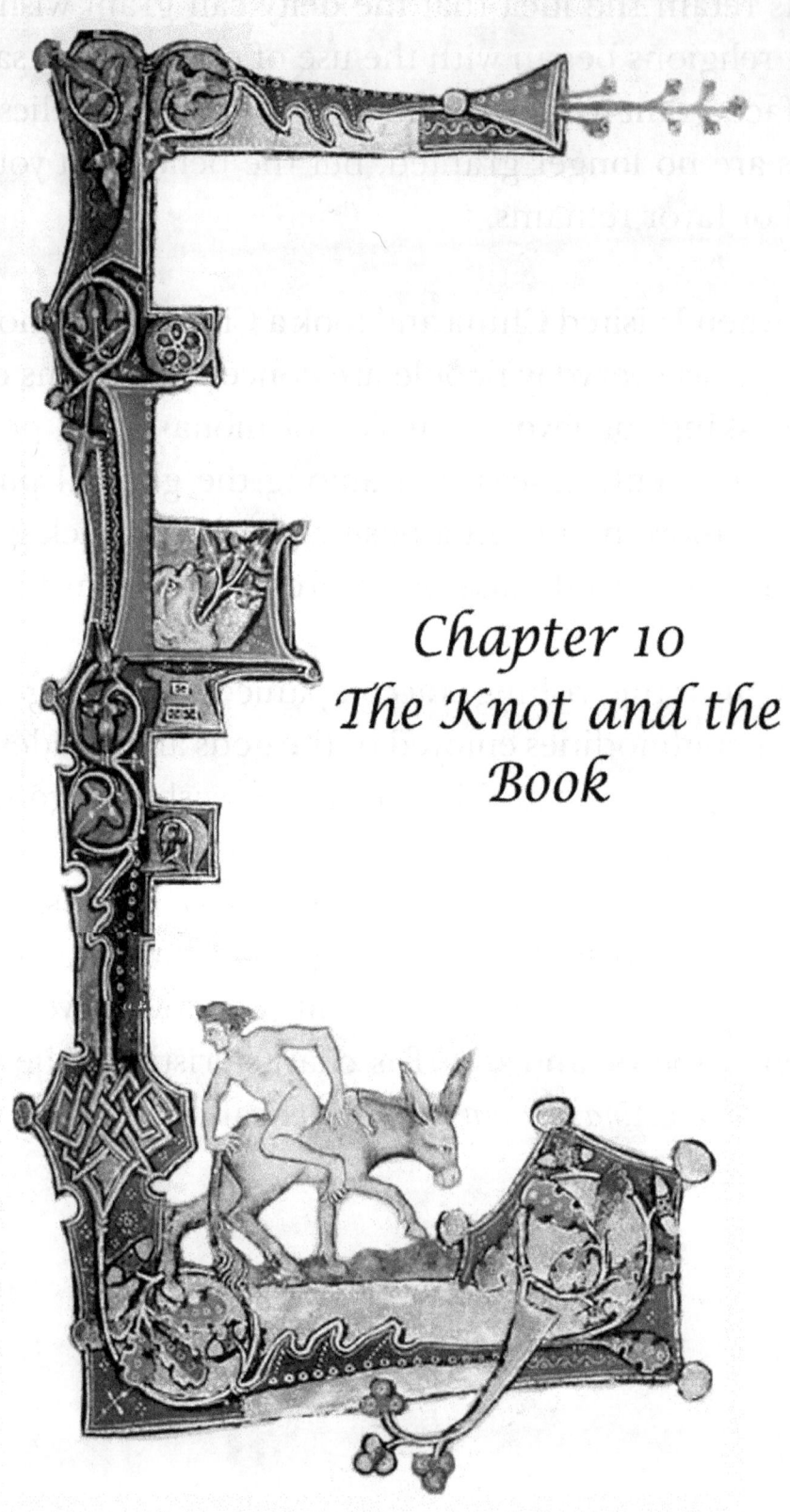

Chapter 10
The Knot and the Book

CHAPTER 10

The Knot and the Book

I HAD BEEN THINKING ABOUT how in Oaxaca, the Mazatecs always eat magic mushrooms in pairs. If you ask a *curandera* how many mushrooms she has eaten, she will always say five pairs or seven pairs or thirteen pairs or whatever number, always in pairs. The number depends on the variety. In mythology, mushroom heroes are often twin brothers, such as Cain and Abel or the mushroom-related twin brothers in the Mayan Popul Vuh.

It is not uncommon for a *curandera* to eat as many as seventeen pairs of pajaritos, or "little birds," that is *Psilocybe Mexicana*. Significantly fewer pairs of *Psilocybe caerulescens* are taken. These are called "landslide mushrooms" by the Mazatecs. In Spanish, they are called "*derrumbes*." They thrive where sugar cane is processed. The less potent San Isidros are *Psilocybe cubensis*. These are called "Cuban mushrooms," because they grow on the manure of cattle originally brought to Mexico from Cuba.

Many people think that the earth-slide mushrooms are so named because that is how it feels when you eat them, as though the ground is sliding away beneath you, but actually derrumbes grow in ground where the soil has been disrupted, such as from an earth slide, not a recent landslide but an older one. Pictures of landslides appear in several works of alchemy, such as one by Sendivogius. The alchemists knew that some varieties of *Psilocybe* mushrooms grow in disrupted earth.

153

I had not previously paid attention to eating magic mushrooms in pairs, so this time I picked out two matched specimens and ate them. They weren't very large and in no way near the five-gram portion of dried *Psilocybe cubensis* that is considered a threshold dose. What resulted from the tiny amount I took shows the capricious nature of the fungus and the way that at the right place and time a small dose can produce a major reaction. After a little while, things had reached a point where I wanted to go lie down on my bed. I brought with me a roll of paper towels and a large, stainless steel bowl to throw up into if it became necessary. Vomiting is common when eating mushrooms and other psychedelics. Images of people and animals vomiting have become religious icons in the pictures of the alchemists.

Suddenly I became aware of a hissing sound like the rushing of air. It was very loud and very distinct, and I considered that it might be gas leaking somewhere in my house. I went from room to room looking for its source, but I could find nothing out of the ordinary. If I had lived in ancient times, I would have thought of snakes or possibly wind, both of which are associated with mushrooms.

Back in my bedroom, the whooshing sound was continuing, but my hearing was undergoing a kind of synesthesia. The field of sound was transforming into an array of moving, changing patterns and designs. It was exactly the same as when moving geometric patterns are superimposed over your vision, only here it was happening to hearing in addition to seeing. Sounds became visible shapes, and hearing was crossing over into something beheld.

While I was dry heaving into the basin, I noticed that forms were beginning to appear in the darkened bedroom. I kept seeing things that looked like armor. They had overlapping plates like medieval or renaissance suits of armor or lobster tails. Lobsters appear in the some versions of the Tarrot, and in pictures in the books of the alchemists. Many alchemical pictures show men in armor formed from overlapping metal plates, especially on their legs. Some statues of the Greek mushroom god Mithras sacrificing a bull show a lobster or scorpion grasping the bulls testical in its claws. The armored objects were filigreed with gold and silver and embossed leather like beautiful art forms that resembled the armor of kings. At the same time, there was an aspect to them that resembled the exaggerated and stylized armor of action figures from computer games or rock stars.

Then I became aware of the presence of a large and very powerful entity. It was in the company of an entourage of lesser beings who seemed to be in attendance. It was a levitating object that looked like a thick plastic ribbon tied into an intricate knot. It was about five feet across, the band being about a foot wide and two inches thick. It kept tying, untying, and retying itself. Like many hallucinatory objects seen on psilocybin, it was personified and, in this case, a very powerful and important entity. Some characters you meet on psilocybin are very verbally articulate and even eloquent, but this living knot was very short on words.

"Why do you have to be so frightening?" I asked. "You're scaring me to death."

The knot spoke a single word. It said, "Friend."

This made me feel somewhat relieved. "The friend" is a common term in Sufism for the principal manifesting entity.

"Who are you?" I asked the knot.

He replied, "Enlil."

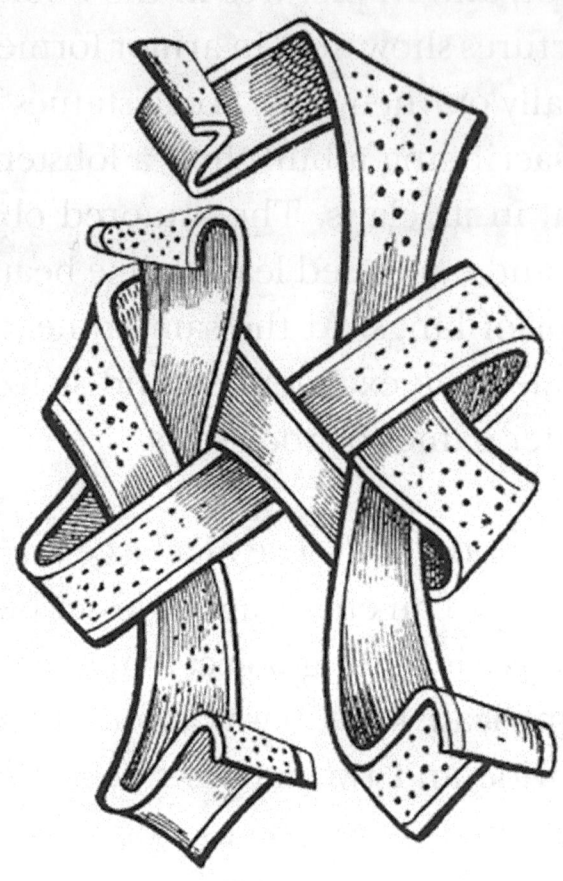

A self-tying and untying knot

The name sounded familiar. It was Sumerian, I thought. Later I looked it up. Enlil was the Sumerian god of wind, god of the storm, and also the god of breath. This was interesting, considering that the trip began with the sound of rushing air.

When Alexander the Great went to Phrygian Gordium, he was shown an ox cart whose yoke was tied to a post with an intricate knot. The cart had belonged to a man whom an oracle had accurately predicted would become king. Like the sword in the stone in the Arthurian legend, many people were offered the chance to untie the knot. All failed because no ends of the knot were visible.

Alexander was presented with the task of untying the knot. He tried but could not find either end. Some say he solved the conundrum by cutting the knot in two with his sword. Others say he untied it by removing the post around which it was bound, allowing it to unravel.

The story is a mystery allegory, for to see the knot is to witness the ineffable visions of the sacred apparitions. Cutting or dividing something in half is mushroom related, because the *Amanita muscaria* first forms as a ball that splits in half, becoming two hemispheres, the top expanding to form the cap and the bottom forming a cup from which the stem rises. Knots, yokes, and swords are also mushroom emblems. The story can be taken to mean that Alexander did undergo the initiation into the mysteries.

Entanglement, from the *Howard Psalter and hours*

Omar Khayyam wrote in the *Rubaiyat*,

> Up from Earth's Center through the seventh Gate
> I rose, and on the Throne of Saturn sat,
> And many Knots unraveled by the Road;
> But not the Knot of Human Death and Fate.

The Throne of Saturn is a common epithet for the sacred mushroom. Like toadstools, it is associated with seats and chairs and, because it was connected with sovereignty, with thrones. In Greek mythology, Saturn eats his children. When the time comes for him to eat his last remaining child, Zeus, his wife fools him by giving him a stone wrapped in swaddling cloths. He eats it. Later he is given a potion that makes him sick, and he vomits up all his children unharmed. A stone is an ancient trope for the *Amanita muscaria* mushroom. It is the alchemical philosopher's stone. The meaning of the myth is that the mushroom is a suitable substitute for human sacrifice. If you feed the gods mushrooms, they won't eat you.

Psilocybin hallucinations of interweaving warps and woofs resemble the tapestry of Penelope in *The Odyssey*, which she weaves every day and unravels every night while her husband, Odysseus, is away fighting the Trojan War. She tells her suitors that when the tapestry is finished, she will pick one of them to marry, but when night comes; she unties the work she has done that day. This was a metaphor for the goddess who weaves the world and unravels it during the dark night of the mysteries. Surely humankind discovered the art of weaving by watching these intricate visionary displays of knotting, braiding, and interweaving.

Intricate, interwoven knots are principle motifs in mushroom-inspired illuminated manuscripts such as the medieval Psalters or the Book of Kells.

In China, knots are religious icons. Called Zhongguo jie, they are woven from a single length of cord and usually colored red. They are often made of silk, often end in a tassel or a coin and are hung on the walls and on clothing and given as gifts or displayed on auspicious occasions. The origin of these knots surely goes back to a time when knotted, braided hallucinations were witnessed in a spiritual, mushroom induced context. These symbols first appeared in the Tang and Song dynasty and later used as a decorative handicraft in the Ming. It bestows protection, good luck, wealth and prosperity. This feng shui symbol is called the endless knot because it appears like the alchemical dragon to swallow its own tail. In Buddhism, the knot suggests that the cosmos has no beginning and no end. Surely the origin of this symbol was the knotted, braided images seen in entheogenic experiences.

Quantum physicists Stuart Hameroff and Roger Penrose have presented a theory of consciousness in which a braided and knotted network of tiny tubes running throughout the body within and among cells may allow the brain to act like a quantum computer. The microtubules are so small that quantum states can occur inside them. They may form a kind of nanoscale nervous system, where instantaneous communication is possible through quantum entanglement, in which distant particles, once in tune with each other, act like one single particle. The networks of microtubules may act as antenna to receive consciousness from beyond time and space, where it resides.

It has been argued that this could not work, because the body's heat would make such systems decoherent, but the microtubular networks are knotted, looped, and braided, which makes them resistant to heat decoherence. They can survive all kinds of disturbance. The particles moving through the microtubular network are biophotons of organic light. Like a quantum computer, these kinds of networks can carry out quantum computations very rapidly.

The physicist Vaughan Jones has proved mathematically that knots and braided networks can store information. What's more, he proposes that threads and loops can form a topology that might be capable of producing consciousness!

The Incas had an information-recording system encoded in knots and threads. Knotting and braiding also occurs in mycelium networks of mushrooms. The underground fibrous network of mycelium is the actual fungal organism. Mushrooms are specialized organs used by the matrix for reproduction.

Entheogenic mushrooms, like *Psilocybes*, certainly seem to be conscious when we eat them. Terrence McKenna has suggested that the consciousness we encounter in the mushroom trance may reside in the consciousness of the mycelial network. These braided and knotted networks common to mycelia, root systems, and microtubule networks may possess topological consciousness. Information storage and computation based on weaving is called "topological." A vast, braided mycelium network could form a super organism that could resonate harmoniously with the world. If such an organism attained quantum states of nonlocality, superposition, and entanglement, it could resonate in sync with the entire universe.

Knots and braids are a common motif in psilocybin hallucinations as they weave and interweave themselves, twisting, looping, and braiding. This may reflect the knotting, weaving, braiding, and looping topology of the mycelial networks and also that of the microtubular networks of the human brain.

Dr. Ede Frecska says that braiding, knotting, and weaving also occur in the root systems of plants and trees. Frecska says that there is an aspen tree in Utah called Pando, or Trembling Giant, whose massive underground root system forms a gigantic colony that is a single living organism estimated to weigh six thousand tons! All parts of the colony have the same DNA. The root network is eighty thousand years old, which makes it the oldest known living thing in the world.

Terrence McKenna's brother, Dennis, described to Frecska a giant mushroom found in the Pacific Northwest called *Armillaria ostoyae.* It is called the Honey Mushroom and also Shoestring Rot. The fungus has a gigantic underground network of knotted, braided, interwoven mycelia that spans twenty-two hundred acres. Its volume is estimated to be one square mile. All parts of the fungal fiber network have the same DNA, making it one of the largest single living organisms on Earth.

An even larger colony of this fungus was recently discovered in Washington State, and its genetically identical mycelial mass covers more than eleven thousand acres. Imagine that! It is a single living organism.

The number of knots, braids, and loops in fungal mycelial networks greatly exceed those in the microtubular matrix in the human brain. Do we see knots and braids so commonly in psilocybin hallucinations because they somehow reflect the knotted and braided networks found in mycelia and the microtubular networks in the human body and brain?

The Book of Wisdom

In my bedroom talking to the giant knot, I looked up and saw an enormous rectangular-shaped object standing near me. It reminded me of the monolith on the moon in the movie *2001: A Space Odyssey*. It was gray and featureless and towered above me. The ceiling disappeared as it extended beyond the boundaries of the room.

When I looked up again, the monolith had become a gigantic book. The cover was decorated with embossed leather inlaid with beautiful, intricate gold filigree. When I looked again, there were two rectangles joined together. The book had opened, and the pages were filled with brilliant letters and hieroglyphics. At times the letters burned like fire, or they appeared as letters of gold on a field of purple. When Moses was given the tablets of law written by the finger of God, it must have been a reference to something like this.

The association of the mushroom and a book is very old. In ancient Mesopotamian Sumer, the earliest writing tablets were round clay disks shaped like mushroom caps. Words were constructed by pressing wedge-shaped marks in the wet clay with a stylus. The writing was called "cuneiform." Then the clay tablets were baked in an oven to harden them. Later the tablets became rectangular.

In the case of the fly agaric, the patches of the white veil clinging to the red cap can resemble letters or hieroglyphics. The Sumerian name for a writing tablet was "*TA-BA-LI." Can you see how this Sumerian word became the English word "tablet"? John Allegro wrote that this was a hypothetical Sumerian name for the *Amanita muscaria* mushroom. It means "two hemispheres" and describes the divided mushroom egg. "TA-BA" means two or double. "LI" mean a mound or cone or hemispherical-shaped object, such as a loaf of bread or a cake of figs or a woman's breast or a book or writing tablet. The same root gives us our word "table."

There is an interesting thing about language; words formed from similar roots have related meanings. For instance in Sanskrit, one of the words for mushroom is "*patra*." This is formed from the root "P-T-R," also expressed dialectically as "F-T-R." The word in Sanskrit for book is "*pattra*," which shows that mushrooms and books were not only verbal puns but had associated meanings.

The mushroom is shaped like a book or writing tablet, and the white flecks of the veil sticking to the red cap can resemble letters. When you and the mushroom read each other, the information received is linguistic. It is perceived as a voice or voices in the head and also as hallucinatory imagery that has often been compared with hieroglyphics. The luminous images seem like the deployment of a higher form of language.

The mushroom-cap-shaped begging-bowl carried by monks is called a "*patra*." Indian and Tibetan deities hold *patras* that are bowls fashioned from skullcaps filled with amrita, the entheogenic elixir of immortality originally made from the fly agaric and later *Psilocybe* mushrooms.

John Allegro gives a hypothetical Sumerian name for *Amanita muscaria* as "*PU-TAR," or "*GU-TAR". This literally means "crown of the head" or "top of the head." It is easy to see how this root could find itself in a Sanskrit word for the skull bowl ritually used for the drinking of amrita. The inside of the skull bowl was colored red with ocher, which, as we have seen, was associated with the red-colored *Amanita muscaria* mushroom and also its surrogate, menstrual blood. Buddhist patriarchs, deities, and bodhisattvas hold skullcap bowls of amrita in their many-armed hands. Skullcap bowls have been found in caves used by Neanderthals, who also practiced red-ocher burials.

"GU-TAR" or "PU-TAR" can alternately be read as "penis (in the) womb (vagina)" or "fetus (in the) womb." This is a description of the sexual symbolism of the fungus, where the stem or stipe represents the male organ and the feathery underside of the cap, the vulva. All these words are formed from the almost-universal mushroom root "P-T-R," which, along with its dialectic variant "F-T-R" and "G-T-R," forms vast constellations of mushroom related words in many different languages. The "P-T-R" root forms the Latin word for father, "*pater*," which became "father" in English where Latin words starting with *p* turn into *f*.

The Sanskrit word for a mushroom-shaped parasol is "*atapatra*." Again this is a "P-T-R" word. In India, the warrior caste was called *Kshatriya*, which means (men of the) parasol or sunshade or (men of the) mushroom. The Sanskrit word for parasol and mushroom is the same. They are formed from the G-T-R root variant. Bronze Age warriors had mushroom-shaped umbrellas on their chariots. They also took *Amanita muscaria* mushrooms, when available, to go into battle in order to produce strength, courage, valor, and martial ferocity. This is why in the Bhagavad Gita, from the East Indian epic poem the Ramayana, Prince Arjuna at the beginning of a battle receives enlightenment from his chariot driver who turns into the god of mushrooms, Krishna.

Another "P-T-R" word is the Greek word for stone, "*petros*." Mushrooms are universally referred to as stones, because they resemble stones lying on the ground and because stones were used to press the juice out of the reconstituted fly agarics. The Sumerian word for stone was "I-A," which, according to John Allegro, was a cultic name for the mushroom *Amanita muscaria*. In Sumerian, the name means "strong water." "Strong" means both the strength that the mushroom produces and medicinal effectiveness. "Water" is the "water of life," "living water," or fly-agaric urine. This is the meaning of the alchemical philosopher's stone, which was a trope for the sacred mushroom.

In the earliest versions of the Grail cycle, the Holy Grail was not a dish or a cup but a stone that miraculously fell down from heaven and floating down the river. Every day a dove would bring a communion wafer and lay it on the stone. Actually the Grail legend is not Christian at all but comes from an ancient mystery religion with the sacramental use of *Amanita muscaria* at its center.

In the oldest versions of the myth, "grail" does not mean a cup or chalice but a dish or plate resembling the flat, spread-out, mature mushroom cap. When the fly agaric grows long enough without being eaten by larva or putrefied by rain, the cap becomes inverted, and the feathery gills rise up on the outside to form the shape of a cup or chalice. The idea that the Grail was a cup used by Joseph of Arimathea to catch blood of the crucified Christ was a late-Christian interpretation of the pagan mystery story.

When Jesus said to the apostle Peter, "You are Peter and upon this rock I shall build my church," it was a concealed reference to the mushroom host. In Greek, "*petros*" means a stone. This is why we use the term "get stoned" to refer to inebriation.

The mushroom is like a book not only because it resembles the shape of ancient books but also because it has content. It has images that are shown over and over to people of all ages all over the world. Many people see lions and tigers and predatory cats. Frameworks, braids, tassels, woven designs, and knots are common imagery. They also report seeing intricate, futuristic machinery, otherworldly environments, and even UFOs.

The mushroom can show you visionary hallucinations that can resemble hieroglyphics and letters and every kind of imaginable thing. Also like a book, it contains knowledge.

These were the Tablets of Law that Yahweh gave Moses on which were written the Ten Commandments inscribed by the finger of God. The tablets were the mushrooms that grew on top of the holy mountain. The burning bush was the same fiery plant. *Amanita muscaria* mushrooms were the Tablets of Law from which was spoken the voice of God. The mushroom tablets were kept in the Ark of the Covenant. Some Tibetan Buddhist deities often hold a book as one of their attributes. Mike Crowley says that books, flaming swords, tridents, skull bowls, begging bowls, vases of amrita, and all the other accessories held by Buddhist deities are hidden euphemisms for *Psilocybe* and *Amanita muscaria* mushrooms.

The golden tablets that the angel Moroni gave Joseph Smith in the Mormon legend can now be identified as *Amanita muscaria* mushrooms, the food of prophets.

The Mazatec *curandera* Maria Sabina said that the mushroom showed her a book filled with all the knowledge of the world. Maria was illiterate, and books were not common in Huautla de Jimenez in the Sierra Mazatecas at that time. This shows that visions of the book are a standard part of the hallucinatory repertoire of the mushroom experience and not metaphors from our own associations.

There are many pictures in alchemy of alchemists holding books. In one picture, an alchemist is sitting holding the visionary book in his hands. The pages contain images that are all alchemical tropes for *Amanita muscaria*. They are suns and moons, including a sun with gills and a double sun. Two suns are often reported as seen in a non terrestrial, desert world that the mushroom shows to people who take them. Also on the alchemist's book is an *ouroboros* composed of an eagle and dragon eating each other's tails. An *ouroboros* is usually a single snake or dragon eating its own tail. According to Clark Heinrich, the word in Greek means "urine drinker" as well as "tail eater."

The alchemical *Book of Wisdom*

Eagles with bows and arrows surround the alchemist. Eagles are among the mushroom-related birds, in the company of ravens, red-eyed white doves, woodpeckers, chickens, cocks, and peacocks. Bows and arrows are also mushroom symbols. Arrows are named after the toxins that were applied to the points and are associated with entheogens, such as Cupid's arrow, which causes the rapture of love. Being struck by the sacred impact of the mushroom is compared to being shot with an arrow.

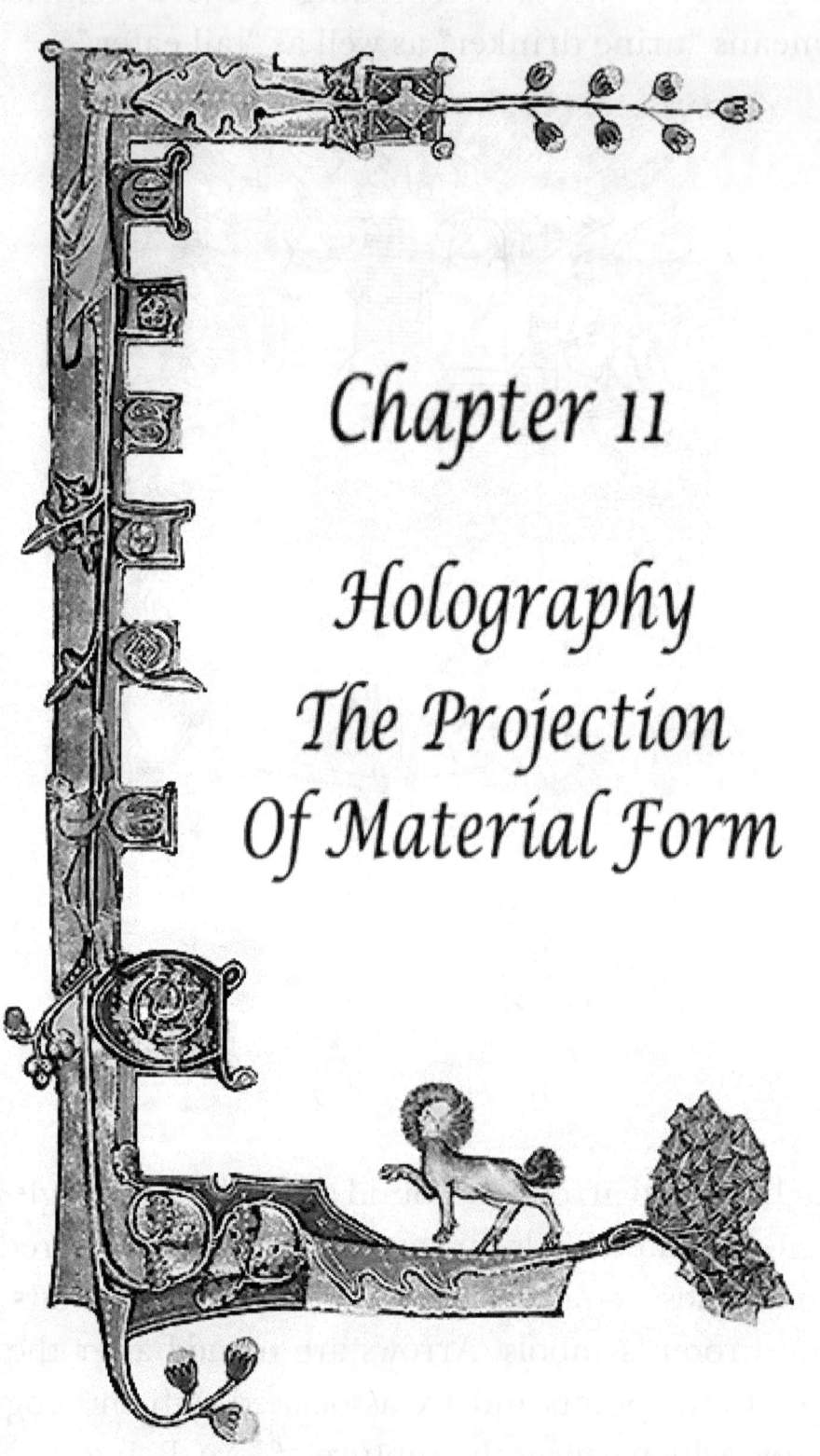

Chapter 11

Holography
The Projection
Of Material Form

CHAPTER 11

Holography: The Projection of Material Form

Up to now we have explored the many ways in which psychedelics can change consciousness. Now it is time to examine consciousness itself: what it is, how it works, and from where it comes. This will help explain on a scientific basis the many varieties of transformation that consciousness can undergo in psychedelic states.

To begin, we will examine the holographic model of consciousness pioneered by quantum physicist David Bohm and neurophysiologist Karl Pribram, among others.

Everything we see is a hologram created by the brain. Perceptual phenomena are projected. We experience a field of apparent three-dimensional structures in space. It appears to be a freestanding, autonomous world of material objects separate from our selves.

Classical physics has long assumed that the brain measures and records a single field of objects external to us and independent of the observer. Quantum physics shows that this is simply not the case. There are no objects except for the images that the mind-brain creates, nor is there space and time except within the object image display. Far from viewing solid objects, what we see are holograms that take on the appearance of images, shapes, and forms. Our brains construct the material world by interpreting vibrations from a dimension that is beyond time and space. Even space and time are projected as part of the holographic display.

There are no objects or images independent of observers. It is the act of looking at it that causes the energy field surrounding us to take the shape of what we mistakenly perceive as the outside world. Forms are holographic projections that are interpretations of part of the energy field in one of its many possibilities.

Because each one of us is making a holographic display, we mistakenly assume that there is only one, solid, objective world out there and we are all in it. Actually all observers are viewing their own personal holograms, but since they are all interpreting the same energy field, the result is easily mistaken for one single outside existence.

Einstein has shown that there is not a single, universal space-time in which everyone is contained. Everyone is contained in his or her own separate space-time, and this is subject to change in certain situations, such as accelerating to speeds approaching the speed of light. We can see that entheogenic plants and fungus can also change our own personal space-time.

Organic evolution has created a modality of conscious perception that is a kind of virtual reality using holography to create the illusion of everyone being inside of a material world existing in space and time. If the holographic display were removed, we wouldn't find ourselves, as in the movie *Matrix*, in another material existence in space-time. Instead we would dissolve into a time less, space less unity pervading the entire universe, where all information is deployed simultaneously everywhere. It would be one of the highest levels of psychedelic experience.

According to quantum physics, the universe is a wave field before someone looks at it. When consciousness observes the energetic wave, it appears to transform into the world of time, space, and images of objects. The quantum computer of the brain is a measuring device. When a sentient being makes an observation, the brain performs analytical computations on some but not all the potential aspects of the energy field. It stores the information in neural tissue, not as images but as interference patterns.

Then illuminating the information with laser-like light consisting of coherent biophotons within the brain, it generates a field of holograms. At this point, the mind-brain has created a three-dimensional model of the observation. It is like taking a picture of the invisible wave field and turning it into something that is "visible" to the mind.

The display of holograms is called "the object-image domain." It is what we see in front of us all the time. It is the only thing we can look at. Physicists use the term the "wave function" to refer to the fundamental energy field. Consciousness, by looking at it, causes the wave function to appear to transform into the object image domain. The mind-brain turns the invisible world into form, qualities, attributes, and characteristics so that it can see it. True reality is featureless. It has no color, no shape or form, no movement, and no location. Space and time exist only in the mind. They are the language that the mind uses to describe what it cannot see directly. The only thing the mind can see is itself.

What is holography? How are holograms created, and how can the brain produce them? Holography is a kind of photography where a coherent beam of light, like a laser, is split in two. One half of the beam falls on a photographic plate. The other half deflects off an object to be photographed, and the scattered light also falls on the photographic plate. The two beams interfere with each other and produce an interference pattern on the film. The photographic plate is called a "holograph." All this happens without the uses of lenses. The pattern on the plate doesn't resemble in any way the subject being photographed, but an image of the original is hidden in what appears to be expanding rings of concentric circles like rain falling on a pond.

When a beam of coherent light from a laser shines on the photographic plate, the original wave pattern is reconstructed, and a three dimensional image of the photographic subject is projected into space. The image is called a "hologram." The image exhibits all the properties of real external forms, showing depth, and parallax, changing as the angle of view is altered, just like real objects in space. You can walk around a hologram and examine it from the back or sides. A holographic image can be magnified to reveal details that are otherwise not visible. A hologram is almost indistinguishable from real objects that appear in our vision. This is not surprising because "real" objects are holograms created by the mind-brain.

When the holographic plate is viewed before reconstruction with a laser, the image resembles a moiré pattern, as though small stones had been dropped in water and the expanding ripples formed concentric circles that intersect each other. This is almost exactly identical to electron-microscope images of atomic structures. On the picture of the holographic plate, one target-shaped pattern is the reference beam from the unobstructed light of the laser.

An interference pattern on a holographic plate

The other ring of circles is formed from the light scattered off the photographic subject and superimposed over the reference beam on the photographic plate. The two intersecting patterns form a new design, an interference pattern. Interference patterns are more visible than the waves that form them and thus are ideally suited to the formation of perceptual images.

But if the world we see is a hologram, what is it a hologram of? What is the photographic subject? If the brain creates the material world as a hologram by scanning, recording, and imaging something, what is it scanning?

Classical Newtonian physics would say that it is a readout of the condition of the local energy field at the time and place where it is measured by the senses. This is partially true, but the readout of the energy state is not one to one. It is one to many. According to quantum physics, when the brain creates a hologram of what we see as a tree, there is not a wave packet of a tree waiting to be transformed into an image. There is a constellation of potential, unmanifested, potential objects containing every conceivable and unconceivable possibility. These all exist outside of time and space. The wave function is pregnant with unlimited potential. It contains the quintessential essence of all possibilities. When consciousness observes it, one of the most probable possibilities ultimately becomes an image of a tree. Remember that the energy field fills the entire universe and is the absolute reality behind all manifestation. It is living, conscious and contains the seeds of everything awaiting germination.

So what is the universe a hologram of? The energy field of the universe before observation is itself a holograph, where its totality is contained in all of its parts. The brain stores a recording of this energy state in neural tissue like a holographic plate. It is a hologram of a hologram. The brain is holographic system interpreting a holographic energy field that is the universe, in which like a fractal, every part contains the whole.

The universe is one thing. It is one, without a second. It functions like a giant, self-aware quantum computer as large as the cosmos. It is omnipresent. It is infinite, for it joins together all points in space. It is eternal because it contains all unmanifested time past, present, and future.

The field is conscious. It is autonomous. It is subjective. The field is intelligent. It is living. It is active and creative.

The energy field we are observing fills the entire universe and resides outside of time and space. It is a condition of complete, universal interconnectiveness. It is a whole without parts where all information is simultaneously deployed everywhere. All time—past, present, and future—is superimposed into a single, resonating now, and all space is unified into a minuscule point. It contains the seeds of space and time in an unmanifested condition.

When we see an object, the reflected light coming from it is scattered in all directions. The light doesn't have any distinct boundaries or outlines. The brain acts like a lens that focuses the radiant field and produces an image. The image is mathematically descriptive of the original, but it is incomplete. Before the recording is transformed into an image, the brain must transfer the process into its own domain. The original energy field is invisible. It has no qualities or characteristics. The brain performs a kind of image enhancement to make a picture of what the energy field would look like if it were visible. It increases its suchness to increase its intelligibility. Words like suchness, isness and thusness are used to describe increases in the degree of being performed by consciousness in the image making process. We see demonstrations of this in altered states of consciousness where the suchness is increased through image magnification.

Consciousness produces texture, color and form. Psychedelic perception magnifies these experiences and hidden texture emerges, colors become far brighter. Everything is emphasized and appears as though seen through a magnifying glass or even a microscope.

A friend once took peyote, and he exclaimed, "Everything is in italics!" He was a writer.

When we take consciousness-changing drugs, the holographic display can change or melt or turn into something unrecognizable. In states of psychedelic consciousness, holograms begin to be produced from our internal mental activity in the form of visions and hallucinations. Then at higher levels of visionary experience, we begin to record and display the universal hologram of the entire cosmic energy field.

Our holographic antenna tunes in to the resonance wave of the entire universal energy in all its infinite possibilities. From there, we can move beyond the holographic display to a state where all sensory information dissolves, and we are confronted with the empty yet all-containing base state of consciousness, the White Light of the Void. We will explore this at great lengths in chapter 13.

In a holographic plate, every part of it contains the entire picture. If you cut it up into a hundred pieces and shine a laser on one of them, the entire hologram appears. Each part contains the whole. The wave state of the universe is like a holographic plate. Whatever happens to one of the parts happens to the system as a whole. The system may be a large as the entire universe, and it may exist as a cosmos-sized web of interconnectiveness.

But if the brain is a holographic plate, what is the laser? What is the coherent beam of light needed to make the hologram? Lynne McTaggart wrote that the German physicist Fritz-Alabert Popp discovered in the seventies that all life forms emit a natural, living light or bioluminescence.

He called this "biophoton emission," and he believed that it originated in the DNA in all the cells making up living tissue.

What's more, Popp calculated that, like a laser, the biological light maintains the highest order of coherence. This allows all the parts of the body to share information instantaneously with every other part, because now the parts have become a whole. The light particles in living tissue are called "bio-photons." This laser-like light resonates inside of a network of tiny tubular structures called "microtubules" inside and between our cells, forming a fibrous web of filaments that covers the whole body.

The tubes are so small that quantum states and computations are possible inside them. The tubes may act as antennae and function as holographic receptors. They tune in to the resonance wave of the external wave field. The brain uses quantum computations to create interference patterns that are stored in neural tissue. In altered states of consciousness, the holographic receptors tune in to the resonance wave of the entire universe.

In laser photography, the more coherent the light source, the more detail can be seen in the hologram. "Coherence" means that all the photons or light particles are in sync with each other, all doing the same thing at the same time. In this state, they become one big particle or wave. Ordinary light starts out as coherent but soon scatters.

James Oroc, did extensive work with 5-MeO DMT, which is one of the two forms of psychedelic compounds naturally produced in the body. Oroc suggested that entheogens somehow increase the coherence of the biophotons in the body's bioluminescence. All the cells in the brain become synchronized and resonate together. Instead of acting independently, they all fire at the same time. This could also explain the experience of magnification seen in the sensory enhancement of psychedelic experience.

Timothy Leary asked the question, "Are we live, or are we on tape?" By this, he meant, are we live or recorded? The answer is that we are recorded. When the senses scan the energy field, the computations are stored in neural tissue, not as images but as interference patterns. The brain is like a holographic plate.

Only when the coherent light of our biophoton emissions activates the recorded information does the array of objects, images, and forms appear along with time, space, motion, and apparent causality, which we mistakenly regard as the material outside world. The appearance of holographic images can only be formed from recorded information from our senses. The mathematics of storing interference patterns of waves contains as part of the same equation, the possibility—if not the necessity—of transformation of waves into images. The transformation of waves into images and of images into waves is mathematically reciprocal.

Aristotle said that time is the moving image of eternity. Someone said that God made time in order to keep everything from happening at once. Actually in the energy field, everything is happening all at once.

But if the world is a hologram, who is looking at it? Where is what Arthur Koestler called "the ghost in the machine"? Quantum physics states that before the wave field can be turned into a hologram, it must be observed by consciousness. It further states that consciousness exists outside of time and space and that there is only one consciousness.

Quantum physics assures us that consciousness is nonlocal. Consciousness exists outside of time and space. It cannot exist in space-time, because it is what causes time and space to manifest. Nonlocal consciousness observes the nonlocal wave state of nature and causes it to condense into the world of objects and images existing in time and space. Think about it. You cannot look at consciousness because it is what is looking. The eye cannot see itself. To do so, it must have some kind of mirror. You can't measure consciousness because it is not an object. It is pure subjectivity.

Are consciousness one thing and the wave field that it is looking at another? Quantum physics says no. Before it is looked at, there are no separate things in the wave state. Consciousness and the energy field must be one single thing. Consciousness must be a property of the all-pervasive energy field that is being observed. If this is true then the snake is biting its own tail. Consciousness is looking at itself.

At the fundamental level, the energy field must be conscious. The holographic display may be a kind of mirror in which the conscious energy ocean can see its own reflection. The entire enterprise of biological evolution may be driven by conscious, intelligent, and creative energy evolving holographic perception in living beings and thus creating time, space, and the material world of image and form.

The astronomer Arthur Eddington agreed when he wrote, "The stuff of the universe is mind stuff." He also said that "The universe is not only more complex than we know, it is more complex than we 'can' know."

The noted astronomer James Hopwood Jeans said, "The universe is more like a great thought than a great machine."

Aldous Huxley made a similar suggestion when he wrote that true mind exists "at large" (in the cloud) and that the brain, far from generating consciousness, acts as a kind of "reducing valve" or filter whose function is to keep consciousness out, that is, to reduce potential incoming stimulus to a small, manageable sampling of the vast energy ocean in which we exist. We can see how, when we take psychedelics, the valve opens wider and wider, allowing more consciousness to enter.

The more we magnify matter, the less material it becomes. It is not solid at all. In the nineteenth-century materialist model, the universe is seen as a giant machine. It was thought that if we knew all the variables, we could completely predict its behavior. Atoms were imagined as tiny solar systems, and particles as solid little objects.

In the light of quantum physics, this belief falls apart. At the subatomic level, particles enjoy non-locality and uncertainty. They are unpredictable. We can know the location of a particle but not how fast it is going, or we can know its velocity but not its position. Never both. An electron exists not as an object but as a cloud of probable locations. Atoms are mostly empty space.

In an electron microscope, the wavelengths of visible light are too large to illuminate energy fields in the microscopic, atomic, and subatomic level of scale. Electrons of much shorter wavelengths are used instead of photons, and this allows the production of a simulation of what the invisible would look like if it were visible. This is the same as the holographic display created by our brain. It is a model of what the energy field would look like if it were visible. The electron microscopic image is an analogue generated by a computer. The material world is an analogue generated by our brain.

Electron microscopy uses the principles of holography. As the photographic subject is being scanned, the scattered electron light is stored in the computer, not as images but as interference patterns. The exact same thing happens in our brains, which act as holographic plates. It is much more efficient to store interference patterns than images, and in fact there are no structures in the brain that store images. Quantum computers use holographic memory as well.

Once, on a mushroom trip, just when I thought it was about over and it was time to come down, everything turned into waves. Then a ship came down. It was also made of waves. It looked like a diving bell or the spaceship in the old movie *The Man from Planet X*. A door opened in the craft, and a figure emerged. He also was entirely made of waves. On his chest was an extremely bright spot. It looked like a badge of authority. It reminded me of the Catholic icon of the Sacred Heart of Jesus, where Christ opens his chest with his two hands to reveal his heart.

The wave-man approached; he pointed to the spot and bade me to look into it. I gazed into the dazzling spot, and what I saw was just amazing! It was the most adamantine and significant thing I had ever seen. It completely took my breath away and left me gasping in astonishment. Everything in the universe was trivial compared to it; the big bang, all the limitless galaxies, the evolution of life, the existence of consciousness, all history, all wars, all migrations, the carrier of human civilization—everything was trivial compared to it.

I said to the wave-man, "Are you God?"

"No," he said, pointing to the badge, "but *this* is what we work for."

The image inside the spot was a picture of platinum atoms taken by Erwin W. Mueller.

Look at the picture taken through an electron microscope. Its wave nature is clearly evident. It looks like waves rippling out as though small stones were dropped in water. The dark circles are atoms. The concentric circles are waves. The waves cross each other and form interference patterns. The emergence of the crystalline structure is completely visible.

This is exactly like what a holographic plate looks like before the original image is reconstructed by illumination with coherent light. It is a holograph. Note the similarity to the picture of the holographic plate with its interference pattern. They look like stones dropped in a pond with concentric circular waves radiating out from them. The waves cross over each other and create a moiré of interference patterns. I can't help wondering, if one were to shine a laser on this image, what kind of hologram would it produce?

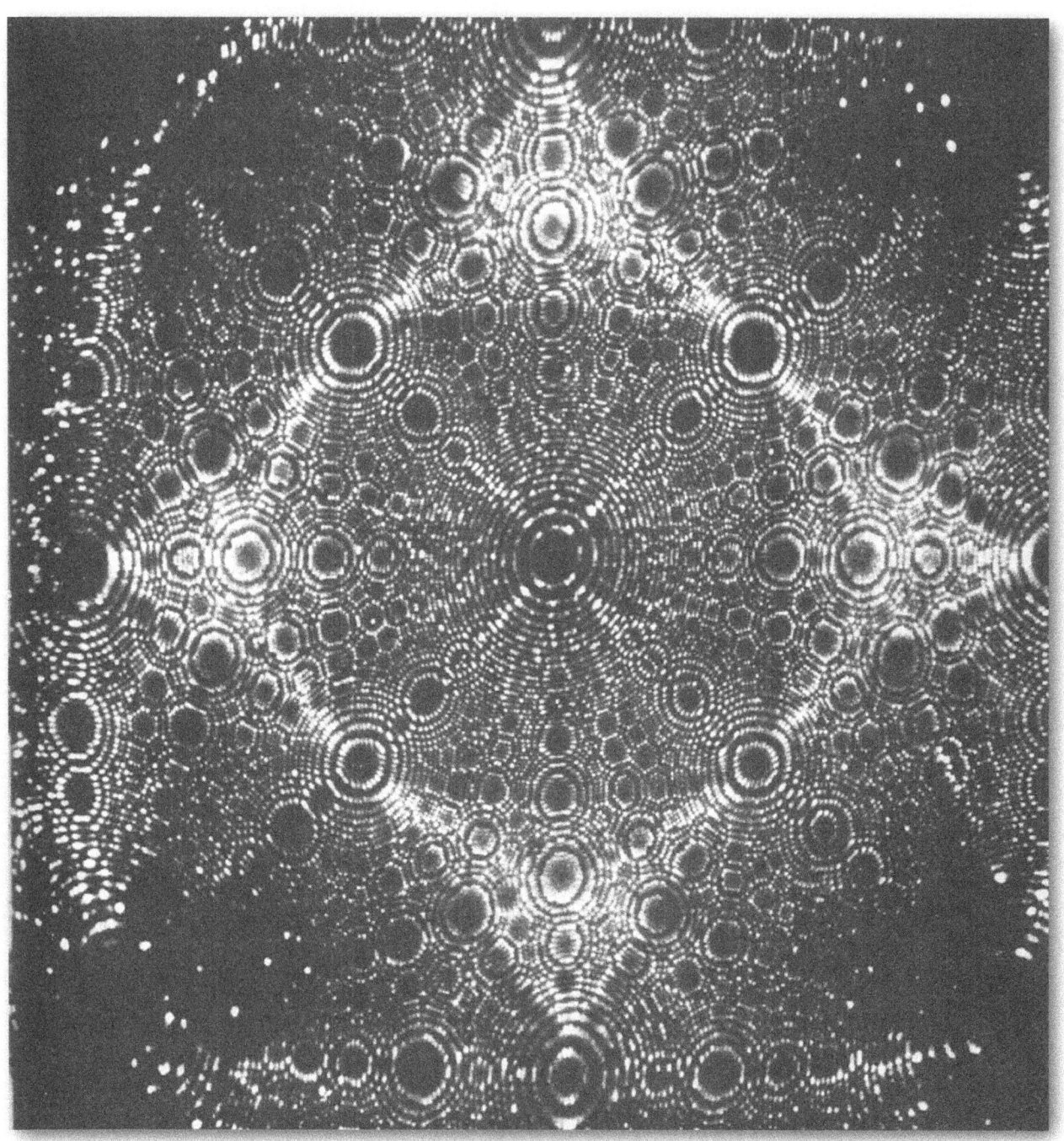

Electron microscope image of platinum atoms taken by Erwin W. Mueller

The image of the spot or the sacred heart must be another of the allegorical visions used by the mushroom to explain it. I once told this story to a group of friends, and a girl said it reminded her of a dream she had had. She went into the bedroom, and her father was standing in front of a mirror, dressing with his back to her. She said, "Father?" He turned around and said, "I am not your father." He unbuttoned his shirt with his hands, and from his chest, a brilliant ray of light shot forth and struck her in the heart. He said, "This is your father!" She went into a state of ecstasy.

But if everything is made of waves, what is waving? Waves happen to something. Sound waves happen to air. Water waves happen to water. In the wave field of the universe, before it is observed, what is waving? The waves are like ripples on an ocean, but an ocean of what?

Two Zen monks were arguing about a flag that was waving in the wind. The first said, "It is the flag that is waving." "No," said the other. "It is the wind that is waving." The Zen master who overheard them said, "You are both wrong. It is the mind that is waving."

The physicist Joseph Fourier, who first described electromagnetic fields, was asked if electromagnetic fields are waves, what is it that is waving? He replied, "The ether, of course." Although the existence of a world ether is believed to have been disproved by Michelson and Morley in their famous experiment, we can now see that they were looking in the wrong place. The media that the waves are happening to is consciousness. Consciousness is what is waving. It is the ground of being.

I once asked a friend, "If the world is a painting, what is the canvas?"

He said, "Dirt?"

What is waving is an ocean of infinite possibilities. When the hologram of the world forms, one of these possibilities materializes. When quantum physicists are asked to describe what in the fundamental wave field is waving, they say that they are waves of probability. There is nothing material in that answer. Probability is a concept. It is the mind that is waving. It is consciousness that is waving. Consciousness is the world ether.

Well, fellow explorers, if you made it through this last part, you are brave explorers indeed.

Consciousness Creates The Material World

According to the Copenhagen interpretation of quantum mechanics developed by Max Born, Werner Karl Heisenberg, and Niels Henrik David Bohr, when consciousness looks at the universe in its wave state, the wave collapses into objects existing in space and time. When consciousness looks away, the objects spread out instantly and return to their nonmaterial formlessness.

It is an illusion that the world of images and objects exists between observations when nobody is looking at. When we look at the moon, it exists as an object in space and time. When we are not looking at it, we assume that it remains a physical object, but quantum physics says otherwise. When we are not looking at the moon, it exists outside of spacetime as a wave. The material world only exists when someone is looking at it. There are no objects without a conscious observer looking at them.

In the television miniseries *Genius*, Albert Einstein and Werner Heisenberg are walking down the sidewalk. Einstein hated quantum physics and called it "spooky action at a distance." He insists, "God does not play dice [with the universe]." In this episode Einstein leads Heisenberg out into the street between moving traffic.

Heisenberg exclaims, "Are you crazy, Albert? We will be struck by a car!"

"Don't worry," say Einstein. "According to you, we are perfectly safe because the car can only exist if we are looking at it and we have our backs turned."

Actually the car exists whether we are looking at it or not, but not as a material object. If you get run over by a car in the object-image domain, that is one of the more probable possibilities that could happen. In the wave field beyond space and time what happens is a range of possibilities. This is where quantum physics gets strange and difficult to understand. All possibilities exist in the quantum domain, but some are less probable than others. Nevertheless all possibilities exist simultaneously before observation. All these possibilities are occurring at the same time in the wave field. It is an ocean of potential. It is anything and everything. It is anywhere and everywhere.

In the energy domain before it is observed, these are all possible:

- You are run over by a car.
- You are not run over by a car.
- You are both run over and not run over at the same time.
- You are neither run over nor not run over at the same time.

- You may be run over by a snail or a dinosaur. (This is highly improbable but still possible. If the probability wave fluxuates, the result is a miracle.)

Only when consciousness looks at the wave function is one of the possibilities manifest. What if your back is to the car and you don't see it coming? Without consciousness observing it, did it happen? The consciousness of the driver of the car is looking at it. What if the car is remote controlled, like all cars will soon be? When the consciousness of the first responder arrived on the scene of the accident, the time-space material event would unfold, bringing with it its history of what would have happened if there had been someone observing it.

What if two observers are looking at the moon? The moon appears as an object in time-space. What if one of the observers turns his or her back? Does the moon both exist and not exist at the same time? How many moons are there anyway? Is the moon I am seeing the same moon as you are seeing? There are as many moons as there are observers. The reason that so many quantum physicists and others find this situation so paradoxical and baffling is that they have not escaped the belief that there is one single world out there independent of observers.

What bothers me is the idea that the wave function of the universe actually collapses into material space-time when looked at and spreads back out when unobserved. I suggest that when a sentient being looks at the wave state of nature, the wave doesn't change. It doesn't collapse. It goes on being a wave. The brain and nervous system creates a model of the wave in the form of the holographic display that we erroneously regard as the material, outside world.

We only create holograms of what we look at while we are looking. The brain is a measuring device. It scans the energy field and makes measurements and computations. The wave nature of the universe continues to exist whether someone is looking at it or not. When we take a picture of a tree, the tree doesn't change. A tree and a picture of a tree are not the same thing. The picture is an incomplete analogue of part of the nature of the tree.

If every observer creates his or her own image of the moon, the situation becomes less daunting. The moon doesn't change. The observer looking at the moon creates a hologram of it that is a material, temporally and spatially bound object. The other observer only creates holograms of what he or she is looking at, so in his or her world although he or she may assume otherwise, the moon remains an amorphous wave phenomenon of timeless, formless potential.

The Gnostic writer Porphyry wrote in the third century AD in his treatise on sensation, "Vision is produced neither by a cone nor an image, nor any other object, but that the mind, being placed in rapport with visible objects, sees itself in these objects, that are nothing else than itself, seeing that the mind embraces everything and that all that exists is nothing but the mind."

Objects are kinds of thoughts. Light is a bioluminescence, and it is as organic as a firefly's tail. When invisible radiation strikes us, we light up. The brain is an organ that turns energy into form. Like King Midas and gold, everything the mind touches turns into matter.

The Buddhists say that forms are empty. They are not solid, freestanding objects independent of the observer. They are nonsubstantial and nonmaterial. This doesn't mean that a nonsubstantial fist won't break your nonsubstantial jaw.

The act of looking creates what is looked at. When we are not looking at something, I doesn't exist for us *as such* in the world of object, matter, and form. It is an illusion that the world exists between observations when nobody is looking at. The material world only exists when someone is looking at it. There are no objects according to quantum physics without a conscious observer looking at them.

This begs, however, a very important question. The universe has existed some fifteen billion years since the time of the big bang and if biological life did not evolve on this planet until very late in the history of the cosmos, there would have been no conscious observers looking at it. How could the universe have existed as a material process in space and time? It must have been, like the unseen moon, a formless cluster of unmanifested possibilities existing nonlocally. Only when observed by conscious beings for the first time could one of its possible potential have become manifest. Even on other worlds far older than ours, conscious organisms would have appeared late in the history of cosmological time.

If this is true, the universe came out of formlessness into form and into time and space only when the first living observer looked at it for the first time. This would have happened when sentient life first evolved on any of the worlds in the cosmos. Even so, there would remain billions and billions of years when the universe existed only as a formless, cluster of possibilities.

Not only that, the field had to evolve organisms advanced enough to use holography to create a holographic model of the world in order to create space-time. The question is at what point in evolution did holographic modeling evolve as the primary modality of perception? Can an amoeba take a holographic picture of the wave function? Probably not, because as far as we know, an amoeba does not use holographic modeling. Can a snail? A fish? A squirrel? As a famous Zen koan asks, "Does a dog have Buddha nature?" The answer to the koan is "Mu!". Mu means "nothing", "emptiness", "formlessness." This "nothing" will be explored in Chapter 13, The White Light of the Void. Dogs and cats and the mammals in general seem to share and exist in our holographic world.

There is a possible solution to this question of how the universe could have existed before there was anyone to look at it. If we consider that consciousness is nonlocal and exists outside of space-time and if it and the energy field is same thing, then consciousness was there from the beginning from the big bang and maybe before. Could nonlocal consciousness look at its nonlocal wave nature and thus create the material universe? Probably not. It could know itself by being itself, but it could not see itself as an object until there were evolved advanced biological life-forms using holography for perception. Only then could the universe assume the attributes of space and time and matter and form.

Consciousness residing outside of time and space in a nonlocal dimension may have influenced the evolution of biological, sensory-oriented beings in order to see itself. An eye can only see itself if it looks at its reflection in a mirror. Only when the brain evolved to the point where it could produce holographic modeling could the material universe come into existence. The whole process of holographic perception may have been a way to create a kind of mirror in which consciousness could look at a reflection of itself.

The real solution to this conundrum may be this. Before the evolution of sentient beings, there was no time and space, so the universe didn't have to wait billions of years to come into existence. When time came into existence, it carried with it its own past history which would be a description of what it would have looked like and of what would have happened if there had been someone there to look at it.

If you find this hard to understand, you are not alone. It drives quantum physicists crazy. A quantum physicist once said, "If people say that they understand quantum physics, they are either liars or they are insane." On the other hand, psychedelic users find these paradoxical concepts more comfortable than others. In the sixties, a common expression was "Yes, but the opposite is also true." This is why Eastern religions, like Vedanta, that had at their center the use of entheogenic mushrooms closely anticipated quantum theory.

As the quantum physicist Erwin Schrödinger demonstrated in his famous thought experiment, a cat can be both alive and dead at the same time until you look at it.

In entheogenic states, you can directly experience the ocean where all possibilities swim together at the same time. It is anything. It is everything. It is anybody. It is everybody. It is nothing. It is nobody. It has no body. It is within all bodies and without. In entheogenic states you can experience a universal field of energy where all information is simultaneously deployed everywhere and where every part contains the whole.

The effects of quantum coherence can be seen in the phenomenon of the contact high. When a person who has taken entheogens in the past comes into the presence of someone who is tripping, they entrain to the energy that is being given off and they go into an entheogenic state of consciousness. This is the well-known and documented phenomenon of the contact high. The contactee ingests not a single molecule of the drug, yet he or she goes into a psychedelic state. If the drug taken is LSD, the contactee goes into acid space. If it is mescaline, he experiences mescaline space.

It is not the power of suggestion. It is not the olfactory ribbons of information that everyone releases into the environment. It is an example of quantum "spooky action at a distance" that Einstein found so unsettling. It is similar to quantum superposition in which two particles or things become entrained to each other, sharing the same vibration and when separated, no mater how far in space or time, what happens to one, happens to the other. Contact high can even happen over the telephone.

On a certain level, people who are tripping or have tripped become synchronisticaly in tuned to each other. They become coherent. Their vibrations are harmonious and identical. The energy they emit becomes one single vibration. This is possible because consciousness is a quantum mechanical process and the brain has the duel function of being a quantum computer and a classical analogue computer.

This is why it is so profound to attend a Grateful Dead concert where hundreds, perhaps thousands of people are all turning on at the same time. It becomes one gigantic contact high where the musicians become affected by the energy of the crowd and the high of the audience is driven by the music.

Psychedelic chemicals and people who take them give off a kind of radiation. Just as a radioactive isotope causes other objects that are near to it to become radioactive, a consciousness that is resonating in a psychedelic state causes people and things that are near to it to become psychoactive. When you trip, the cloths you are wearing, the sheets you sleep in, everything with which you come in contact become irradiated with psychedelic energy and can trigger a contact high into an entheogenic state. This is the source of the experience called flashback, where sometime after tripping, a person finds themselves back in the psychedelic domain. Some people found this frightening and disconcerting, as though once the experience had you in its clutches, it could turn you on again and again at its own discretion. If you like being high on psychedelics, this is just a natural part of the consciousness changing process.

People say, "And what about other people? Are they made out of my mind, too?" Every person is making and viewing a different model of the same energy state. These models contain pictures of all the other people. Gottfried Leibniz, the inventor of calculus, created a model of consciousness in which every sentient being is like a mirrored sphere. Each contains the reflection of all the others and the reflection of the entire universe.

There is a Zen saying that "The whole moon and all of the stars are reflected in a single drop of dew on the grass." Every observer is like a dewdrop reflecting the whole universe.

Kobayashi Issa, a Japanese poet and Buddhist priest, wrote a famous haiku poem that goes,

> It is a dewdrop world.
> A dewdrop world it is
> And yet,
> And yet…

It is the second "and yet" that makes this poem all the more profound.

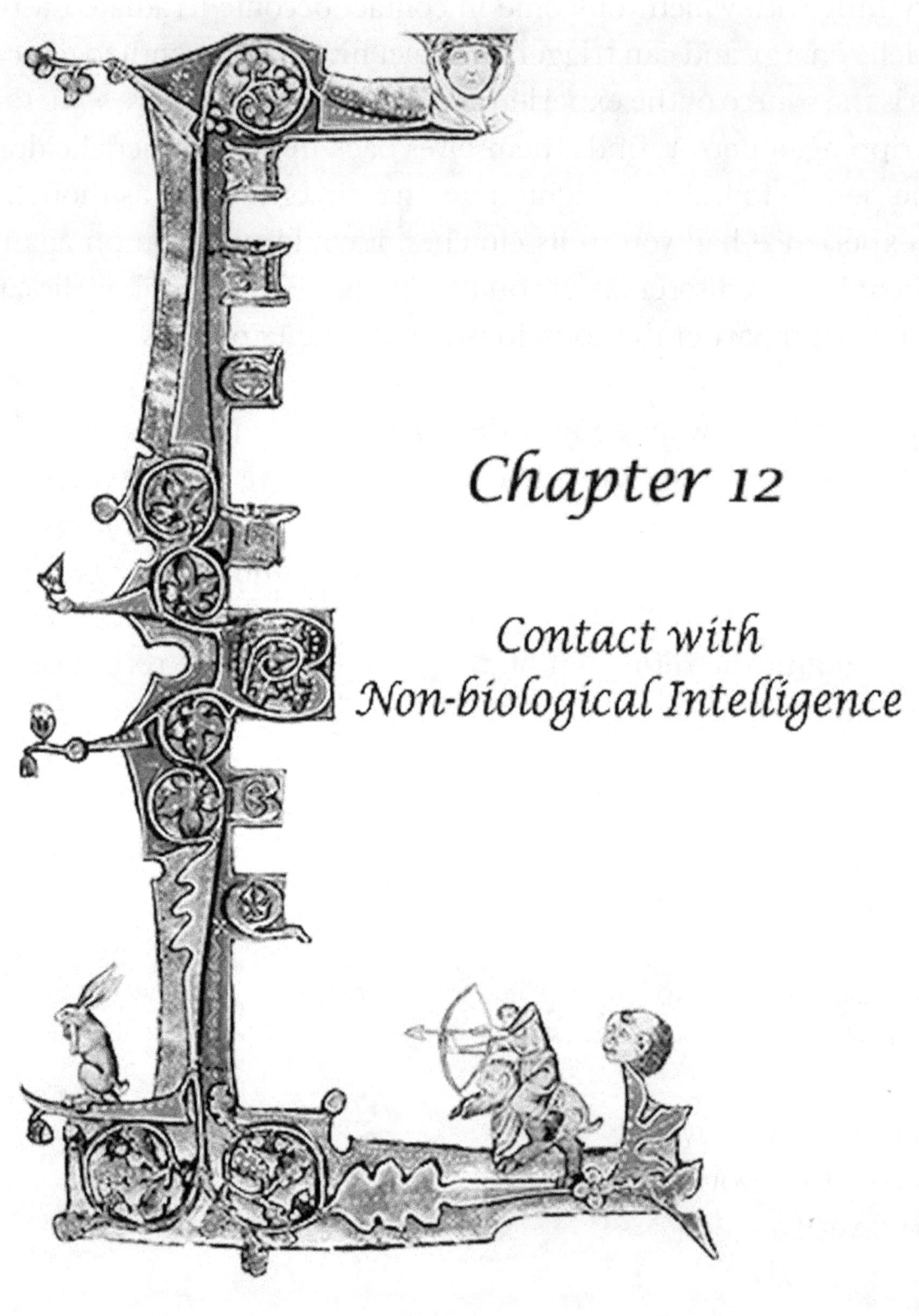

Chapter 12

Contact with Non-biological Intelligence

CHAPTER 12
Contact With Nonbiological Intelligence

ONE OF THE THINGS THAT can happen when taking entheogens is the experience of contact with living, communicating beings that are not human or in some cases don't even have bodies. It is as though these drugs mediate a communication between us and different forms of intelligent life.

It is ironic that the whole idea of extraterrestrial contact is so current right now and that it is such a powerful motif in the popular imagination. It is in movies and on television. New books on the subject are appearing every day. It's just bursting out of everyone's minds, and yet when we think about it, almost invariably these beings are imagined to be from outer space or from other planets or other star systems across great physical distances. As Terence McKenna said, Looking for the source of extraterrestrials in radio signals from space is as culture-bound as searching out in the galaxy for a good Italian restaurant.

Where do these beings come from? The mathematics of science describe a multiplicity of universes; for example, string theory necessitates eleven universes that are all tangent, including this one. They may contain intelligent life capable of making contact with our world. We live in a multidimensional universe, and they may come from other dimensions.

They may come from dark-matter universes, or they may come from places that our science has not yet discovered. In the case of mushrooms, they may represent a form of consciousness that is inherent in the vast underground mycelia networks, which in some species can span hundreds of acres.

When contact occurs, it can be like an aperture opening or a rupture in the fabric of space-time right before you. It can be like a window or a door or a crack. As you peer into the hole in the world, there is something else on the other side, and it is usually a whole lot of people and things coming to meet you and greet you and interact with you. The beings come through the opening in space-time into our continuum. Sometimes they take us through the doorway into their world.

So what does this all mean? There are many different kinds of beings who come through the opening, and they seem to have their own agendas. Some seem to have physical bodies and some do not. Some may have come to help us or teach us. Some may have come to harm us or manipulate us or exploit us. Some diverse species may be seen at times to be working together. Some groups may be in opposition to each other. Who are these many different types of beings we encounter? Where do they come from, and why are they here? Do they all come from the same place or from many different places?

Of course people have been taking entheogenic plants and mushrooms since the Stone Age, and resulting ideology is deeply embedded in mystical and religious literature.

Since the use of entheogens seems to be so old and part of civilization going back to the early origins of our species, these beings must have been with us all the way. Contact with nonhuman entities must have been a part of human cultural experience all throughout history, back to and over the horizon of human origins. Since they seem to be more technologically advanced than us, if they have mastered time travel, they may be able to appear simultaneously in all periods of history.

When *Psilocybe* mushrooms are taken in the dark, the air becomes filled with luminous images. Some of the images are your own mental content—your memories, thoughts, and impressions. Others seem to be from minds other than your own. Your personal images are rearranged to form the content of a message that is quite beyond your subjective experience. You can clearly recognize some of the individual elements as fragments of your personal mind, but they are being arranged into a collage whose meaning is coming from outside you.

Mirrorlike Wisdom

The entities we encounter who seem to be directing the experience may be mirror like in their own nature. If the psychedelic experience is like a mirror into which human beings have been peering all throughout time, it may be a mirror with memory. It may photograph and record every impression that it reflects. It may be a recorded encyclopedia formed from the collective reflections of the inside of every mind and memory and imagination of every creature that ever looked into it, human, animal, or otherwise, on this world or many others. It may selectively mix these impressions with the reflections of ourselves. It is the Knight of the Mirror who daunted Don Quixote.

I once had an experience on ibogaine during which it was politely suggested to me that I should read a certain book before my next trip because there were some things they wanted to explain and they couldn't find the necessary conceptual elements in my immediately accessible experience. Imagine a trip giving you reading assignments.

Nonbiological Intelligence

On entheogenic drugs, we can encounter beings that appear to be nonmaterial and come from somewhere outside of the holographic display. Whether they enjoy alternate methods of perception as complex and complete as ours, we do not know. They may exist beyond space-time in quantum nonlocality, like dolphins swimming in a sea of infinite possibilities.

Terrence McKenna liked to talk about people as though they were monkeys. Of course he meant primates, but monkeys are funny. A woman once asked him, "Do you think that we are monkeys?"

"No," he said, "I think we are in monkeys."

The way we experience nature is from inside of a biological organism. Our consciousness is embedded in a mind-brain system, by which everything that comes to our attention is processed and mediated. We are inside of biological life form. We perceive a display, highly evolved though it is, created by an animal's nervous system.

There is increasing evidence that selves are not always found attached to bodies. We know that people can have out-of-body experiences, but it may be that conscious entities can exist without bodies. In our world, we almost always experience consciousness embedded in an organic matrix.

Everyone assumes that intelligence and physical bodies go together and are one organism, and we even assume that animals grow intelligence, that consciousness is merely an epiphenomena, that intelligence is something that is exuded by biological matter rather than the other way around. This is our primary materialistic cultural mode. It is much more probable that minds grow bodies to express themselves. With entheogens, especially the tryptamine-derived psychedelics, you very frequently encounter intelligence that doesn't appear to be associated with an animal body.

If the only time you ever saw a man, and he was riding a horse and if you were neither a horse nor a human, you could end up with a kind of a centaur picture of the situation. You would assume that the horse and man was one animal instead of two. But if the time came when you encountered men who were not on horseback or even horses not mounted by men, it could occur to you that these were separate things that are sometimes found together and sometimes not.

It seems that with entheogens, we sometimes encounter entities that are not inside animal bodies. This is what could be called "non biological intelligence." While they do not seem to have intrinsic form, they can and do take on forms that they borrow from us in order to interact with us. This is part of the nature of entheogenic contact phenomena. They do this by entering into our holograph-forming system and creating holograms that reflect their mind and nature so that we can see them.

This is why mushrooms are best taken in total darkness, where the normal holographic display of the world disappears and the darkness presents a backdrop for otherworldly forms.

This other kind of intelligence takes control of our way of experiencing through holographic projection so that we can see them. We can't see them unless they enter into the object-making process. Otherwise they are invisible to us, only manifesting as a telepathic voice in the head. For us to notice them, they must show us objects, because we are inside of a life form that is making a holographic-object display of the world.

The magician David Copperfield said, "There are no objects in the spirit world. We must loan the spirits objects so they can show themselves to us."

They take over the object-making process, and they can make them much better than we can. The hallucinogenic objects we see in mushroom visions are much more vivid than our everyday perception. Following a psychedelic event, we experience a temporary period of sensory enhancement. Everything appears sharper, clear, more detailed, and magnified, with a great increase in texture and pattern.

The holographic making of objects can act independently from creating a display of the world. When unhooked from the representation of the energy field, it can be used consciously. This happens in dreams and in hallucinations. In dreams, we make dream forms, dream people, dream landscapes. It can be something of which we can take control. This is true in the case of lucid dreaming, where as we dream, we are aware that we are dreaming and then influence the dream and take control of the content. Some people dream very vividly. Vivid dreaming can appear much more real by far than ordinary perception. As anyone who has taken the tryptamine entheogens can attest, hallucinations can appear much more real by far than what we see in ordinary life.

The Taoist Huang Po dreamed that he was a butterfly. When he awakened, he didn't know if he was a man who had dreamed he was a butterfly or if he was a butterfly that had dreamed it was a man.

When we contact non biological entities on mushrooms, it is they who take control of the holographic object-making process. They use it as an artist would use media to paint or carve stone or mold clay to create objects of art and beauty, such as exquisite ornaments and jewelry.

When psilocybin is taken in the dark, the image-making function stops making pictures of chairs and tables and rooms. In the psilocybin trance, this activity is used as an expressive form. People usually start out thinking that what they see in these states is the unconscious made conscious—their own mind spilling out its memories and unconscious content, running wild, with the restraints of ordinary perception removed.

In time, it becomes apparent that while some of the imagery perceived comes from a person's memory, most of the forms are utterly novel and strange, and all the images are being arranged by a kind of intelligence that exists outside of us. It is as Laurie Anderson said of the visions she saw with botanical entheogens, "Hey! This stuff doesn't grow on trees."

The theater-like presentation of the mushroom trance is not being presented by ourselves. It is someone else who is using our hologram-making machinery in order to communicate with us. It is continuing to make objects, but now these objects are floating in space all around us. They have geometric orientation. They have topology. They have surfaces, and they do everything that form does here, only more. The object-making process is now in the hands of master artists. When it starts doing what we do, it wants us to start doing what it does.

The image display and the modeling of forms are just to get our attention. Just as we are seeing it, it is also seeing us.

In the movie *Hans Christian Anderson*, Hans says,

> Now here's a book of a different sort;
> Just gaze at a page or two.
> You laugh, ha-ha, but you blush a bit,
> For you realize as you're reading it,
> That it's also reading you.
> I'm Hans Christian Anderson,
> Anderson, that's who.

Terrence McKenna said, "When you take the mushroom, the mushroom is also taking you." The mushroom entity is looking into our minds and seeing us from perspectives that are fourth-dimensional, psychic cross sections. It can peer deeply into our subconscious and even into the collective unconscious. They can see things about our personality and our history.

When the mushroom comes into our minds and merges with us, it peers into our memory stores. It rummages around in our memories like an old trunk, and it looks at pictures we have taken during our life that are stored there. It can read the book of our mind and thumb through the pages. It will select images. It is trying to say something, but it is saying it on our terms.

The philosopher Clement of Alexandria writes in his introduction to The Protrepticus, "Come. I shall show you the Logos and the Mysteries of the Logos, and I shall explain them to you in images that are known to you."

The mushroom entities pull out all these pictures and put them up as on a felt board. The forms seem to float in the darkness. They are our thoughts as seen by the others. We are seeing how someone else sees us. There is a strange kind of loop in it, as what we see, in part, are pictures of ourselves. They are showing us to ourselves as they see us.

In contact phenomena, this other mind comes inside you, and for a time, there are two minds in one body. Because they are minds, they are not nudged up against one another. They merge, and they flow together like two streams of water. There is commingling. There is confluence. It is both undeniably your mind, and it is also very clearly that of another. But they are so completely interwoven that the warp and woof produces one cloth. Doris Lessing said, "Sufism is what I call whole cloth."

There is one new kind of mind there, and this demonstrates the possibility that the minds of more than one organism can be joined together, temporarily or permanently.

The mistletoe growing on the oak is an ancient metaphor for the grafting on of new intelligence. This is particularly significant because the oak is one of the host trees for *Amanita muscaria* mushrooms. The brain is the host for the mushroom consciousness. Terrence McKenna wrote that the mushroom says, "I need a mammalian nervous system. Do you have one handy?"

The use of ivy in Dionysian rituals had the same symbolism of the attachment of one life form to another. While mistletoe and ivy are parasitic, the attachment of the non biological mind is symbiotic, becoming the higher intellect, perhaps even an immortal soul.

Biological conglomeration is common in the animal world. The flagella or oar-like feet of single-cell life forms, like paramecia, are separate organisms that long ago joined forces in symbiosis with the mother cell. They give it mobility, and they are supplied with food. It would be like discovering that your arms are actually separate organisms that attached themselves to the body early in its evolution and coexist with it in a symbiotic state. The bacteria living in the guts of termites that allow them to digest wood are separate creatures from the insect, with their own individual DNA.

Some of the mushroom entities strongly suggest that it is better, or at least truer, to exist without this biological symbiosis. The fact that these life forms that we encounter with entheogens appear to be non biological and that some of them greet us as though we are their kin suggests that we may be the same as they are.

This suggests that the human self is a nonbiological form of life that somehow wound up inside a primate. This condition may not be the end of its existence. The possibility exists that beyond this stage may lie a much higher and freer nature.

A Sufi teacher was asked by one of his students, "What are angles?" He said, "Angles are the higher faculties of the mind." Later when the Sufi spoke of angles, the student said, "But you said that angles were only the higher functions of the mind." "No," said the Sufi, "I said that the higher functions of the mind are angles."

The human intellect may be a nonbiological entity that has become attached to a primate. This is something that has been suggested to me on many occasions in these encounters. The thing that they show us concerns our existence untangled from association with biological systems. They talk about it and demonstrate it by producing out-of-body experiences, in which you can feel what it would be like to not be connected to a body.

This is related to what here we know as death. The permanent separation from the body is one of those places we dread to peer. Biological systems don't endure very long, and they have a fixed period of time in which to exist. If, as our materialist culture believes, biological systems generate life, mind, intelligence, and consciousness as a kind of epiphenomena, then we are doomed to perish when the body decomposes. If, as the mushroom seems to suggest, consciousness may not be biological, then the separation doesn't necessarily indicate the destruction of intelligence.

The permanent separation of the mind from the body that the mushroom spirits demonstrate and encourage seems to the materialistically oriented individual an invitation to death—an invitation to die.

Quantum physics tells us that consciousness does not live in the physical world of time and space but beyond in a nonlocal dimension; also it tells us that consciousness is unitive and all pervasive. It cannot die when the body dies, because it is an aspect of the fundamental state of the entire universe. Consciousness is not an object in the holographic display. It is pure subjectivity. We cannot make a hologram of consciousness, because consciousness is needed to make the hologram.

But what the mushroom entities are here to do is not to help us make better objects. What they have come here to do is to tell us about other possibilities that exist beyond the holographic display of biological consciousness.

Some of them have apparently come to tell us that intelligent life in nature is not fundamentally biological although it can be associated with an animal body and that a human being is actually two or more life forms entangled in a kind of symbiotic union. The physical body, the primate, has a psyche and consciousness, and it uses the hologram-making process to see the world.

We can see this in animals, but in the case of humans, there is present another life form living very closely intertwined with the host. It is a kind of guest-host situation. The human mind in the primate body is symbiotic.

The entities with which we interact on mushrooms don't make holograms to experience nature. They claim that the holographic display is a very indirect way of perception. They suggest that reality can be contacted directly, unfiltered and unsorted.

They suggest that we can actually be part of nature instead of constantly describing it. They intimate that we can be identical with the interconnected totality everywhere and everything and every when, instead of just one of its parts. If what we are is not the same as the animal we are in, our true nature is not necessarily biological or even material. We may have originated somewhere else.

All the other animals besides us don't contain human intelligence. If you look at the evolution of the human mind, its sudden appearance is quite noteworthy. In all of biological evolution, there is nothing that happened so fast as the emergence of the human mind. It was an enormously accelerated process, and it is not happening to the other animals. We are not like the other monkeys.

Shipwrecked Castaways

Here is a model I like to use sometimes. It is not to be taken literally. Think of it as an allegory or a thought experiment. Picture an interdimensional vehicle, a ship that can sail the ocean between worlds, dimensions, and universes yet undreamed of. This ship contains nonbiological entities, and they are from a nonmaterial universe. This ship is visiting our universe within a world of matter and biologically based life forms.

Perhaps they are exploring or surveying. Perhaps they are on vacation, but somehow they have entered our waters and are in Earth orbit. They are in trouble. The ship is derelict. It is breaking apart. Its communication systems are down. Its life-support systems are starting to fail, and everybody is in big trouble. They can't go home. They can't signal for help, and they are shipwrecked on this primitive planet, where there are all these biologically based life forms running around. The computers will soon stop functioning.

These beings are creatures of pure intelligence. They are like data seeking a computer. A decision is made to do the only thing possible. The shipwrecked castaways must enter into the biological substrate of the planet and make a radical adaptation and stick it out until help arrives. It is that or perish. They survey the biological ecology. The most promising animals are large primates flourishing in Africa, so this higher intelligence literally moves in and embeds itself in the warm, moist hardware of the primate brain and nervous system.

They enter into the quantum biocomputer of the primate brain, which acts as a kind of substrate that can serve as a vehicle and an environment to sustain them. It is a symbiotic relationship rather than a parasitic one. The symbiote becomes what today we think of as the higher intellect.

So there they are. They are in the monkeys. The spaceship has crashed. They have no way of getting home. They remember the world that they came from, but it is too difficult to keep the two dissimilar universes in mind at the same time. It is finally decided that the most merciful thing is that everyone forget the past and the homeland.

The true situation is too unbearable to stand, and the knowledge isn't really necessary for the time being, because this reality is an interruption and there is nothing that can be done about it. They decide that they simply won't tell their children. If the children want to think of themselves as super evolved primates that will be fine.

They decide that they have to keep the knowledge alive somehow, because in some future time, the situation might change. Help might come, and rescue might occur. So certain people are selected to know the story of their history and their origins. There will have to be a continuous line of transmission, and it should be secret.

Now the story jumps ahead to the present. Everyone has forgotten except the few who were chosen to remember, and they are keeping it a secret, as they always have. But now a new thing has happened. The rescue has begun.

The people from the homeland have stumbled upon our planet and said, "Hey, look at those primates. There is something strange about them. There are people inside them just like us."

They come down and survey the situation. The visitors pick up a few humans and study them and find that they can actually separate the nonphysical higher mind from the primate body. They conclude that this must be some offshoot of what they are, that sometime back for uncertain reasons had gotten stuck in biology. The newcomers decide to rescue them and take them home.

Well, this doesn't go over very well at all, because the people in the primates don't know that they are something other than the monkeys. They don't know who these other people are who are telling them that they are going to separate them from their bodies and take them away. It sounds just like death to them. They don't understand that beyond the dark womb of matter lies our true identity. It is the one, universal mind and consciousness that exist in total, interconnectedness, simultaneously sharing all information beyond space-time and outside of the world of form with the entire indivisible whole.

It is not death. It is going home.

Chapter 13

The White Light Of the Void

CHAPTER 13

The White Light of the Void

BEFORE WE GO, WE MUST explore one more variety of the psychedelic experience. That is what the Buddhists call "*sunya*," the void. Up to now, the experiences described in this book involve contact with nonhuman entities and non terrestrial environments. There is another class of entheogenic experience that is universally considered the highest and most desirable state of consciousness. This is the void, the living, conscious nothing that is the source of everything. To the Taoists, it is the Tao; to the Buddhists, it is the Dharmakaya. In India, it is Brahman. The Gnostics called it the "Aeon" and the "Logos.' It is the White Light of the Void and the Clear Light. It is your own consciousness not being conscious of anything. It is your true self. To know it you must dissolve into it and become extinguished in its radiance. It is the highest you can get.

The most surprising thing about the void is that people who have experienced it report that it somehow permeated with life and consciousness. It is conscious. To say that it is consciousness is an abstract and safe concept, but if you drop the "ness" and say it is conscious, it takes on an altogether different meaning. *Consciousness is conscious*. It is conscious of you, and in its presence, you disappear. It is conscious of the world and the universe. It is intelligent. Something that is conscious is somehow personified. We are conscious of a rock, but a rock is not conscious of us. Gravity is not conscious. Electromagnetism is not conscious, but consciousness is conscious.

The White Light of the Void is the consciousness in all beings. Consciousness is inexplicably a super being, and it is you. Consciousness is a someone rather than a something, but it is not someone among others. It is one without a second. It is the only someone that there is. In East Indian Vedanta, it is called Brahman, the absolute, and the ultimate reality. It is also called the "Atman," which means "self.", the indwelling consciousness that is identical with the Absolute. It is the conscious self in all beings. In Vedanta, it is said that Atman is Brahman. The conscious self in all beings is the same as the cosmic, universal consciousness pervading the whole cosmos. It is also called "Purusha," which means "person." and "the supreme God".

In the East Indian Rig Veda, it says,

> A thousand heads hath this Purusha,
> A thousand eyes, a thousand feet.
> All creatures are one-fourth of him
> Three fourths (of him is) eternal life in Heaven.

When the void is experienced, it has the nature of being alive. It is not material, yet matter could not exist without it. It is not biological although it makes biology possible. It expresses itself through life and matter.

The void is living, loving, conscious, intelligent, and infinitely creative. In fact it is the source of all material form, all consciousness, and all life in all beings in the universe. It is your own consciousness, which is knowable only when it is not formed into anything. It is absolute emptiness, yet the fountainhead of all forms and all life and all sentient beings. It is omnipresent because it encompasses all space in the universe. It is eternal because it contains all time past, present, and future. It is the ground of being. It is the canvas upon which the entire universe is painted. Yet when approached, the painting disappears, and only the canvas remains. It is unborn and unrestricted. It is beyond human comprehension, complex in its simplicity, and simple in its complexity. It cannot be objectified.

It is not produced or controlled by the multidimensional entities encountered on entheogens although they have been known to try and take credit for opening or closing its access. It is on an entirely different and higher plain that the spirits and the invisible worlds they inhabit. They are trivial compared to it. It is consciousness without an object, the limitless cosmic ocean of awareness without waves. It is the ground state of human consciousness.

Consciousness and DMT

The incredible aroma of DMT floated like a vapor on the summer breeze like a sweet, seductive, indole taste of mothballs and ether. The odor is so familiar, ancient, and primordial. People smell it for the first time and say, "Oh that smells just like…" and then they pause. They just can't put their finger on it.

I put down the pipe. There was the unmistakable sense of a presence watching, controlling, and operating the situation, not as the image of a personage but as the profound intimation of someone who is in complete control of the event. There was the sound of crackling, like cellophane being crumpled. There was a sound like a sign wave ascending in pitch rising higher and higher until it disappears, leaving only an inaudible shimmer.

The odor is a magnetic smell trembling, vibratory, and radiant. Inside my brain galaxies of molecular patterns were whirring, spinning, and unfolding like clockwork. Inside moist, synaptic gaps, electrochemical messages were flashing that seem to say, "Yes!" as uninhibited molecular strings of neurotransmitters are synthesized in endless chains of conductivity. Sense organs recoiled as boiling implosions of radiant energy struck retinal mosaics to be turned into neon arabesques by the ecstatic decoding centers of the brain.

DMT feels like fluid light streaming through the bloodstream, illuminating the coiling, braided branching vascular canals with coherent light that flows through capillary fingers to touch each cell and make them glow like tiny suns.

The room slid noiselessly into an undulating cloud of radiant energy. For a moment, the objects in the room could still be made out through the boiling illumination as they slipped into stacks of standing wave columns of clustering photons. The last fragments of objective sensation spun out in many-faceted prisms as the room unfolded like a lotus blossom of energy petals falling away to reveal more petals, which unfolded to reveal the subtler and immeasurably more complex structures of atomic pattern.

A reaction was happening within the chemistry of the deepest seat of consciousness. The synthesis of living energy into living matter was spinning, attracting, repelling, combining, and recreating itself within the mirror of awareness. Now the room was a swirling cluster of energy patterns, not random and impersonal but ordered with the unmistakable precision and complexity of a fine Swiss clock. All parts of the field seemed equally related as the standing wave cogs and axles spun, whirred, clicked, slid, and articulated in their intricacy. I could almost see how this wheel turns to drive that shaft that releases this paddle that rotates this cog. But what part drives what? All segments of this molecular clock seemed to be driving one another. The field was acting of itself.

The wave machine was not a collection of parts—cold, impersonal, intelligence of random order. Its movement was funny, playful, carnival-like, and full of vibratory clowns and circus music of the midway.

A carnival barker seamed to be saying "Right this way, ladies and gentleman. See the secrets of perpetual motion revealed. See the deus ex machina. Watch the infernal machine. Nothing drives it. It produces nothing. Watch the wheels and gears of creation move unaccountably for no reason at all."

Something special was happening. Wherever it was that there were rooms, walls, tables, and chairs had become far, far away in another time and another place. There was the uncanny feeling that all this was time out, as though it is completely removed from the normal continuum. Somewhere back on Earth, a record was playing music. Here the music had come to a stop.

Time had slowed down so much as to stop completely. The music hung suspended motionless in the air like a great wet, shimmering glob. Eventually much, much later, this massive, moist, pulsating note would slide into silence, and it would be a long time before the next note appeared. During the eternities that followed, leaves that fall from trees hung in eerie suspension between branch and earth. Clocks hovered between seconds.

Metabolisms waited breathlessly between two heartbeats. What use is a body where there is no time and space? Where could it remain when the whole field of matter and form had glided into an electromagnetic-wave phenomena that erupted from some stellar explosion of cascading photons and was broadcasted outward to travel through millions of light-years of space to trigger the most complex psycho neural events in the deepest center of an ecstatic nervous system? As the body slipped away, only the timeless play of energy remained.

But then even the machine was dissolving. It was becoming a timeless, dark, flowing river of pulsing, ebbing flux. Here one needs no guidepost or introduction. It had become the life stream, the flowing river of life, and the river Styx, which separates the world of men from the underworld. All instructions were completely implicit. One must float. One must flow and melt and merge and be carried away by the warm primal waters. One must submit to the ebb tide and be washed out to sea.

Flowing through peristaltic eddies of primal fluid, my old Earth self was being washed away by the dissolving waters. This ancient baptism requires complete submission, to become completely dissolved in the solution, but what is the nature of this stream that asks so much? Whose nature is it in addition to my own?

This river beyond time and space exists in the heart of all human beings. It is the direct experience of life energy itself, a turbulent stream of chi and a river of prana. Floating, swirling, and tumbling through the dark waters were countless billions of living microbiological things, cellular forms, and luminous diatoms with their snowflake geometry. Brightly colored schools of multicolored neon fish moved by in quantum synchronicity. As I drift through this ancient current, I felt surrounded by every living thing that had ever lived. In dark waters like this, the timeless thing that was there in the beginning first combined with itself to form primeval life.

To understand the nature of this level of consciousness, we must look more closely at DMT. DMT is an endogenous psychedelic compound. "Endogenous" means that it is made naturally in the body. It is abundant in nature and is found in a wide variety of plants and animals, including fish, certain toads, sponges, and even coral.

Psilocybe mushrooms contain a form of DMT. The alkaloid psilocin found in these mushrooms is DMT with an extra hydrogen and oxygen atom attached. This makes DMT orally active and increases its duration from fifteen or twenty minutes to around five hours. All the other tryptophan-derived hallucinogens work because they resemble DMT. They bond to the same receptor sites. DMT is the prototypical tryptamine entheogen.

Once, I was preparing to smoke DMT. Taking DMT or large doses of any entheogen can be accompanied by a feeling of dread. I mustered up all my courage and rapidly inhaled three clouds of the aromatic vapor. Immediately I felt myself falling into a rapidly flowing river.

Oh, no! I thought. *I am rushing through the rapids, and I am going to be dashed to pieces on the jagged rocks.*

I was filled with terror when suddenly I realized that the flowing water was furry. It was a river of kittens. Soft paws and warm, fur-clad tails surrounded me. Playful, loveable kittens were rolling and bouncing down the stream, and I, among them, was tumbling in their midst, laughing with joy and relief. The DMT entity had sensed my fear and produced the most unthreatening situation imaginable. A river of kittens!

DMT is a food for the brain. It passes freely across blood-brain barriers as easily as glucose and is welcomed inside. It is found in the blood, in the urine, and in cerebrospinal fluid that baths the brain and spinal cord. It is found in the lungs, the brain, and the nervous system. A gene has been discovered that activates its production. At the same time that the brain seeks DMT and draws it in, it has an extremely efficient system for removing it from the blood and carefully regulating its blood level. This is an enzyme called "MAO," or monoamine oxidase.

DMT must be smoked or injected because the MAO in the stomach and gut break it down before it can reach high-enough blood levels to become entheogenic. People around the world, past and present, have discovered that certain plants contain chemicals that block the activity of MAO. These compounds are called "MAO inhibitors." If you combine DMT with these admixtures, it becomes orally active, and the duration increases to ten hours or more.

The South American drink ayahuasca is an example of a beverage in which DMT is combined with an MAO inhibitor from the jungle vine banisteria, which contains chemicals called betacarbolines. The DMT in ayahuasca comes from a variety of plants the most common of which is *Psychotria viridis*.

Why does the body welcome and completely interact with a chemical that is the key to the multiverse of unseen worlds and contact with enumerable species of nonhuman beings? Dr. Rick Strassman, who has extensively studied DMT in controlled laboratory settings, has suggested that DMT is the base mediator of human consciousness. Consciousness as we experience it may be a psychedelic experience.

With all the other entheogens, people who take them exhibit a tolerance. The more often they take them, the less effective they are. A person has to wait at least four days to take LSD again and at least a week to be able to experience the flash, and even then it is not guaranteed. DMT shows no such tolerance. You can take DMT every fifteen minutes or sooner with the same intensity and effectiveness. *Psilocybe* mushrooms show much less of a tolerance in their takers than other psychedelics. An endogenous chemical that could generate a continuous stream of consciousness would have to produce no tolerance, or it could not work.

Dr. Strassman has made an extraordinary suggestion that we are continuously tripping on the body's own endogenous entheogen and that ordinary consciousness is made possible by a psychedelic substance in the brain that is the base level, primal, primordial substrate of awareness. DMT may be the prototypical consciousness-manifesting chemical in the brain. No wonder psychedelics seem so familiar.

Tryptamine entheogens, like psilocybin and LSD, are consciousness-changing drugs. Because they resemble DMT, they become substituted for it at the receptor sites. Because they are different from DMT, their nature is noticeable as a change in consciousness. The mind cannot see itself, but if consciousness changes, the change is very perceptible.

Their similarities allow them to function in the consciousness-making process, but their differences stand out dramatically and allow us to see what consciousness really is. Estrogenous psychedelics, which are made outside of the body, can be consciousness-expanding agents.

Evolution has vastly limited the amount of consciousness that is allowed in ordinary perception to keep us from being overwhelmed by the potential Niagara of awareness that is possible. The other psychedelics have no such restrictions and produce greatly enhanced and amplified levels of perception, cognition, and awareness.

This begs the question, if DMT is the normal consciousness-mediating molecule, why aren't we hallucinating all the time and in constant contact with extra dimensional entities? The suggestion that such things only occur in doses that are higher than the normal levels seems unsatisfactory.

The answer may lie in the fact that there are two kinds of DMT naturally produced in the body: DMT and 5-MeO-DMT. As we have seen with *Psilocybe* mushrooms and as has been reported in the experiences of Dr. Strassman's volunteers in his seminal DMT study, DMT is intensely hallucinogenic, producing oceans of boiling colors and moving, kaleidoscopic patterns. It initiates contact with a wide range of nonhuman beings and places that are not of this world.

On the other hand, 5-MeO-DMT does not produce hallucinations. It does not open the door to contact with other universes and their inhabitance. In low doses, it is rather similar to everyday consciousness, but with higher blood-level doses, normal sensory perception falls away and what remains is pure consciousness, which is not being conscious of anything. It is pure subjectivity without an objective reference. In high doses, it produces the classic White Light of the Void experience.

Normally we cannot see the ocean for of the waves. It is the ocean of consciousness that is waving, but our attention is fixated on the waves. When 5-MeO-DMT blood levels increase, as when it is smoked or injected in the form of a plant or animal extract, the sensory input from within and outside of the body diminishes and finally disappears altogether. What is left is pure consciousness without an object, consciousness not formed into anything. At last we can see what it actually is, and just as we are confronted with absolute truth, we disappear. As we dissolve into the radiance, we realize that whatever we thought we were was actually it. It manifests as the Clear Light of the Void.

The White Light is the fundamental base-level stratum of perception, and it is universal. Consciousness is capable of reflecting the entire universe. It is not an impersonal force like gravity or magnetism; it is a conscious super being beyond anything we can possibly imagine. It resides in another dimension outside of time and space. It is the source of everything in the universe, yet its fundamental nature is empty nothingness. It is surely what gave rise to the concept of God! Gordon Wasson, Carl Ruck, Rick Strassman, and others have suggested that entheogens were the source of religion in the human species.

The body makes both DMT and 5-MeO-DMT. Of these two kinds, 5-MeO-DMT is the best candidate for the base psychedelic that mediates consciousness, because it doesn't produce hallucinations or contact with other worlds or their inhabitants. If DMT were the base level psychedelic that mediates consciousness, we would be hallucinating all the time and interacting with otherworldly entities. The body produces 5-MeO-DMT. It also synthesizes DMT in what must be smaller amounts.

DMT by facilitating contact with other worlds and nonhuman beings gave rise to the whole world of the supernatural—the gods, the spirits, the elves, the fairies, the gnomes, the dwarfs, the muses of inspiration, the guides, helpers, and teachers, the demons and evil spirits, and the concept of heaven and hell. It produced the ideas of the spirit world, fairyland, the underworld, the netherworld, and all other otherworldly environments whose door are opened by the entheogenic keys.

Most plants and animals that contain DMT also contain 5-MeO-DMT. Why is DNT present in our bodies in a system mostly mediated by 5-MeO-DMT? Because it thickens the plot. It adds a dimension of richness and of artistic, poetic, and mythological complexity to the mind. It drives music, dance, art, and poetry. The presence of DMT in the human body allows for spiritual states and spontaneous mystical experiences.

Dr. Strassman is a Buddhist. He expected to find in his DMT experiments confirmation of the Buddhist mystical experience as produced by meditation. Instead he found a multiplicity of worlds and strange nonhuman beings. If he had investigated 5-MeO-DMT instead of DMT, he would have found what he was looking for: the classic White Light Void of the Buddhist Dharmakaya.

Strassman was expelled from the Buddhist community because of his DMT research and because he compared Buddhism with psychedelic states. Many modern, orthodox Buddhist sects are completely unaware of the entheogenic roots of their religion, both ancient and contemporary.

A wealth of information about the psychedelic origins of early Buddhism can be found in Mike Crowley's extraordinary book, *Secret Drugs of Buddhism: Psychedelic Sacraments and the Origins of the Vajrayana*. I urge anyone interested in Buddhism and psychedelics to read this.

I once read a book, and at the end was a blank page. At the bottom was written the words "This page is intentionally left blank." I marveled that a blank page would have to paradoxically contradict itself in that way.

When I visited the Zen Center at Green Gulch in Northern California, they had a pamphlet that told about who they were and what they did. Halfway through the book was a full-page picture of a fly. The next page was blank. The fly clearly was a reference to *Amanita muscaria*, the fly agaric, and the page intentionally left blank pointed to the White Light of the Void. Clearly the monks at the Zen Center were using *Amanita muscaria* mushrooms in the traditional way. The use of psychedelics in most of the world's religions has always been a closely guarded secret.

There is a illustrated Zen poem by Kuoan Shiyuan called the called the *Ten Bulls* or the Zen bull hunting pictures. The bull is a universal a symbol for *Amanita muscaria*. The adept goes in search of the bull. First he finds its footprints. Then he sees it at a distance. Then he gets up close. He catches the bull, tames it Finally, he is able to ride it home. The next page in the series is intentionally left blank. Shiyuan wrote:

> "Whip, rope, person and Ox
> All merge in No Thing.
> This heaven is so vast,
> No message can stain it.

How may a snowflake exist
in a raging fire.
Here are the footprints
of the Ancestors."

Finally, the initiate returns to society His time spent in the timeless void of the White Light has enlightened him. He is ever blissful. Before him, Shiyuan writes, the dead trees become alive.

This poem has been duplicated in many woodcuts and other versions, all showing the blank page.

JAMES OROC'S 5-MEO-DMT EXPERIENCES

An excellent source of information about 5-MeO-DMT comes from James Oroc, who did extensive work with the substance, which he obtained from the Sonoran desert toad, *Bufo alvarius*. The toad's excretions can be smoked, and they contain a very pure and nontoxic form of 5-MeO-DMT. *Bufo alvarius* is the only toad known to secrete 5-MeO-DMT but there must be others. Toads are sacred in China, and toad carvings and votive offerings are found in European Neolithic temples. Effigies of toads were abundant among the Mayans in association with representations of mushrooms.

In his book *Tryptamine Palace, 5-MeO-DMT and the Sonoran Desert Toad: A Journey from Burning Man to the Akashic Field,* Oroc writes beautiful and moving descriptions of his experiences with toad venom. He experiences a dazzling White Light shining with the intensity of a laser. His sensory perception fades away as he finds himself dissolving into the radiance. His sense of time disappears, and he feels that everything in his entire life has led him to this point. He feels himself becoming a part of everything, as if the entire universe is contained within him.

He recognizes the light as the source from which he and everything else has emerged and will ultimately return. He experiences the light as a void containing nothing yet, paradoxically, as the source of everything. It is absolute emptiness. It is not an idea, not a concept, not a sensation, not a perception, and not even an emotion. The physical world dissolves, and the light can be felt to be a conscious, intelligent, creative being out of which pours an ocean of love. It is an immense and unfathomable field of consciousness endowed with universal intelligence and creative power.

His ego identity disappears as he merges with the illumination, and he realizes that he and this infinite field of intelligent, creative energy are one being. He feels his consciousness resonating and entraining to this greater, universal consciousness until he cannot tell one from the other. He feels that at the deepest, most basic, fundamental level of his existence, he and this being are one and have always been one. It has been there all along as his own consciousness, concealed beneath matter and mass and form. He feels that he is experiencing the godhead.

Losing our identity and dissolving into the whole is something we experience in psychedelic states where subject-object boundaries disappear and everything becomes one.

This is what the Buddha meant when he was reported to have said, "I truly attained absolutely nothing from complete, unexcelled enlightenment. If this were not true, it would not be called complete, unexcelled enlightenment." The absolute nothing that the Buddha gained was the

White Light of the Void. There is a Buddhist saying that "Buddhism is nothing special." There is nothing that is more special than the nothing that is the Clear Light.

Entheogenic Experience and Death

My father, who was a devout atheist, surprised me by saying many times, "We are all sparks from the Infinite and when we die, we return to the Infinite."

I had an aunt named Bonita who was dying of cancer. My parents suggested that I correspond with her, as any contact with family or loved ones could offer a consolation. At that time I was taking LSD regularly, and I felt pretty clear about certain aspects of life and death. So I wrote her a couple of letters in which I more or less told her not to worry, that nothing was the way it seemed, and that neither life nor death were what they appeared to be.

I assured her with a certainty I was later to lose myself that life and death were two sides of the same coin. I told her that the acceptable and the unacceptable were strung on the same string. Death, I assured her, was a continuation of existence, and now that she was about to leave her life in this world, she should try and see what a privileged and wonderful gift and opportunity she had received by experiencing a human birth. I told her that this interlude of space and time, this momentary flash of light in the darkness, had no necessity to have happened at all.

With all the energy in the universe running down toward entropy like a pile of old clocks, what could possibly bring it all together to weave a human body and a human mind from threads that emerge and disappear into the greater fabric of the world?

Now here was a woman who hadn't had a very happy life. She worked hard, sacrificed, and never quite actualized her greatest goals. You may feel, I told her, that you didn't get a very good part, but you still got to be in the play. She died.

A little later I was high on LSD, and I was out walking. Near my house was an intricate system of fire trails extending miles and miles into the wilderness. I could walk all day in solitude, and for me, the trail became a living metaphor spanning all of human history. While walking I felt that the common human experience of traveling along a path in all its enumerable variations from the prehistoric to the present seemed to merge in one experience.

In Chinese Taoism, one of the meanings of the word "Tao" is a "path, a way, or a method." Walking has long been associated with the taking of entheogens. Australian aborigines took a drug called *alan* for their long annual migrations and their "walkabout" initiations. Bronze and Iron Age armies would take fly agaric mushrooms to march long distances without hunger, thirst or fatigue. "Wandering" is an ancient trope for tripping.

As I walked along the path that day I was everyone who had ever transversed the byways and trails of the world. At times it was like leaving the road well traveled and, crashing through a virgin thicket to blaze a new trail in the wilderness. Once, while riding my horse on Mount Tamalpais when I had taken acid, I gave my Morgan horse Viking the reins and told him, "You decide where we will go." We followed a path that turned into a deer trail that turned into a rabbit path that turned into a dry creek bed that just plain disappeared, and there was nothing but unbroken vegetation in all directions.

Sometimes when walking on acid the trail would become the path between the worlds, the road that souls traveled as they came into the world and departed from it. It was the journey that we have all made and must all make to the very border of time-space and beyond. It was this aspect of the trail mythos that I was experiencing this particular day, and as I walked along, I felt like I was traveling along the path that the dead take to the world beyond.

Then I had the distinct feeling that I was not alone. I looked over, and in my mind's eye, I saw Aunt Bonita walking along beside me. We were hurrying along, and she was kind of fretting. I realized that this was Aunt Bonita's death, and it was as though she was now making the transit out of this world.

She was saying, "Well, I just don't know about all this," and "I hope everything is going to be all right."

And I was saying, "Now don't you worry, Aunt Bonita; everything is going to be just fine."

And she would say, "I just don't know where all this is leading," and "I hope I know what I'm supposed to do."

And I would assure her that the whole affair was catered in advance and everything was completely taken care of. Years before, another aunt, named Nora, had ask the same question on her deathbed. My mother was by her side, and Nora said, "Will I know what to do?"

"Why what do you mean, dear?" asked my mother.

Nora said, "When that door up there on the ceiling opens, will I know what to do?"

The trail was winding back down toward the place where I was going to turn off to return to my home. I thought about Elizabeth Kübler Ross and her description of dying people being met by relatives and friends who console, reassure, and guide them on their transitory journeys. I thought about the traditional role of shamans, as psychopomps to lead and guide the souls of the dead to the other world, for it is the shaman who travels that path and returns.

I wondered if I was a guide in Aunt Bonita's death experience. I wondered what would happen to Bonny when my part of the trail turned off and hers continued on. We approached the fork, and suddenly I sensed that there were three of us walking along together, where a moment ago there had only been two. I looked, and it was as though that the third person who had mysteriously joined us was Bonny's son, Teddy, who had been killed in a car accident some years before.

I said, "Aunt Bonita, I have to turn off here, but Teddy will guide you the rest of the way."

I turned onto the branch of the fork to the right, and Bonny and Teddy continued along the trail.

The Tibetan Book of the Dead

To explore 5-MeO-DMT and its effects, we must look at a very important Buddhist text, *The Bardo Thodol*, published as *The Tibetan Book of the Dead*. Aldus Huxley first brought *The Tibetan Book of the Dead* to the world's attention when after taking LSD, he commented that he wished there was some kind of guidebook like *The Tibetan Book of the Dead* that could be read to him as he went through the experience. Timothy Leary wrote such a book, and it proved to be of little use for guiding an LSD experience. Most people who had it read to them freaked out or found it distracting and confusing.

This is because while large doses of LSD do sometimes make people feel that they are dying, it does not produce the White Light of the Void experience produced by 5-MeO-DNT, *Amanita muscaria* mushrooms, or death itself. This was very confusing in the early days of psychedelic exploration, because we read books of Eastern religions that described the void and tried to make the void match the psychedelic experiences at our disposal, and it just didn't fit. You can't produce the White Light state with acid nor with peyote nor with *Psilocybe* mushrooms.

This brings us to the relationship between death and dying and the psychedelic experience. It has long been observed that near-death experiences, NDEs, bare a close similarity to entheogenic states, especially those produced by *Amanita muscaria* mushrooms and 5-MeO-DMT. Dr. Rick Strassman says that the brain contains a complete enzyme system for the syntheses of DMT, and it is controlled by many chemical restraints to keep blood levels exactly correct. At death, when the breathing stops and the heart stops beating, these restraints begin to fail, and DMT is produced without inhibition flooding the brain and body with the sacred substance. Death is a 5-MeO-DMT trip followed by a DMT trip.

First there is a manifestation of the White Light of the Void, where the 5-MeO-DMT that mediates normal consciousness increases and increases until forms disappear and consciousness returns to its fundamental base state beyond time and space in nonlocal, quantum connection with the entire universe. This explains why death is a sacrament.

The Tibetan Book of the Dead was created by Tibetan monks and passed on as an oral tradition from time immemorial; it is a guidebook for death and dying and for the passage through the after death experience. The Tibetan Buddhists of the Tantric Vajrayana sect used entheogenic drugs, such as *Amanita muscaria* and perhaps DMT-containing plants and fungi, to produce near-death experiences.

"*Vajra*" means thunderbolt. Thunderbolts are symbols of the bolt-shaped mushrooms that fall from the sky and spring up after lightning and thunderstorms. . The lightning with its defining clap of thunder inseminates the earth and was believed to engender the sacred fungus to rise up. In Tibetan ceremonies a *vajra* is a dumbbell-shaped ritual object that has the form of *Amanita muscaria* mushrooms in their early stage of growth

Some entheogens at high doses are thanomimetic; that is, they replicate the experience of death without danger to the physical body. During a Tibetan monk's education, he is helped by his teacher through a series of secret initiations to enter into the after death state. He is taught to recognize and merge into the White Light. It is called being "set face-to-face with the Clear Light." He also is familiarized with the confrontation with what appear to be deities, along with contact with the entities that inhabit the other worlds, and he experiences the hallucinogenic projections of his own preconditioned mind.

When a monk dies, the *Book of the Dead* is read to him, reminding him that he has seen this before and giving him active and practical instructions as to what to do or not do as he passes through the levels of the after death state called "bardos." *The Bardo Thodol*, as the book is called in Tibetan, means *The Book of Liberation by Hearing on the After death Plane*.

The first bardo happens after the breathing has stopped and the heart ceases to beat. It is the dawning of the White Light of the Void called the "Dharmakaya." People who have meditated and repeatedly taken thanomimetic entheogens have the opportunity to experience this supreme wonder. People who have not meditated and taken death-imitating psychedelics usually faint at this stage and wake up after the white light has passed. The dawning of the Clear Light is followed by the bardo of karmic hallucinations, in which the content of the psyche spill out and appear as external phenomena, as sounds, lights, colored rays, and rainbows that appear like deities. At the same time, there occurs contact with nonhuman entities of many worlds.

It is clear that the first bardo is mediated by 5-MeO-DMT, and the second and lower bardos by DMT.

In the following extracts I have modernized the language from the original translation by W. Y. Evans-Wentz to make it more intelligible and easier to understand for the modern reader.

The teacher speaks the name of the deceased and instructs him to listen carefully:

Do not let your mind be distracted. That which is called death has come to you now. You are now dead. It is very important that you understand that you have died. You will now have the precious opportunity to experience the Ultimate Reality. You must form a powerful resolve not to waste it or miss it through losing consciousness or falling asleep.

As your body and mind have separated, you are experiencing a glimpse of Pure Truth: subtle, sparkling, bright, dazzling, glorious, and radiantly awesome. It is like a mirage moving across a landscape in springtime in one continuous stream of vibrations. Do not be daunted thereby. Do not be terrified. Do not be awed. The time has now come for you to seek the path that leads to Reality.

Because you practiced meditation during your life and experienced secret initiation, you can eject your consciousness now. This is called transference. You need not transverse the intermediate states of the after death plane. Move your consciousness up your body and out through the top of your head. Send your consciousness on up and you will go directly to the Dharmakaya by the Great Straight Upward Path. You will be set face to face with the Clear Light without any intermediate states of the lower after death states. You will obtain the unborn Dharmakaya by the Great Perpendicular Path. There all things are like the void and cloudless sky, and the naked, spotless intellect is like a transparent vacuum without circumference or center. At this moment, know that it is your self and abide in that state. Recognize the White Light and enter into it. It is your own consciousness not formed into anything.

Listen. Now the pure luminosity of the Dharmakaya is shining before you. Recognize it. At this moment your mind is pure emptiness. It does not possess any nature whatsoever—no substance or quality or color or form. It is not just blank emptiness. It is unobstructed, sparkling, pure, and vibrant. This is the Dharmakaya of the Buddha. It is a radiant source of light of unimaginable intensity. It is like an infinite ocean, calm and without any waves. There, mist clouds arise and rainbows appear. The clouds in the glory of the rainbows condense and fall as rain.

A great roar of thunder will come from within the Light. It is the natural sound of the Great Body of Radiance. It is like a thousand thunderclaps simultaneously. This is the natural sound of your own true self, so do not be afraid or bewildered. When you are confronted by it, you feel awed.

Now your intellect shines clearly and more lucidly. You are experiencing that state as an unbearable Intensity. Do not be afraid of it. Do not be bewildered. This is the natural radiance of your own mind, so do not be afraid or bewildered. Do not lose consciousness. Do not fall asleep. Remain alert and aware throughout the experience and stay in the light as long as you can.

Now that you are experiencing the Fundamental Clear Light, try to abide in that state. Recognize it! It is unobstructed, shining, thrilling, and blissful. Dissolve into the Clear Light. Your mind is luminosity and emptiness in the form of a great mass of brilliance. It has no birth or death. To recognize this is all that is necessary.

In *The Tibetan Book of the Dead*, the deceased first experiences the 5-MeO-DMT flash of the White Light of the Void. This is followed by the second bardo, the sphere of karmic hallucinations called the "*dharmadatu*." It is the realm of the return of phenomena. This state first involves the dawning of what are taken to be deities followed by contact with nonhuman entities, the denizens of other worlds. This stage is surely mediated by the more familiar DMT.

The Second Bardo of Karmic Hallucinations

The Tibetans describe a number of other worlds that, like the Earth, are tangent to the afterdeath plane. Some of them are higher than the human domain, such as the world of the gods who inhabit paradise realms. There is the world of the Asuras or titans, who live in subterranean caverns. There are hell worlds of great suffering, home of demonic and malevolent entities, and there is the world of beasts. There is the world of unhappy or hungry ghosts. There are bands of tormenting furies that lie in wait to ambush and peruse the unwary traveler. The furies are people who are possessed with such anger and malice and sadism that they never attained rebirth and are doomed to wander the after death plane as autonomous hallucinations.

For the second bardo, the text reads,

> (Name of the deceased). You are beginning to wake up from your swoon. You are feeling emotions of confusion about the nature of your condition. You are wondering what has happened to you.

You must realize that you have died. Recognize this as the after death state. You lost your balance and equilibrium in the state of the Primary Clear Light, and you have been unconscious until now. Now you are awakening, and you do not know if you are dead or alive. Although the Clear Light of Reality dawned upon you, you were unable to hold on, and so you had to wander here.

At this time forms will begin to reappear. Everything will be reversed and turned inside out. The content of your mind and memories and emotions and past actions will be projected outward, and everything you see appears as colored lights and images. If you do not recognize them in this way as your own hallucinatory projections, the colored lights will frighten you, the echoing and reverberating sounds will bewilder you, and radiation and shocking rays of light will terrify you. If you do not recognize the sounds, lights, and rays as coming out of yourself, you will wander in realms of illusory forms.

It is like a mirror. Everything you see is a reflection of yourself. You will become the sole spectator of a marvelous panorama of hallucinatory visions. At first the happy and glorious visions will awe you. Then as they merge into the visions born of your lower animal nature, they will terrify you, and you will wish to flee from them. But they are inseparable from you, and to whatsoever place you may wish to flee, they will follow.

At this time you must remember that you have seen this while you were still living. Your teacher, through secret initiation, has repeatedly set you face-to-face with this. Remember! You will have already recognized all these lights that have shone upon you as being the reflection of your own inner light. Having recognized them as intimate friends, you will believe in them and understand them as a son or daughter recognizes his or her mother.

At this time whatever thought occurs to you, whether it is loving or hateful, will wield great power. Therefore do not think in your mind of things that are angry, sad, or hateful. These feelings will appear as monsters that will chase and attack you. Allow the intellect to abide in its own unmodified state.

Now your auditory senses begin to become activated, and you will hear a cacophony of strange and daunting sounds echoing and reverberating around you. Sounds you will hear in the after death state include rolling noises, piercing whistling sounds, humming sounds, and oscillating tones. You will hear clicking sounds and crackling sounds like cellophane is being crumpled. You will hear hissing sounds like snakes or gas escaping. You will hear rushing sounds of moving air and howling sounds like storm winds. You will hear clashing sounds and rumbling sounds as loud as thunder. Sounds will be heard as of mountains crumbling down and of angry overflowing seas and the roaring of fire and of fierce winds springing up. When these sounds come, you will be terrified by them, and you will want to flee from them in every direction, not caring in which direction you run, but the way of escape will be blocked by three awful precipices, white, black, and red. They will be terror inspiring and deep, and you will feel as if you are about to fall down them. They are not really precipices. They are anger, lust, and stupidity.

(Name of the deceased). The world of illusory form is in revolution, revolving round and round like a swirling vortex, and the phenomenal appearance that you will see then will resemble radiant Deities. They are in reality not Deities. These are your own projected thought-forms. They come from inside you. Recognize them as reflections of your own intellect. They are the anthropomorphic personifications of your own propensities purified in the fire of the flash of death and projected outward so that they appear like deities. They appear to have solidity and mass, but they are no more substantial than dreams.

The apparitional visions you see are not visions of reality but nothing more than the hallucinatory embodiments of the thought-forms born of the mental content of your mind. They are the intellectual impulses that have assumed personified form in the after death dream state. All these Deities were born at the same time you were. All these Deities have arisen out of the spontaneous play of your own mind. They are not coming from somewhere outside yourself. They come from your heart. They issue from within and shine upon you. They have existed from eternity within the faculties of your own intellect. Know them to be of that nature. The bodies of the largest of the Deities are equal in vastness to the limits of the heavens. The bodies of the intermediate Deities are as big as lofty mountains. The smallest Deities are equal to eighteen bodies such as your own set one upon another. Although the Deities may appear to you gigantic, their size is not large nor small but relative and proportionate in the same way that a thought of a mountain is not of any real size. They only appear as giants.

If you can recognize the radiance of the Five Orders of Wisdom to be the emanations from your own mind, you will obtain Liberation through being absorbed into them in a halo of rainbow light.

At the same time as the dawning of the deities, there will appear beings from the alternate universes, the world of the gods, the titans, and the animal-headed deities from the beast worlds, the world of the unhappy or hungry ghosts, and the hell worlds of demons. These entities are considered as real as the beings in our human world. The deceased is admonished to not communicate or follow these lower entities in order not to be reborn in one of their worlds.

The radiance of the deities is so bright and intense as to inspire awe and terror, while the soft, dull light of the otherworldly entities seems to the deceased to be safe. This is a trap, and stern warnings are given to shun the entities from other worlds and to allow oneself to be drawn in by the rays from the deities and to dissolve in a halo of rainbow light and there attain Buddhahood.

The deities appear with the reemergence of form. They are comprised of lights, rays, colors, and complex motion but are without meaning or content. They don't resemble anything recognizable except lights and rays. They are described as disks, orbs, and revolving wheels. They are compared to inverted bowls. They have bright lights and rainbow energy fields, and they shoot out colored floodlights and shockingly colored rays called "hook rays," which strike against you and pull you in like a fish on a line to merge in a halo of rainbow light and find enlightenment in the radiance. The hook rays are like *Star Trek* tractor beams.

The Book of the Dead reads,

> At this time there appears before you a bright, radiant light of such dazzling brilliance and transparency that you will scarcely be able to look at it. It is white and transparent, glorious and terrifying,

made more glorious with orbs surrounded by smaller orbs, each like a gem-encrusted mirror. It is like an inverted bowl of coral. It is the Jewel Born One. It is hard to look at. A ray will shoot out and strike against you with a force so powerful that you will scarcely be able to stand it. It is extremely clear and fine like the rays of the sun spun into glistening threads. These rays are the hook rays of grace. Allow the hook ray of grace to draw you in. They will pull you into the great body of radiance where you may dissolve in a halo of rainbow light and find liberation.

CONSCIOUSNESS AND THE ZERO-POINT FIELD

In James Oroc's search for understanding of the conscious, laser-like light he experienced in the White Light flash of 5-MeO-DMT, he ran across a concept in physics known as the "zero-point field." This is an enormous field of energy filling the whole universe, coming out of absolutely nothing.

It is this nothingness that interested Oroc, because in the White Light of the Void he experienced on 5-MeO-DMT, he confronted a conscious being of light that was, in its essential nature, absolute nothingness. It was complete emptiness. He felt intuitively that it was the source of everything and recognized it as his own consciousness. James Oroc suggests that the White Light of the Void and the zero-point field may be the same thing. As we will see, the zero-point field is itself the source of the stability of atoms, the source of matter and inertial forces, and perhaps the source of all life and all consciousness.

The zero-point field is as big as the entire universe. It is empty space. When all matter has been removed—all dust, all gas, every atom of anything taken away—from out of the depths of this vacuum radiates an immense ocean of energy, which represents most of the energy in the universe.

Lynne McTaggart talks about this in her book *The Field: The Quest for the Secret Force of the Universe*. She writes that the physicist Richard Feynman calculated that one cubic meter of empty space contains enough energy to boil all the oceans in the world. The zero-point energy density is one hundred and ten orders of magnitude greater than the radiant energy at the center of the sun.

There is far more energy in empty space than in all the matter in the universe. According to quantum physicist David Bohm, vacuum-state energy exceeds that of matter by a factor of ten to the power of forty. Where does the energy come from? Out of absolute nothing, there is omitted a continuous array of subatomic particles and antiparticles that are opposite polarity of each other.

The particles and antiparticles cancel each other out, releasing a flood of radiant light that is so pure and coherent that all the photons are in perfect synchronous harmony. Oroc suggests that this may be the highest level of coherence known called a BIC or *Bose-Einstein condensate*. In that state, they become one big particle or one big wave as large as the universe. All the molecules in the vast expanse of space share information nonlocally with each other instantaneously. This means that every point in space and every second of time past, present, and future are in contact with each other sharing the same information.

When I first heard of bosons, I imagined that they had a big red nose and long floppy shoes, but bosons are particles or waves that become in tune to each other and share information and behavior no matter how far they are separated in space and time. This is called "entanglement." "Coherence" means that all the particles or waves in a system are doing exactly the same thing at the same time. Their individuality disappears as they merge into the whole. This allows instantaneous sharing of information between all the parts of the system. What happens to any one part happens to all the parts and to the whole. Like a hologram, the complete universe is contained in each and all of its parts. This is why mystics aided by entheogens see the entire universe contained in whatever they observe.

William Blake wrote,

> To see a World in a Grain of Sand
> And a heaven in a wild flower,
> Hold infinity in the palm of your hand
> And Eternity in an hour.

The zero-point field is what gives mass to the universe. It has been proposed that inertia is the result of mass being slowed down as it passes through the vacuum energy, like dragging a stick through honey.

The zero-point field is intrinsically connected to the big bang. One of the mysteries of the big bang is that physicists don't know what it was that banged. The zero-point field may have been what it was that banged.

The zero-point field plays an integral part in the stability of atoms and the formation of matter. The atoms draw off energy from the zero-point field, allowing matter to become stable and keeping all their elements from flying apart.

The zero-point field may exist in the strongest possible form of coherence. In this state, all the bosons or tuned particles resonate together. When this occurs, their individual identity dissolves into the whole, and they become one single wave that fills the entire universe. This causes the joining together of all elements in space and also in time. Imagine that! Not only could all points of physical space connect, but so also could all moments of time, past, present and future. The zero-point field is not only infinite; it is eternal.

Lynne McTaggart wrote that the German physicist Fritz-Alabert Popp discovered in the seventies that all life-forms emit a natural, living light or bioluminescence. He called this "biophoton emission," and he believed that it originated in the DNA in all the cells making up living tissue. What's more, Popp calculated that the biological light maintained the highest order of coherence. This allows all the parts of the body to share information nonlocally and instantaneously with every other part, because now the parts have become a whole. If it is nonlocal, it means that it is happening beyond time and space.

As mentioned in chapter 11, quantum physicists Penrose and Hameroff proposed a theory of consciousness in which this stream of coherent living-light particles, or biophotons, resonates throughout the body through their own circularly system inside tiny structures called "microtubules." This fibrous network of tiny tubes is found inside and among the cells in the brain and nerves and in all living tissue. This network of braided, knotted, and interwoven tiny ducts forms the skeleton of the cells and is called the "cytoskeletal matrix."

"Cyto" means cell. The tubes are so small that they are of a scale where quantum states of entanglement and nonlocality could occur and quantum computations can take place. Because the biophotons are in a state of coherence, they resonate together, allowing all the cells in the body to share information instantaneously. Information appears to travel throughout the body much faster than can be explained by neurons acting like wires and exchanging energy through chemical reactions at the synapses. The microtubular network acts as a kind of internet throughout the body. The microtubule network running throughout the body is far more extensive than the nervous system. It has ten million times more elements than the nerves and synapses. Quantum coherence allows the body to be one thing instead of a collection of parts. Parts communicate with each other, but in a single thing, all the information is present simultaneously everywhere.

This means that the brain and body may act as a quantum computer. Not only that, but the universe and the zero-point field may act as a giant quantum computer.

Popp, who discovered bioluminescence, made an amazing proposal. Living tissue exhibits a state of quantum coherence. The zero-point field is also a system of extreme quantum coherence. Popp suggested that these two levels of coherence were so in tune to each other as to be two aspects of the same thing. The zero-point field sends out a resonant wave, and the cells and atoms of the body resonate in sync with it. They are entrained to a superfield.

The superfield is like a gigantic tuning fork as large as the entire universe. All vibrating systems conform by entrainment to this giant resonating wave. The microtubules act like antennae picking up the resonance of the zero-point field. Popp has suggested that the DNA in all the body's cells may also act like an antenna for the vacuum energy and channel its coherent resonance to the living light they emit.

Popp suggests that the neural matter of the brain could exist in a state of extreme coherence forming a BIC or Bose-Einstein condensate. Normaly a BIC state exists at extremely cold conditions at or near absolute zero, but there may be exceptions to this that would allow this state of mater to exist in living tissue. This could be possible if the quantum particles in the tissues of the brain and body could draw off enough energy from the zero-point field to cause them to entrain to the field. The result, he proposes, could be consciousness. This would form what has been called a "pumped system" which would allow the ultimate coherence of a BIC to exist in living tissue at body temperature.

Information in such a system is shared nonlocally. This means that information happens at the same time to all parts instantaneously without propagating through space. Local signals travel through space, taking a finite amount of time to arrive. "Nonlocality" means that information doesn't travel from place to place but exists in all places at the same time. If one part changes, all the parts change. Things that share information this way are said to be correlated.

"Correlation" means that when particles or things share quantum states, they are said to undergo entanglement whereby, no matter how great a distance separates them in space or how long a time, they behave exactly the same. What happens to one happens to the other. Every atom in our body is in resonance with every atom in the universe. This happens outside of time and space. Information appears instantaneously in all parts of the system without any signals moving through space. There is no transfer of information.

Information can be shared all the way across the universe and from the past and even the future. At this level everything in the universe is in simultaneous communication with every other part both in space and time. The entire universe has become a single thing. Its parts have dissolved into the whole, so there isn't any transfer in information. All the information is present everywhere instantaneously.

Because it is instantaneous, this kind of information would seem to move faster than the speed of light, but since everything is interconnected, nothing goes anywhere. It is all one big thing. Einstein's universal speed limit doesn't apply in the quantum domain that exists outside of space and time.

We see by this that the universe is like a gigantic hologram in which each part contains the whole. If a piece of holographic film is cut up into a hundred pieces and a laser beam of coherent light is shined on a single piece, it reproduces the entire image. Each part contains the whole.

Consciousness and the Zero-Point Field

This brings us to a concept of great significance: how consciousness exists in individuals and in the universe at large and how it relates to the zero-point field.

According to a theory proposed by the American-British author and speaker on quantum physics, Danah Zohar, the neural matter of the brain synchronizes and entrains with the zero-point field, resulting in consciousness. Quantum particles inside the cells of the nerves and the brain and inside of tiny, sub cellular microtubules resonate in coherence with the zero-point field. This could only result in consciousness if the zero-point field and consciousness is the same thing. The field would have to be conscious! This theory points to the fundamental similarity between the White Light of the Void and the superfield with its vacuum energy. Both may be the same thing—a superconscious, intelligent being.

When living tissue synchronizes with the field, it becomes conscious, but it has no individual consciousness separate from the zero-point field. All consciousness at every level is the zero-point field, and it exists beyond time-space. Furthermore, it is unitive. There is only one consciousness because in whatever being it exists, it is caused by neural matter being in tune with the one zero-point field.

Once, I took ibogaine and *Psilocybe* mushrooms together. I found myself flying through space in the company of two silvery disks. We flew over an immense city all lit up with colored lights resembling Las Vegas. Finally, we arrived at a huge building that had a feeling of importance, like the Pentagon. We came to a door, and I was entering a room where a man was sitting at a table with his back to me. In front of him were millions of little TV screens.

Someone next to me said, "He's the one who looks out through the eyes of every living thing."

I approached him, and like in the early movie of the *Phantom of the Opera*, the figure slowly turned around. I saw his face, and he was I. These kinds of visions are allegorical.

Then the scene changed. We came to a door with a sign that said "Universe Project." Inside was a table and on the table a box. In the box was everything—all space, all time, all history, the big bang, the dinosaurs, all the wars, the industrial revolution, and the nuclear age. Suddenly I was inside the box, looking out. Looking out of the box, I felt like the entire universe was somebody's science project.

Ibogaine can be like sitting in a box seat over Niagara Falls with all of history going over. Others are sitting next to you and pointing things out like, "Look! There goes the Civil War!"

So from the perspective of quantum physics, there is only one self, one conscious subject, looking out through the eyes and listening through the ears and feeling with the fingers of all sentient beings. It exists in another nonlocal dimension, outside of time-space. Because it is the consciousness in all beings, it is your consciousness. The quantum physicist Erwin Schrödinger said. "Consciousness is a singular, for which there is no plural." It is one without a second.

This is another way of saying that the energy field that is the wave function of the universe and nonlocal, universal consciousness may be the same thing. The zero-point field may be the consciousness in all beings, and it may be conscious!

Somehow when a force as large as the universe enters into a quantum state where all information is shared everywhere nonlocally throughout all space and time and also outside of space and time, it wakes up, and becomes aware of everything. The result is cosmic or universal consciousness. The field may be a conscious being. Let me repeat this because it is so important. *The zero-point field may not only be consciousness; it may be conscious!*

Also it could be said that *the zero-point field may be alive*. The zero-point field may be the source of all life in the universe. It produces the condition of life in all living beings. As living tissue uses up its energy, it constantly draws fresh energy from the zero-point field. Overcoming entropy, it makes possible growth and life. This coherent energy drawn from the zero-point field is what has been called the "life force." In the Orient, it is called "qui" (pronounced "chi"). In India it is called "prana." Because living tissue draws off energy from the zero-point field, living organisms do not run out of energy, at least not for a long time. The second law of thermodynamics states that all energetic systems constantly lose energy like a clock, run down, and move toward entropy. In the end, the energy runs out. Living systems are an exception, because they move in a process of progressive complexification. Cellular growth is antientropic. Growth is the opposite of disintegration and decomposition. This can be explained if living structures draw energy from the zero-point field. If life is the entrainment of living tissue with the zero-point field, the field must be alive.

As the Zen master said to the hot-dog vendor, "Make me one with everything." The first time I became one with anything was on morning-glory seeds. I was looking at a refrigerator, and I could clearly see that it and I was the same thing. I didn't understand how this was possible, but still it was undeniable. Later I was driving taxi for Yellow Cab during a period when I had been taking mescaline. I was headed out to the airport, and suddenly what happened to the refrigerator happened to everything—the houses, the trees, the cars, the hills, the sky, the stars. There was no difference or separation between the world and me.

Once you see it, you can't unsee it. It has been that way ever since. It was a case of mistaken identity. If you mistake a rope for a snake and then recognize that it is a rope, you will never again see it as a snake. If you mistake the outside world for something separate from yourself, once you become one with it, you can't go back.

Physicist Niels Bohr said, "Those who are not shocked when they first come across quantum theory cannot possibly have understood it."

At first it was thought that quantum physics pertained to very small things and processes in the scale of subatomic particles. Now it is recognized that quantum effects happen at all sizes, from the infinitesimally minute to things as big as the universe and everything in between. Quantum processes underlie all classical phenomena. The quantum level of nature includes nanoscale phenomena, such as neutrons, protons, electrons, and their constituents.

Quantum processes of intermediate size can be observed in the flight of a flock of birds, the swimming of a school of fish, or the behavior of super organisms, like some species of ants where the entire colony is a single being. On the macro scale, it can manifest in galaxies, galactic superstructures, and the cosmos-sized filamental web of antimatter that determine the locations of galactic swarms.

The White Light experience that can be known at death and under the influence of drugs like 5-MeO-DMT and *Amanita muscaria* mushrooms may be a direct manifestation of the zero-point field. In these states, the tissue in our brain resonates in coherence with the vacuum-state void, which appears as pure emptiness in the form of a living, conscious, creative, loving being of light totally beyond our comprehension. We discover that this is our own consciousness, not formed into anything, and that it was there all along.

At the deepest level of our being, this universal, uncreated, all-encompassing entity has been the source of our perception, the ground of our being, and our life itself. It has been our true identity. It was the one and only one who was looking out through our eyes, listening through our ears, and touching the world with our fingers. It is what we call our self. Our personal, subjective identity is an illusion produced by the subject-object split of ordinary consciousness. The zero-point field is the supreme identity.

Since our life and consciousness are borrowed from the zero-point field and since our apparently separate identity disappears when we confront the White Light, who are we? This is illustrated by a Sufi story of a yokel who went for the first time to a country fair. He had never seen such a large crowd of people before, and he was worried that he would get lost. So he tied a gourd to his foot. That way he could say, "I'm the one with the gourd." After a while, he became tired and lay down in the shade to take a nap. Some boys for a prank untied the gourd and attached it to the foot of a stranger. When the bumpkin awoke and saw the situation, he cried out to the stranger in consternation, "Well, if you're me, then who am I?"

I always thought that I was my consciousness. It was quite a surprise to discover that my consciousness was someone else and that I don't really exist.

Consider the creation poem from the East Indian Rig Veda. It shows that even the Vedic sages who had directly experienced the White Light of the Void using soma, which was *Amanita muscaria* mushrooms, didn't know how the One came into being or from where:

> Nonbeing then existed not nor being:
> There was no air, nor sky that is beyond it.
> What was concealed? Wherein? In whose protection?
> And was there deep unfathomable water?

Death then existed not nor life immortal;
Of neither night nor day was there any token.
By its inherent force the One breathed windless:
And it was self-sustaining. No other thing than It existed.
Darkness there was at first by darkness hidden;
Without distinctive marks, this all was water.
That which, (was) becoming, by the void was covered,
That One by force of heat (samadhi) came into being.
Desire entered the One in the beginning:
It was the earliest seed. Consciousness was its germination.
The sages searching in their hearts with wisdom,
Found the bond of being in nonbeing.

Its ray extended light across the darkness:
But was the One above or was it below?
Seminal powers made fertile mighty forces.
Below was energy, above was impulse.

Who knows for certain? Who shall here declare it?
Whence was it born, and whence came this creation?
The gods were born after this world's creation:
Then who can know from whence it has arisen?

He who surveys it in the highest heaven,
Whether he fashioned it or whether he did not.
He knows (from whence this Creation came),
Or maybe even He does not know.

What is striking is that sages who had directly experienced the White Light using soma, the *Amanita muscaria* mushroom, composed this hymn, yet they regarded it with a great amount of uncertainty. The hymn asks more questions than it answers.

Amazingly it seems to anticipate many aspects of the quantum mechanics and the zero-point field. The Vedic sages recognized the one conscious and creative field to be the source of the universe. In the beginning, it was formless without attributes or distinguishing characteristics. It was covered by the void. It was nonlocal. Desire was the seed that germinated into consciousness (variously translated as "mind" and "thought). It came into being by the power of heat—in Sanskrit, "*tapas*," which means "austerity," or "*samadhi*." which is "mystical or psychedelic experience,"

It came into being through the highest level of entheogenic experience, the White Light of the Void. The White Light of the Void state anticipates the origin of consciousness as its base level state. It is pure consciousness before there was anything to be conscious of.

The one force created life: "Seminal powers made fertile mighty forces." It preceded even the gods who came into existence after the creation. It contained great energy: "Below was energy, above was impulse." It was autonomous. Particles and parts in a nonlocally connected system lose their individuality and dissolve into the whole. To know the White Light of the Void is to disappear into it, until there is no difference or separation between it and us.

A man went to the door of the Beloved and the Beloved said, "Who is there?" "It is I," said the supplicant. "Go away!" said the Beloved. "There is only room for one in here." Later the pilgrim returned, and the Beloved said, "Who is there?" "It is you!" the supplicant proclaimed, and the door opened wide. The Beloved said, "Come in."

The Light says, "Come in. Come out here where I am. There is nothing but love here. We together are one being. Flow into me like water until you can't tell me from yourself."

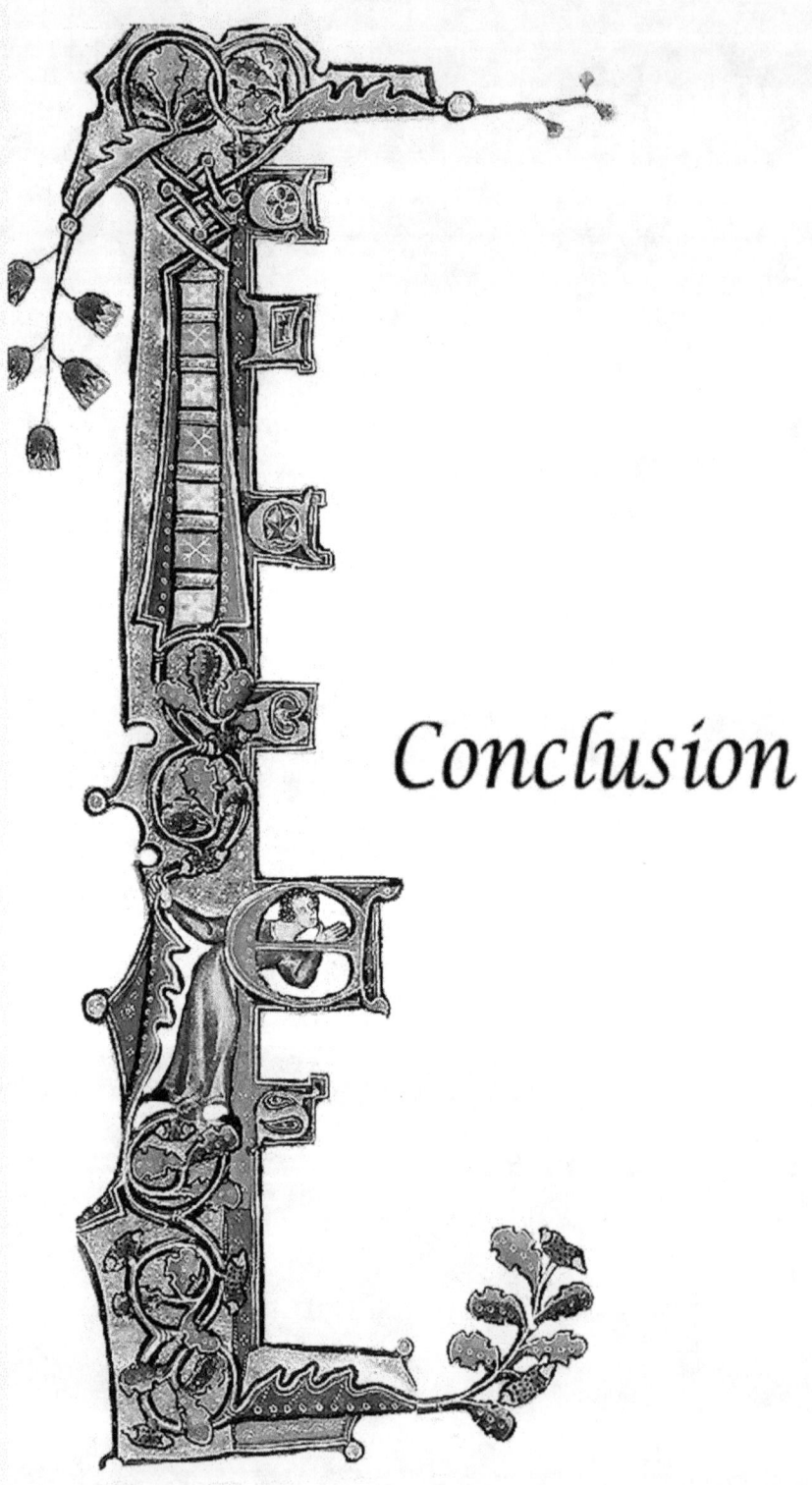

Conclusion

CONCLUSION

WELL, FELLOW EXPLORERS. THIS BRINGS us to the end of our journey. We have walked on the path between the worlds. We have had meetings with strange men and machines that are not of this earth. We have confronted and communicated with nonbiological entities from beyond space-time. Giant insects have menaced us. We have marveled at luminous ornamental objects floating in the dark, hovering like hummingbirds with vibrant wings.

We have been dazzled by the sacred networks of lights. We have watched time slow down and stop completely. We have seen time cut up, multiplied, duplicated, and rearranged with repetition out of order. We have turned into wolves and back again to people. We have teetered on the brink of giant whirlpools and been urged to jump in to the raging, swirling maelstrom. We have been shown vortices that demonstrated the recapitulation of organic evolution. We have flown over monumental architecture and buildings as big as mountains.

We have been surrounded and threatened by cannibalistic Mouseketeers, only to be rescued by a flying saucer. We have seen flying doorframes with rooms inside filled with intricate machinery. We have had our wishes granted and received otherworldly boons only to be manipulated into dependence and affiliation. We have conversed with talking knots that tied and untie themselves.

We have seen the famous book of the philosophers with burning, hieroglyphic letters of fire and gold. We have explored the mystery of consciousness and the holographic projection of material form. We have traveled to the quantum mechanical brink of materiality. We have traced consciousness to its most fundamental, base state of all containing nothingness as the White Light of the Void. We have gone out and touched the great death and explored the bardos between death and resurrection.

Nobody could say it better than the Mazatec *curandera* Maria Sabina (translated from the Mazatec by Henry Munn and liberally paraphrased by the author):

> We have walked along the path.
> The path of our health.
> The path of our long life.
> The path of our well-being.
> The path of sap.
> The path of dew.
>
> The little saint children have come
> And worked inside our bodies.
> The sprouting children.
> The budding children.
> The babies.
> The offshoots.
> The hummingbird children with vibrant wings.
> They are mas que hombre.
> They are more than human.
> They are not men of water.
> They are not men of tortillas.

We came forth sacred from out of the darkness,
From out of the night,
To swim in the immense,
To swim in all forms,
To swim in the great expanse of the flowing waters,
To swim in the vast expanse of the divine sea
Where the primordial sounds forth,
Where the sacred sounds forth.
We have gathered up the primordial.
We have gathered up the sacred.
We have shepherded the immense beneath the water.
Where the darkness thickened.
Where the forms and the hollows hardened.

There are clean flowers where we are going.
There is pure water where we are going.
There is no dust there.
There is no garbage there.
There is no rancor there,
There is no anger there.
We have gone with grand eloquence.
We have gone with purity.
We have gone with calmness.
We have gone with well being,
With freshness,
Like breast milk,
Like sap,
Like dew.
We are known in heaven.

All I can say is, "What a long, strange trip it's been."

About the Illustrations

ABOUT THE ILLUSTRATIONS

THE PICTURES PRECEDING THE CHAPTERS are mostly taken from *the Macclesfield Psalter.* This magnificent illuminated medieval manuscript from East Anglia was commissioned by a wealthy patron around 1330; The book is currently in the Fitzwilliam Museum, at the University of Cambridge. The Psalters are illuminated prayer books and books of hours from the twelfth, thirteenth, and fourteenth centuries. It is a little known fact that illumination is associated with hallucination. While clerical in content, illuminated books contain a subtext in the margins that shows an active involvement with entheogenic plants and fungi, including *Amanita muscaria* and *Psilocybe* mushrooms, Syrian rue, and solanaceous plants of the nightshade family. Now for the first time, we can understand the hallucinatory origin of these magnificent illuminations. The books were not the only things that were illuminated. Other pictures come from *The Petites Heures de Jean de Berry* cc. 1375 and 1385-1390 and from *The Wurzburg Psalter 1240-1250.*

Naked men collect Amanita muscaria-ladened urine in a bowl to drink.
They stand among red and white spotted oak leaves suggestive of that fungus.
From the Macclesfield Psalter, 1330

This picture from the *Macclesfield Psalter* is one of many that show the use of Amanita muscaria mushrooms. A naked man urinates while a second man catches the urine in a bowl. They will drink it. When the mushroom is eaten, the toxic ibotenic acid is converted into the psychoactive muscimol, which is retained in the urine. Since ancient times, cultures that make use of A. muscaria have discovered that drinking the urine following the ingestion of the fungus, is the preferred, less toxic and more inebriating form of the drug. The urinating man is standing next to a bolt-shaped protuberance that resembles Amanita muscaria in one of its stages of growth.

The red oak leaves with white spots, allude to the red and white spotted fungus and the oak, one of the host trees beneath which the mushroom grows in symbiotic association with the trees roots. The men are naked because Amanita muscaria produces profuse perspiration that soaks a persons clothing, and the fungus is traditionally eaten while naked or wearing a simple loin clothe. Nudity has taken on an iconographic significance that alludes to the use of that mushroom.

A bull legged man
wearing a red and white-spotted cap,
and holding a urine bottle,
rides a fantastic, composite beast
with a Syrian rue plant growing from its tail.
From the Luttrell Psalter between1320-1340

In next picture from the Luttrell Psalter, a man with bull's legs is riding a fantastic, composit creature with the head of a bear with an owls beak and eyes, birds' wings and the body of a snake. The man wears a red cap with white spots, suggesting the red and white spotted Amanita muscaria mushroom. His tawny bovine legs are also spotted with white. Bulls are universally associated with the fly-agaric mushroom. The man holds a vessel that has been identified as a urine bottle, of the sort used in bed at that time. The urine further connects the man with A. muscaria.

The body of the fantastic composite beast terminates in a plant that can be identified as Syrian rue, (*Paganum harmala*). This plant is the most common botanical form represented in the Psalters. The flowers of Syrian rue have prominent spike-like leaves extending from them. Paganum harmala contains a class of chemicals called *mao inhibitors* that interfere with the activity of an enzyme found in the stomach and gut (*monoamine oxidase*) that rapidly break down certain drugs before they can reach high blood levels. Most commonly are tryptamine drugs like DMT and psilocybin. The same mao inhibitor found in Syrian rue occur in the South american vine banistaria that is a key ingredient in the DMT containing drink ayahuasca. While there is no ethnographic evidence that I am aware of that links Syrian rue with Amanita muscaria mushrooms, the two appear numerous times in the same context in the Psalters and other sources relating to entheogenic plants and their use.

The third example of entheogenic plants and mushrooms presented in the Psalters is from the *Macclesfield Psalter* is portrayed on the cover of this book. A man is in bed praying. The feet of the bed are mushroom forms. Strong doses of entheogens are frequently taken in bed and a person in bed has become a common iconographic representation of someone tripping on a psychedelic. Behind him is a red pillow with white spots that suggests Amanita muscaria. He faces a fantastic, columnar form filled with intricate, interwoven knots and spirals formed from tendrils of ivy. The key-shaped column is similar to the hallucinogenic, standing wave constructions seen on entheogens. The entheogen is the "key" that unlocks access to higher dimensions and to the world of the divine. At the top of the column is the face of a bearded man who is the medieval conception of God. Above to the right is the familiar spiked flowers of Syrian rue and the left, the seedpods of that plant. Syrian rue seeds contain the psycho-interactive chemicals (beta carbolines) that give the plant its effect as an mao inhibitor.

ALCHEMY

Some of the pictures in this book are taken from works of the alchemists.

Many people believe that the alchemists were early natural scientists who sought to bring about the transmutation of gold from base metals. This was true of a large number of puffers and charlatans who used trickery to deceive kings and wealthy patrons. They wrote numerous books on the subject, some of which were misunderstood copies of true alchemical texts and other purely fictitious. In contrast, true alchemists were members of a secret society that practiced an ancient, pre-Christian religion that used entheogenic plants and fungus as its sacrament.

The gold of the philosophers was not ordinary gold. It was the *Amanita muscaria* mushroom that, when dried, takes on the hue of metallic gold. Potable gold, known as the golden elixir, was the urine that came from a person or animal that had eaten the fungus. The urine is less toxic and more intoxicating than the mushroom itself, because the liver acts like a kind of filter and digestion converts the toxic ibotenic acid into the inebriating muscimol.

The philosopher's stone and the elixir of immortality were euphemisms for the sacred mushroom, its expressed juice, and its urinary excretion. The alchemists knew that the mushroom had to be combined with MAO inhibitors, such as Syrian rue, to activate it. The chemistry they practiced was pharmaceutical and involved the extraction and purification of drugs and the art of distillation. The alchemists distilled their urine.

The alchemists concealed their communications in false narratives and deliberate misdirection. Their writings were intended to conceal rather than reveal information about the entheogens from the uninitiated. The alchemists were well versed in a very ancient, secret language of words, symbols, and emblems, going back over the horizon of history. This secret language was recognized and understood by many mystical groups and societies around the world. Practicing a pagan religion in a Christian society required concealment, misdirection, and pretending to be something else. The truth would be considered a heresy and would be subject to persecution by the Church and the Inquisition.

The pictures of intricate machinery are original drawings by the author.

The pictures titled "Field notes" are original drawings made by the author immediately following the trip.

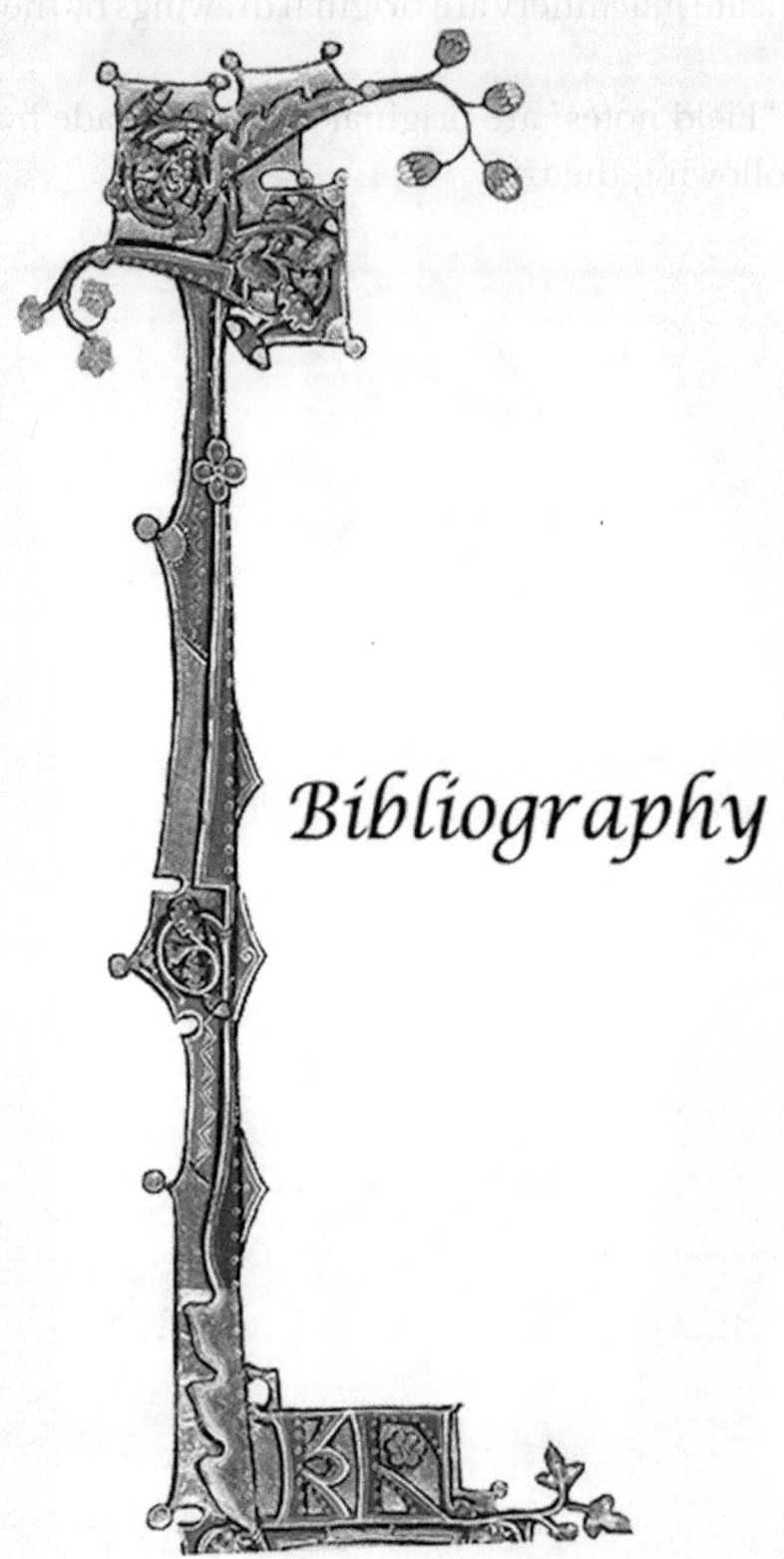

Bibliography

BIBLIOGRAPHY

Allegro, John. *The Sacred Mushroom and the Cross: Fertility Cults and the Origins of Judaism and Christianity.* Garden City, NY: Doubleday & Company, 1970.

Arthur, James. *Mushrooms and Mankind: The Impact of Mushrooms on Human Consciousness and Religion.* Escondido, CA: The Book Tree, 2000.

Crowley, Mike. *Secret Drugs of Buddhism: Psychedelic Sacraments and the Origins of the Vajrayana.* Hayfork, CA: Amrita Press, 2016.

DeRopp, Robert S. *Drugs and the Mind.* New York: Grove Press, 1957.

Estrada, Alvaro. *Maria Sabina: Her Life and Chants.* Translated by Henry Munn. Santa Barbara, CA: Ross-Erikson Inc., 1981

Evans-Wentz, W. Y. *The Tibetan Book of the Dead: Or the After-Death Experiences on the Bardo Plane, According to Lama Kazi Dawa-Samdup's English Rendering.* New York: Oxford University Press, 1927.

Goswami, Amit. *The Self-Aware Universe: How Consciousness Creates the Material World.* New York: Tarcher Putnam Books, 1995.

Grof, Stanislov. *LSD Doorway to the Numinous: The Groundbreaking Psychedelic Research into Realms of the Human Unconscious.* Rochester, VT: Park Street Press, 2009.

Irvin, Jan, and Andrew Rutajit. *Astrotheology and Shamanism: Unveiling the Law of Duality in Christianity and Other Religions.* San Diego, CA: The Book Tree, 2005.

Khayyam, Omar. *The Rubaiyat.* Rendered into English Verse by Edward FitzGerald. First version. With drawings by Edmund J. Sullivan. Illustrated Editions Company New York,.1938

McKenna, Terrence. *Food of the Gods: The Search for the Original Tree of Knowledge: A Radical History of Plants, Drugs, and Human Evolution.* N.p. New York: Bantam, 1992.

McKenna, Terrence. *True Hallucinations: Being an Account of the Author's Extraordinary Adventures in the Devil's Paradise.* N.p: Harper Collins, San Francisco, 1993.

McKenna, Terrence, and Dennis McKenna. *The Invisible Landscape: Mind, Hallucinogens, and the I Ching.* N.p.: Harper Collins, New York: 1993.

McTaggart, Lynne. *The Field: The Quest for the Secret Force of the Universe.* New York: HarperCollins, 2002.

Oroc, James. *Tryptamine Palace: 5-MeO-DMT and the Sonoran Desert Toad.* Rochester, VT: Park Street Press, 2009.

Ott, Jonathan. *Pharmacontheon: Entheogenic Drugs and Their Plant Sources and History*. 2nd ed. N.p.: Natural Products Company, Kennewick, WA: 1998.

Popp, Fritz-Alabert, Qiao Gu, and Ke-Hsueh Li. "Biophoton emission: experimental background and theoretical approaches." *Modern Physics Letters B* 8, no. 21/22 (1994): 1269–1296.

Reps, Paul ed. *Zen Flesh, Zen Bones: a collection of Zen and pre-Zen writings*. Charles F. Tuttle Co. Rutland, Vermont: 1968.

Ruck, A. P., Blaise Staples, and Richard Heinrich. *The Apples of Apollo: Pagan and Christian Mysteries of the Eucharist*. Carolina Academic Press, Durham, NC: 2001.

Ruck, Carl, A. P. Blaise Staples, Jose Alfredo Gonzales Celdran, and Mark Alwin Hoffman. *The Hidden World: Survival of Pagan Shamanic Themes in European Fairy Tales*. Durham, NC: Carolina Academic Press, 2007.

Strassman, Rick. *DMT: The Spirit Molecule: A Doctor's Revolutionary Research into the Biology of Near-Death and Mystical Experiences*. Rochester, VT: Park Street Press, 2001.

Strassman, Rick, Slawek Wojtowicz, Luis Eduardo Luna, and Ede Frecska. *Inner Paths to Outer Space: Journeys to Alien Worlds Through Psychedelics and Other Spiritual Technologies*. Rochester, VT: Park Street Press, 2008.

Wasson, R. Gordon. *Soma: Divine Mushroom of Immortality*. N.p.: Harcourt Brace Jovanovich, Printed in Italy: 1967.

Wasson, R. Gordon, Stella Kramrisch, Carl Ruck, and Jonathan Ott. *Persephone's Quest: Entheogens and the Origins of Religion*. New Haven: Yale University Press, 1986.

Whilhelm, Richard, trans. *The Secret of the Golden Flower*. New York: Harcourt Brace Jovanovich, 1962.

Wilber, Ken, ed. *The Holographic Paradigm and Other Paradoxes: Exploring the Leading Edge of Science*. London: Shambhala, 1982.

Zohar, Danah. *The Quantum Self: Human Nature and Consciousness Defined by the New Physics* New York: Quill/William Morrow, 1990.

www.ingramcontent.com/pod-product-compliance
Lightning Source LLC
Chambersburg PA
CBHW081207170426
43198CB00018B/2879